McCARTNEY

McCARTNEY

CHRIS SALEWICZ

ST. MARTIN'S PRESS
NEW YORK

Design by Larry Kazal

Library of Congress Cataloging-in-Pulication Data

Salewicz, Chris.
   McCartney, the definitive biography.

   1. McCartney, Paul. 2. Rock musicians—England—
Biography. I. Title.
ML410.M115S24 1986   784.5'4'00924 [B]   85-25115
ISBN 0-312-52369-6

First Edition
10 9 8 7 6 5 4 3 2 1

For Alexander

McCARTNEY

That summer of 1956, the first the McCartney family had spent in their neat, new government-subsidized home in the almost pastoral Liverpool suburb of Allerton, Mary McCartney had been troubled by chest pains. Dismissing them as symptoms of a prickly digestion, the slim, petite woman would dose herself with Bisodol and carry on with her meticulous housework, or immerse herself with industrious dedication in her job of health visitor, to which she had graduated from full-time nursing.

At the beginning of August her two sons, Paul, who was just

1

fourteen, and Michael, eighteen months younger, went for ten days to their school's annual summer scout camp in nearby North Wales. When a spell of dry, hot weather—during which both boys managed to suffer from sunstroke—ended in the kind of continuous torrential rain that is so characteristic of that mountainous region, Mary and her husband Jim felt considerable concern for the health of their two sons.

Sympathizing with their anxiety, Olive, the daughter of Bella Johnson, a friend of Mary's who worked at the same health clinic, offered to drive them to the camp for the weekend. There they found that, as always, their eldest son was playing his familiar part as life of the party, his distinctive doe's eyes glistening with gleeful enthusiasm as, with his pert wit, he ceaselessly held sway over his fellow followers of the Baden Powell Boy Scout ethic. The boys were obviously experiencing little difficulty in weathering the inclement elements. So, after liberally dispensing cakes and sweets, Mary, Jim, and Olive began the drive back to Liverpool.

It was on this return journey that the nagging ache that Mary had felt in her chest for some weeks suddenly erupted into shrill agony. So far, she and Jim had dismissed the small lump that had appeared on one of her breasts as just one more irritating symptom of the "change of life" that Mary, at forty-six, was beginning to undergo. But on that drive back to Allerton the pain she suddenly experienced was so intense that she had to lie down on the back seat of Olive's small car.

With this physical hurt almost matched by an excoriating mental anguish caused by the fact that her worst secret fear was perhaps being realized, Mary went straight to bed as soon as the car pulled up outside their trim, terraced house at 20 Forthlin Road, Liverpool 18. After a few hours, however, the pain subsided, and, with a nurse's distaste for symptoms of hypochondria, Mary stubbornly refused to mention it to any of the doctors she worked alongside.

But Mary's symptoms would not be ignored, and a few weeks after the boys' return from scout camp, twelve-year-old Michael surprised his mother one afternoon in his parents' bedroom.

Clutching a crucifix and a photograph of a relative who was a Catholic priest, Mary McCartney was quietly sobbing to herself: the pain was returning sporadically, each time with an increased anger.

Within a month, even Mary had run out of excuses for not seeking medical assistance. After an emergency consultation with a specialist, she was promptly admitted to Liverpool's Northern Hospital. Cancer of the breast was diagnosed: a mastectomy was immediately prescribed. Exploratory surgery, however, revealed that the cancer had spread far beyond the area where the symptoms had manifested themselves; it was decided that removal of her breast would accomplish little, if anything.

The probings of the surgeon's scalpel, moreover, seemed to have unleashed the worst, final fury of the disease. Mary received the last rites and had rosary beads tied around her wrists. "I would have liked to have seen the boys growing up," she whispered to Dill, her brother Bill's wife. Within a matter of hours of being admitted to Northern, Mary Patricia McCartney's life had ended. It was October 31, All Saints' Day, the day when, as Mike McCartney later wrote in typically worshipful tones, "all her sins were washed away and her soul went straight to heaven, which it did."

Jim McCartney, who had found his true love in Mary at the comparatively late age of thirty-nine, was beside himself with grief; all he wanted to do, he would tell anyone around him, was to join his wife on the other side.

To spare the boys from the harrowing sight of their father's anguish, Paul and Michael were taken to Huyton in North Liverpool, to stay with their Auntie Jin; there they were tucked in at nights in the same single bed by their father's small, rotund sister, her habitual jolliness curbed by the tragedy. After she had switched out the light, the boys would cry themselves to sleep.

This hidden mourning was in complete contrast to the way in which, in a clumsy attempt at a mature, joking acceptance of her loss, Paul had responded to the news of his mother's death: his initial reaction had been to blurt out, "What are we going to do without her money?" (Twenty-five years later, similar circumstances were to lead him to make an equally apparent faux pas, this time before the self-righteously critical eyes of the world's media. "It's a drag, isn't it?" was the only response he was capable of giving to the murder of the man with whose destiny his own had been so inextricably linked. Yet in the very brevity of that understated reply was exposed every screaming nerve end running amok beneath the impenetrable blankness of his shock as—in what had become a chilling pattern—yet another person suddenly vanished from his life.) For months, even years, afterward, Paul McCartney was to be haunted by that remark about his mother, his glib flippancy hardly in accord with his nightly prayers, in which he would beg God to return her.

To all who saw them, Paul had been "Daddy's boy" as a small child; his younger brother, more closely resembling Mary, physically, had seemed intellectually nearer to her as well. But to a considerable extent this impression was a consequence of Mary McCartney's innate fairness: her sense of balance instinctively asserted itself so that a potentially harmful rivalry for parental affection between the two brothers would never develop.

In fact, Paul, who early on had learned to conceal the depth of his feelings as a means of survival, was at least equally in love with this gentle soul, whose aura glowed through their various homes. And Mary McCartney's death was the most devastating experience of his young life, its dark, paralyzing shock waves sweeping with resounding effect over all his succeeding years. Ultimately, it was to prove the principle motivating factor behind all that he became; indeed, fourteen years later, the final album from the Beatles would be released with a title song, "Let It Be," that was a direct hymn to Mary McCartney.

At an age when Paul McCartney was breaking away from childhood, he still desperately needed her support, to be able to lean on the solid foundations she and Jim hand-in-hand had consciously created for their boys. Now his father was in a state of mourning that, in one form or another, would remain with him for the rest of his life. And his brother, whom everyone felt an urge to protect, was visibly shattered. Yet no one saw signs of great woe in Paul McCartney: instinctively, he knew that to get through this time he had to distance himself from feelings of grief.

He had to be strong, for his father and brother, *and* for his mother. And he had to be successful.

CHAPTER TWO

Some claim that the cause of the thick, nasal Liverpool accent is the constant breeze—icy on all but the very hottest days—that blows off the River Mersey, gifting each of the city's inhabitants with a thick wad of catarrh lodged resolutely at the back of the throat. Whatever its origins, that unmistakable Liverpool vocal tang is one of the cornerstones of Merseyside mirth. There is, in fact, no other collective body of Britons with a more keenly developed sense of humor than Liverpudlians; one result of this reputation is that even the most serious Scouser —as natives of Liverpool are

7

known—may find that outside of his home city he is considered a dry, laconic fellow, due to the Scouse knack for larding every phrase with apparent ironic understatement.

A simple, almost self-evident explanation is invariably offered for this inability on the part of most Liverpudlians to consider their lives with any great degree of seriousness: that the reality of existence in this northwest English port is so hard and rough, the only way to get through life is with a joke and a grin. In fact, such a view has been so commonly expressed that it has come near to entering the realms of myth.

Certainly the early life of Jim McCartney, Paul's father, can be seen as perfectly fitting the stereotype of the underprivileged. With his parents and three brothers and six sisters, Jim McCartney lived in a minute back-to-back terraced house in a cobbled street in one of the worst working-class slums in the city—Solva Street, in the Everton district. His father, Joe McCartney, earned so little from his job as a tobacco cutter that the family's vegetables would be obtained each weekend by trading the tobacco Joe had filched from his firm—he would sneak the contraband home at night by hiding it in the cuffs of his pants.

The Macs, as the McCartney family referred to themselves, were of Irish descent. At one time they had been one of the largest families in Belfast, and it was only in the middle of the nineteenth century that some family members had moved across the Irish Sea to Liverpool. Joseph McCartney had been born on November 23, 1866, to James McCartney II, a general handyman, and Elizabeth, his wife. Joe's son James was born on July 7, 1902.

Joe McCartney was a man of strict regimentation not atypical of Northerners: a teetotaler, he went to bed every night of his adult life at ten o'clock. He was also something of a musician, playing his beloved big brass tuba in both the Territorial Army's brass band and the one sponsored by Cope's, the tobacco firm he so loyally served all his life. Whenever the opportunity arose at home, Joe would practice and play his brass tuba, all the while encouraging his children on their chosen instruments. Joe was also blessed with a fine singing voice, though he never aired it in public; he was, however, once left £40 in the will of an old woman who had learned of his secret talent and had persuaded Joe to sing to her once when she was sick.

Jim McCartney began work in 1916, at the age of fourteen, for the local cotton brokers, A. Hannay and Co., earning six shillings a week. Before then, however, he had illustrated his initiative in his attempts to bolster the meager amounts of money coming into the family home. After school he worked at the nearby Theatre Royal, a music hall where he would sell programs and act as limelight boy (he followed the star around the stage with the spotlight). When the auditorium had emptied, the enterprising Jim—obviously a true canny Northerner—would pick up the programs left under the seats, take them home, iron them crisp, and resell them the next day.

It was not long after he began work at Hannay's that an upright piano was installed in the McCartney parlor, purchased with what might be seen as some measure of prescience from one of the NEMS furniture stores that were peculiar to Liverpool. At the encouragement of his father, Jim taught himself—and anyone else in the neighborhood who cared to benefit from his suddenly discovered expertise—chords and musical notation. From then on, Jim's eldest sister Jin recalled, she would never go to bed without some form of communal music wafting up the stairway from the parlor or even, on warm nights, from the street outside. Sometimes this jollity would form the tail-end of one of the frequent McCartney "pound nights," so named because each friend and relative invited was expected to arrive with a pound of some commodity—sugar, tea, or whatever. The picture suggested of life in Solva Street, with its laughing singsongs and undercurrent of often elusively indefinable suffering, is almost an archetype of the urban British working-class family in the early twentieth century.

The choice of music played in the house, however, was always a source of some contention. Joe McCartney was a lover of brass band music, like any Northern workingman should be, a sound that is at once pompously portentous yet somehow self-deflating. He held no truck with the new-fangled big-band sounds of the likes of the Henry Hall and Tommy Dorsey bands; "a load of old tin cans" was his favorite description of this music.

In that seemingly perverse way that sons and daughters almost inevitably take the opposite course of that favored by their parents, such an adverse reaction to his favorite music may well have spurred on Jim McCartney. For by the time he turned seventeen, in 1919, Jim had formed his own ragtime band, with a repertoire that included such classics as "The Birth of the Blues," Jim's own favorite, "Stairway to Paradise," and his own composition, "Walking in the Park With Eloise." In early rehearsals, and for their first show, the band was known as the Masked Melody Makers.

Jim McCartney knew that if his band wanted to get ahead, it had better get a gimmick, and so it was deemed that onstage the musicians would wear highwaymen's masks over their eyes. At the Masked Melody Makers' first date, however, Jim and his fellow players were sweating so much from their efforts that the black dye from the masks started to run down their faces before they had even reached the first break.

From then on, they were known as Jim Mac's Jazz Band. Dumping the faintly rakish highwaymen's masks, Jim McCartney aimed for a more formal image, one that was very close to his own well-scrubbed, pristine, daytime appearance. For their performances the musicians would don dinner jackets with paper shirtfronts and cuffs, purchased at twelve for a penny.

Though it was never considered that they might become anything more than merely semipro, the group stayed together until the mid-twenties, and played at the first local showing of the silent movie *The Queen of Sheba*. Uncertain as to which songs in their repertoire would best suit the occasion, Jim selected a popular song of the time, "Thanks for the Buggy Ride," for the chariot race sequence, and "Horsy Keep Your Tail Up" for the Queen of Sheba's dramatic deathbed scene.

Unlike the straitlaced Joe McCartney, his son Jim was inclined to be a lad about town, one of the reasons why he didn't marry until comparatively late in life. Something of a ladies' man

—his reputation only enhanced by his being a local bandleader—Jim McCartney also enjoyed a drink, but would never permit himself to become so intoxicated that he was no longer in control of his own actions. That he should always maintain his self-respect was one of the principles of his existence, and one which he later passed on to his sons. As tends to occur in large, close families, many other rules of life were taught to Jim and his brothers and sisters: among them, such superficially simplistic yet vital adages as "fend for yourself," "always soldier on," and "if you don't at first succeed, try, try again." Again, years later, such maxims were firmly drummed into his own sons.

Though given such a strong foundation, Jim could not be spared from a further vice. For Jim McCartney was something of a gambling man, fond of betting on the horses. He once got badly into debt, though for reasons that at least had motives other than selfishness; his mother, Florence McCartney, who was capable of coupling a strongly matriarchal role with a fondness for humor of a most prurient nature, was badly in need of a holiday. With confidence so great that it might well be seen as a mark of his desperation, Jim attempted to raise the necessary funds with what he believed was a series of well-placed bets at the racetrack—with inevitable results. So deeply was he in debt that his employer, Mr. Hannay, learned of his plight; however, instead of giving his employee an unproductive verbal flaying, Hannay offered not only to pay off Jim's debts, but also to loan him the money to send Florrie on vacation to Devon. For the next year, in order to repay the cash, Jim McCartney walked every day the five miles from his home in West Derby, where the family had moved, to the Cotton Exchange in the City of Liverpool.

By now, however, Jim was enjoying a sufficiently improved status for it not to seem some arrogant, grandiose gesture that he should contemplate paying for his mother to go on holiday—so long as he didn't stoop to flashy, instant money-making schemes, that is. In 1930, after fourteen years as a "sample boy," showing prospective pieces of cotton, Jim McCartney had been promoted to cotton salesman, with a salary of £250 a year; the weekly wage of a miner at the time was only £1.50. Perhaps even more crucial than the actual increase in pay for this neat, dapper man—so ostensibly serious yet whose lurking sense of humor was liable to erupt at any time—was the fact that cotton salesman was considered a middle-class job, a position of some status in the community. Cotton salesmen were rarely recruited from lads with lowly working-class backgrounds. In the viciously class-conscious country that was England, with the ever-implied statement that you should "know your place," Jim McCartney was unable to avoid blessing his good fortune and noting the significance of this upward step. Though in years to come his fortunes were to fluctuate —largely due to World War II—he was never to lose hold of the sense of self-worth that this new position brought.

One effect of Jim's new relative affluence was that it enhanced his status as an eligible bachelor. And, at the same time, the spare cash in his pocket provided him with freedom and a desire to hang on to that liberty. Joe and Florrie McCartney, all the same, would fret about the gold-digging females who would come casually calling on their successful son.

Mary Patricia Mohin, however, did not appear to be a similar threat. Born in Liverpool on September 29, 1909, to Owen and Mary Teresa Mohin, she had been brought up a strict Catholic, something that gave a hint of her Irish ancestry. There was, indeed, something extraordinarily Irish about the way the Mohin family had arrived at its surname, which was a corruption of Mary's father's original family name. He had been born in Ireland as Owen Mohan on January 19, 1880. At the school in Owen's small village, however, so numerous were children of the vast Mohan clan that the headmaster had trouble keeping track of them. Accordingly, he arrived at an expedient solution: the children on one side of the class would forthwith be known as Mohan; those on the opposite side would become Mohin.

Mary's father moved to Glasgow, Scotland, at the age of twelve. Thirteen years later he again uprooted himself and traveled down to Liverpool, where he met and wed Mary Teresa Danher in Saint Charles Roman Catholic Church in Toxteth.

They had three children—Wilf, Mary, and Bill. But in 1919, Mary Teresa Mohin died, and Owen took his children back to Ireland for a time, although his attempt at farming there failed.

Shortly after, he returned to Liverpool, where he set up his own coal delivery business and soon owned five horse-and-carts. Not only was this a sign of some appreciable status, but the income from the rigs allowed the family to live in the very best part of the working-class slums. Using his horse-and-carts to double up as a moving business in the summer months, Owen Mohin quickly earned large amounts of money, and at one stage was so successful that he owned four race horses.

Owen Mohin, a teetotaling nonsmoker, had one vice, however: gambling. Eventually all he had would be lost at the race-track.

On a journey to Ireland in 1921 to buy horses for his carts, Owen met a woman called Rose. Perhaps persuaded in his decision, so family legend has it, by her £100 dowry, Owen returned to Liverpool with Rose as his new bride. Mary Mohin, however, was unable to accept the idea of a stepmother; when she was thirteen, she moved away to stay with relatives in the Liverpool district of Litherland. The next year she became a trainee nurse, first at Alder Hey Hospital, then at Walton Hospital, where, dedicated to her vocation, she became a sister when she was twenty-four. By the age of thirty-one, the trim, peaceful figure of Mary Mohin was employed as a district health visitor by Liverpool Corporation.

That year she met Jim McCartney, who was eight years her senior. They fell in love and were married soon after, on April 15, 1941, at Saint Swithens Roman Catholic Chapel, Gill Moss, Liverpool. After their wedding, the couple moved into furnished rooms in Anfield.

By now the Liverpool Cotton Exchange had closed for the duration of the war. Too old for military service, Jim McCartney still had to participate in some form of war work, and so he was sent to Napier's, the aircraft factory that produced the Sabre aircraft engine, where he was made a lathe-turner. At night, meanwhile, Jim became a fire fighter, struggling to deal with the almost nightly infernos caused by the German bomber attacks that attempted to smash not only Liverpool's heavy industry, but to destroy the city's importance as the most crucial British port for Atlantic crossings. Even when the raids briefly ceased, the newlyweds were unable to avoid a constant, ominous reminder of the fate that the Nazis would like to befall Liverpool: close by their first home were the mass graves in which victims of the bombing had been buried.

The war also brought a temporary end to Jim McCartney's musical endeavors: the piano, one of the few items of furniture taken by him to his new lodgings, was stuffed with sandbags for the duration of the war. It was into this inauspicious, infinitely modest setting that, fourteen months after their wedding, Jim and Mary McCartney brought their first baby son.

CHAPTER THREE

James Paul McCartney was born on June 18, 1942. A warm, clear night, it was ideal weather for Luftwaffe raids, and Jim McCartney, busy watching to warn of the blazes from bombings that never came, missed the birth of his first child.

From the beginning Paul was blessed with a superior environment to that of most of his contemporaries, something that was to become a subtle but significant pattern in his life. He was born in a private ward at Walton Hospital, an honor bestowed upon Mary McCartney because she had once been the sister in charge of the maternity ward.

An advantage of Mary's privileged status was that Jim McCartney was not restricted to hospital visiting hours, but could visit whenever he wanted. Coming off his fire-watching night shift, Jim received the news of the birth and made straight for Walton "Hozzy," as hospitals are termed in the ever-abbreviated Liverpudlian dialect.

Rushing to his wife's bedside, Jim McCartney was horrified at what he found in his wife's arms. Somehow he had managed to reach the age of forty without ever having learned of the wrinkled, raw state of babies when they first emerge from the womb. Jim thought that his longed-for son resembled nothing so much as "a horrible piece of red meat." So great was his disappointment that when he got back home to Anfield, Jim burst into tears, the first time in years that he had cried. With each subsequent visit to the hospital, however, the baby's redness lessened. Very soon, it was clear to everyone that the young Paul McCartney was a baby with perfect features, dominated by exquisite round eyes, as moon-shaped as his father's face, that were at once dreamily wistful and precisely penetrating.

One day, not long after Jim and Mary McCartney had brought their baby son home, his mother put him in his pram out in the garden to enjoy the weather that had continued warm for much of that summer. Going out later to bring him into the house, she was aghast to find his face coated in light flecks of dust. Fearing what he might be breathing in, she demanded of her husband that they move home.

As Jim's employment at the Napiers factory was classified as Air Ministry work, the family was able to move into a small government-subsidized house. However, these dwellings were so small that they often were disparagingly referred to by their occupants as "half houses." Jim and Mary McCartney were forced to concede that the houses were far better for bringing up a young family in than their previous furnished rooms. Moreover, this new address at 92 Broadway, Wallasey Village, had the advantage of being on the other side of the Mersey to Liverpool itself, and therefore away from the main targets of the German bomb crews.

16

Soon, however, Jim's work with Napiers came to an end. But with a small child and much of Liverpool destroyed, there was no question of the McCartneys losing their house. Jim was transferred to work as a temporary inspector for Liverpool Corporation Cleansing Department, a job that consisted of checking how efficiently the city garbage collectors were doing their duty. For such a dignified figure as Jim McCartney, so aware until quite recently of how he had managed to escape his lowly background through his salesman's job at the Cotton Exchange, this employment, which carried none of the romantically patriotic connotations of his war work at the aircraft factory, seemed demeaning. What's more, the pay was bad. To help out, Mary McCartney went back to health visiting. Her salary, however, turned out to be more than her husband's.

This situation would remain for the rest of their life together, apart from a brief period in 1944 when she again stopped work to have a second child, Peter Michael McCartney, born on January 7 in the same private ward at Walton Hospital as his older brother. By now, the McCartneys had moved again, back across the Mersey to an area called Knowsley on the northern outskirts of Liverpool. Almost as soon as she had brought Paul's baby brother back to their new home, a prefab bungalow in Roach Avenue, Knowsley Estate, Mary returned to the hospital to be treated for mastitis, a breast disease.

Soon Mary McCartney was home again. With the family's urgent need for more money, she wanted to get back to work as quickly as she could. But the officelike routine of health visiting made the job seem dull, compared with nursing. Although she knew she would rarely be able to get a full night's sleep without being called out to assist in a birth, Mary McCartney took a job as a domiciliary midwife; this entailed caring for the pregnant women on one of the large housing projects now being built all around the outskirts of Liverpool.

A major perk of this work was the council house that, for a nominal "emolument," or rent, went with it. So the McCartneys moved again, to 72 Western Avenue, Speke, a housing project largely intended to provide homes for workers at the nearby

17

Ford factory. Here the McCartneys were able to establish some roots.

A hardworking, dedicated woman, Mary McCartney considered her fractured sleep to be almost part of her birthright. In homes and at bus stops and on corners of the wide, spanking-new streets of Speke, however, Mary's ceaseless devotion to her vocation was the subject of frequent, admiring comment. She often brought home small gifts from grateful new parents. Moreover, Mary did not allow her involvement with her midwifery to interfere with the upbringing of her two young sons, although her absences from home strengthened the bond between Paul and Michael and their father. Always immaculately groomed, the well-mannered boys were the objects of envy and admiration from friends and neighbors. Jim McCartney, meanwhile, was going through rapid adjustments, from affluent bachelor-bandleader to devoted husband to pipe-smoking, slipper-wearing father. But he would shower his wife with wondering praises over Paul and Michael's appearances and over her creative administration of their still-rationed food supply. And in both large and small details he was as much an example to his sons as his wife: among the shirts and sheets in the linen closet and wardrobe he would place small bags, hand-sewn by Mary, filled with lavender, whose scent would intermingle with the musty odor of mothballs dangling from coat hangers.

Watching out of the corner of a smiling eye as Mary slipped the boys the first succulent cuts from the Sunday roast, or gazing in repose across the kitchen at the sight of Paul and Michael "helping" push newly washed, dripping wet clothes through the wringer she was operating, or scrubbing and pumice-stoning away in the bath at the pair's thick layers of garden dirt, Jim McCartney must certainly have mused on how blessed with good fortune he had been in his choice of partner.

Even so, there was a tinge of sadness, even of guilt, in such reflections. With the war's end, Jim had left his job with the Corporation and gone back to selling cotton for Hannay's, but it was a different financial world altogether. No longer was the cotton trade a secure market: if Jim McCartney could take home

£6 at the end of a hard week's work, he was doing well. Such wages were approximately the same as his wife brought in, and it was through Mary that they had their home. When he compared their respective contributions, the proud, honest Jim McCartney felt shame.

Not that this was discernible to his sons, whose rapid progress he viewed with something close to adoration. Paul, who took after him the most, would sit on his father's knee, rocking with boisterous glee, as Jim spun through a selection of favorites on the piano. The more vulnerable, more sensitive Mike, meanwhile, would sway back and forth on the carved steel foot pedal of the sewing machine as his mother—whom he most resembled—sewed on, keeping a watchful eye out lest his tiny fingers stray too near the galloping needle.

Mike's closeness to his mother was partially at Mary's instigation. As befitted her gentle, compassionate nature, she would always champion the underdog, though the lack of great affection in her own childhood made it difficult from time to time for her to openly express love. Eighteen months old when Mike was born, Paul—big-eyed, chubby, and cheerful—was not at an easy age for accepting a new baby into the household. Accepting the undiluted affection of his relatives and neighbors, Paul attempted to turn in his direction those unexpected torrential floods of pure love that poured the way of the newly born child. His intuition, rather than any contrived guile, taught him at this early age the benefits that charm could bring. Such sibling rivalry is hardly unique, though the benefits to which in later life Paul McCartney was able to put the lessons he learned were rather more so.

In time, the experience that Mike in his turn had learned from the psychic jockeying for position with his brother taught him how to present a facade of almost aggressive confidence. Very early in his school career, he became known for his argumentative nature. But, as always, Paul was one jump ahead of Mike. Paul had learned to stay out of trouble by keeping quiet; one of his earliest memories was of hiding from another child and then hitting him over the head with an iron bar.

19

Such an act, if discovered, would have provoked intense disfavor from Jim McCartney. Though he may have been unable to provide financially for his family as much as he might care to, he was still unequivocally the head of the household. Outwardly placid, he would not hesitate to punish an unruly son by giving him a good walloping, the threat of which was often invoked by Mary at times when Paul and Mike were approaching insurrection. Even here, Paul soon had figured out a simple way of coping with his father's wrath. Once when Michael was being physically brought to order by their father, Paul, standing on the sidelines, demonstrated his fondness for the expedient solution. "Tell him you didn't do it," he advised his bellowing brother, "and he'll stop."

A somewhat troubling flaw in Paul's otherwise apparently perfectly formed character was demonstrated by a petty desire for vengeance that even he later pinpointed as "pretty sneaky." When, from time to time, all his tact and diplomacy would run out, and the appropriate punishment would be meted out by Jim McCartney's hand, Paul would display no evident ill will toward his father. But later, he would creep upstairs to his parents' bedroom and rip the slightest tear in the bottom of their prized lace curtains. Such willful destruction of a fond object is revealing; it seems as though rather too much affection had been larded on this prettily plump child, and in many ways, he had become spoiled. The resulting self-love, however, would serve him well in time.

Excepting such aberrations, however, the McCartneys were an almost archetypal, provincial British family in that shadowy no man's land between working-class and lower middle-class. Jim's embarrassment at the imbalance of their financial setup notwithstanding, he gravitated naturally to the role that he had witnessed his own father play. He was a good dad, playing his masculine part with relish; his baggy trousers tightly clipped, he would take his kids on long bike rides through the country that surrounded the Speke estate. Leading Paul and Mike, he would go armed with a bucket and spade in hunts around the neighboring streets for horse manure. As evening approached each Saturday in winter, the two brothers, sworn to total silence, would sit at their father's feet as he religiously listened to the soccer results on the radio. Racing Paul and Michael with giant strides to the bus stop, he would lure the reluctant pair onto the bus that took them down to the barbers in Penny Lane, where a "short-back-and-sides" would be briskly administered.

At every opportunity he would attempt to broaden their experience: each day as he sat in his favorite armchair, doing the crossword in the Liverpool Echo, he would convince the boys that he needed their help, insisting that they look up in the dictionary all the words that they didn't know. Yet the education that Jim McCartney offered his sons was not always conventional; they couldn't help but notice his inability to pass a slot machine without putting a coin in it, or the way he would give quadruple measures of undiluted alcohol to guests. Later, when the boys were in their teens, he would show them how to get away with drinking underage in pubs, slipping them the cash to buy rounds of drinks.

It was, however, the glow from Mary McCartney's good soul that really dominated the household. Her close friend, Bella Johnson, whose daughter Olive worked at the Law Society close to the Cotton Exchange and who would travel to work with Jim, recalled how important was the atmosphere established by Mary's presence. Olive, meanwhile, was able to clearly observe the strength with which Jim loved her.

Linked to Mary's appreciation for quiet, unassuming dignity, and a belief in the need to better yourself, were her assiduous efforts to eliminate every trace of the local Liverpudlian accent from her sons' speech. Imitating the other children on the estate in Speke, Paul, in particular, had quickly assumed thick Scouse intonations. At her informal, do-it-yourself elocution classes, Mary McCartney persevered until every last trace of Scouse was exorcised from her eldest son's speech.

CHAPTER FOUR

Like his birth, the atmosphere in which Paul McCartney was educated was advantageous. In 1947, while a certain John Lennon was starting his third year in the efficient but spartan and Victorian Dovedale Primary School with its concrete playground, Paul McCartney began his school career at Stockton Wood Road Primary, a model new school less than two hundred yards from his parents' home. Both Paul and his brother had been christened as Catholics; however, Jim McCartney was adamant that his boys should not attend a Catholic school, institutions that he believed did not provide enough of an education.

23

The only school on the Speke estate, Stockton Wood had been opened in 1939. A wide, two-story brick building, Stockton Wood was surrounded by an expansive stretch of green playing fields that extended almost as far as the boundary of Liverpool Airport, just beyond the school's perimeter fence. Only the whine of light aircraft lodged there by their wealthy Northern industrialist owners and the occasional roar of larger cargo planes disturbed the area's rural calm. The airport may have had some influence on the Stockton Wood schoolkids; the school's black-and-yellow badge featured a design of a Spitfire flying over the Mersey.

Under its enlightened head teacher, Miss Margaret Thomas (who was later rewarded for her efforts with a British Empire Medal), the children at Stockton Wood Road were given a grounding in far more than the usual three Rs. A progressive educationalist, Miss Thomas insisted her staff remain undaunted by classes of forty and more pupils—something akin to a record figure in those times—and that they provide their charges with a broad education.

Paul and, later, Michael McCartney didn't only learn to read, write, and add at an early age; they also received the foundations of an education in music, crafts—Miss Thomas herself made the toys for the children—and, most important of all, in "attitude to life." At "Stocky Wood," to which the school's name was shortened in the inevitable Liverpudlian abbreviation, Paul and Michael, who joined his brother at school when he was nearly five, watched their first film together, a black-and-white Dick Barton movie, based on a character whose serialized radio adventures already had established the detective as a firm favorite with the boys. It was then, with some bewilderment, that midway through the movie Mike observed his brother fleeing the auditorium in terror. Not that Michael in any way considered Paul to be spineless; on several occasions he had already given the measure of his mettle in the school playground, defending his younger brother with his fists from school bullies.

Seemingly precocious—or adventurous—beyond their years, it was during their last summer in the Infants School at Stocky Wood that Paul and Mike discovered for the first of many times the delights of "sagging off school," as playing truant is known on Merseyside. Cutting through the grounds of Speke Hall, the pair would head for the banks of the Mersey where, stripping off their clothes, they would plunge into the river's waters (unpolluted that far inland from the docks) and, like some Liverpudlian variant on Mark Twain characters, happily swim the day away.

With a socialist government in power, the late forties brought a period of sweeping social change in Britain. But such legislated shifts in the country's makeup as universal free health care existed alongside such more primally rooted developments as the baby boom around the end of World War II.

By 1949, the Junior School at Stockton Wood had to cope with teaching over a thousand children, too many even for such an exemplary establishment. (By 1953 it was the biggest children's school in Britain.) Consequently, at the end of August 1950, Paul and Michael McCartney joined the two hundred or so other children from around Speke in the great adventure of a half-hour ride by specially chartered buses each morning to an area known as Gateacre (pronounced *Gatt-ekker*). There they were dropped off at the brand-new Joseph Williams Primary School.

Joseph Williams was the first school to be built in Liverpool after the war ended, and consequently it was of a very high standard. Comprised of four one-story wings that linked to form a rectangle, the school was set in a conservation area that at the time was intended to be a permanent green belt; the only other buildings in the vicinity were prefabs housing people whose homes had been bombed. It was so rural that as Paul and Mike McCartney stood by the bus stop on a summer's day they could hear the warm wind rustling through the corn. And the local farmer, a Mr. Rimmer, once stormed into Joseph Williams to see the headmaster, one John Gore, with the threat that he would shoot any of the school's pupils who wandered through his wheat fields; these city children were unable to distinguish between what was and what was not valuable in the countryside.

This model educational institute also had a model headmaster. A cultured, well-read history graduate, Gore was intensely committed and an ardent proponent of primary education. The school's relationship with the local farmer somewhat restored, classes of children would be taken into the surrounding countryside for work on local studies.

Appreciating this, Jim McCartney brought home to 12 Ardwick Road—to which the health authorities had recently moved the McCartneys from their place just around the corner in Western Avenue—an empty beer barrel, which he lodged in a hole in the garden. His sons filled it with assorted weeds, water lilies, and eggs. At first the boys would diligently inspect their pond to see whether the frog spawn had turned into either tadpoles or, even better, frogs. Soon, however, other distractions grabbed their attention. It was only when another "Joey Williams" pupil told them how many frogs *he* had that the pair remembered to check on those in their own garden. By then the spawn not only had become tadpoles, but the resulting frogs had escaped. Vowing revenge at such disloyalty, Paul, Michael, and their dog Prince went down to a nearby stream on the weekend and, in an act of cruelty reminiscent of Paul's ripping the lace curtains, hung all the frogs they could find on a nearby barbed-wire fence.

The bad karma the boys set in motion for themselves swiftly came back upon them. On the way home the pair passed an apple orchard, into which they jumped. Busy filling their pockets with fruit, the brothers failed to notice the arrival of a pair of farm laborers. Michael managed to flee. But Paul, who was known as "Fatty" during this period, got stuck at the top of the orchard gate, where he was captured and one of his arms shoved up behind his back until Michael agreed to return. Both were then locked in a barn until Jim McCartney was sent for, and threats of calling the police were forgotten.

Such boyish mischief was commonplace. Once when the boys were over at Auntie Jin's Huyton home, the police actually did become involved as a result of a prank perpetrated by the pair. Ever eager for fresh information, the two brothers experimented to see whether gas from a can in their Uncle Harry's garage would actually burn up the garage wall. The flames were scorching the top of the bricks and beginning to lick along the tarpaulin roof when a member of the local constabulary passed by on his bicycle. Smacked behinds resulted.

The image Paul presented at Joseph Williams hardly suggested someone likely to be involved in such pranks. Both brothers were always immaculately dressed in regulation school black blazers, with their ties neatly knotted. "Paul had a habit," remembers Muriel Ward, his headmistress at the school, "whilst waiting to go into the hall for assembly, of leaning against the wall and gazing upwards at the teachers passing by with his eyebrows raised up above his neatly trimmed fringe. He would always make people laugh. Paul was very vivacious, really much more lively than his younger brother, who was far quieter: Paul had darker hair, darker eyes, and was certainly vividly distinguishable. But each day of my life I would see children who were equally beautiful."

All the same, Muriel Ward never had any doubt that, in the jargon of the time, "he was an eleven-plus," referring to the examination taken at that age that determined whether a child would go to a school that would push him toward high professional or academic attainment, or one of more modest ambitions. Around a quarter of those children taking the exam would pass. In 1953, however, only four of the ninety boys who sat the eleven-plus at Joseph Williams received sufficiently high marks to be awarded places at the city's top boys' school, the Liverpool Institute—and one of those was Paul McCartney.

In the fifties, the Liverpool Institute was an academic force to be reckoned with, one of a handful of select Northern England grammar schools that offered largely free (in the case of Liverpool Institute, entirely free to all pupils) education of a classical, liberally academic sort that rivaled that provided by the great private schools like Eton, Harrow, and Winchester. (In fact, Liverpool Institute regularly was the top British free state school in terms of Oxford and Cambridge scholarships: in 1957, nine Cambridge open scholarships in mathematics were won by the school, a figure that has never been equaled by any other British school.)

Until 1944, the Institute, which had opened in 1837, *had* been a fee-paying school. As a consequence, certain "public school" attitudes remained, not the least of which was a sense of superiority to less fortunate contemporaries. The school bestowed on its pupils a sense of their own importance; all the same, it drew its thousand pupils from all over the city and from all social classes. And though its headmaster, J. P. Edwards, was something of a martinet, his draconian regime was counterpointed by a lackadaisical, laissez-faire ambience that arose from nowhere else but the very nature of the school itself.

It was by no means a neighborhood school, like the self-consciously "posh" Quarrybank Grammar in Woolton. It was, in fact, the largest school in Liverpool. Situated on the edge of the city center in Mount Street, the Institute was a broad-shouldered, stone building highlighted by the Greek facade of its stone-stepped entrance. That, however, was for the sole use of "sixth formers" (or high-school seniors): younger pupils were permitted to enter their school only by the side gates.

Adjacent to the Institute was its sister school, Blackburn House, with whom any association was actively discouraged by the staff of both establishments. Not that this overly concerned the boys from the Institute: immediately opposite the bottom gate of their schoolyard was the Sheila Elliott School of Dance and Drama, a convenient situation for the more sexually precocious boys, who would devote their lunchtimes to loitering by the gate and waving and calling to the Sheila Elliott girls, considered greater prizes than those from Blackburn House. Adjoining the Institute, meanwhile, was a center of learning that contained females of such glowingly mysterious legend that only the most self-possessed and sophisticated of the Institute's pupils would attempt to pick them up: this was the Art College, once controlled by the same board of governors as the Institute, and linked physically to the school by a small interior courtyard.

Briskly attired in the school's uniform of blazer, cap, white shirt, tie, shorts, socks, and highly polished black shoes, Paul McCartney joined the ranks of the Institute in September 1953, three months after his eleventh birthday. He quickly fit in, his natural charm assisting him. If he created any impression at all on his teachers, it was that of his very ordinariness: he was also considered polite, quiet, and—most important—*helpful*. This last

28

quality seems to have led to his consistently being voted "head boy" by his thirty or so classmates. "This gives you a measure of his character," says his English master, Alan "Dusty" Durband. "He was always respected by the other boys. I don't remember him playing the fool; he was a well-behaved sort of fellow. But I think he was privately what he became publicly—the person always ready with a witty comment: he would make all his mates and peers collapse with laughter at the *sotto voce* remark, rather than the public one. It was very much the Liverpool wit: he would be very much like a joker would be, making a nuisance of himself on the front row. He was hardly a withdrawn figure."

His function as class head boy included taking the register (or roll call) at the beginning of morning and afternoon classes, fetching piles of fresh textbooks, and delivering notes to the staff common room. "He was responsible for organizing the class," Durband explains, "but never in any bootlicking way—he was just a good executive."

A further mark of distinction was that in a school that still adhered to old world values, the still chubby Paul was one of the very few pupils referred to by the other boys throughout his school career by his Christian name.

Alan Durband, a scholar who was a disciple of the iconoclastic Cambridge professor, F. R. Leavis, was a gnomelike figure with an all-consuming, idealistic passion for literature and the theater. At one stage he was desperately trying to raise money to save a Liverpool theater from closure. "If I'd got it, I'd give it to you, sir," he remembers a young Paul McCartney promising him. It was Durband, who was Paul's form master for the three years leading up to his taking his O level GCEs, who in 1956 sent a letter around to the other teachers, suggesting tolerance of any sense of strangeness emanating from Paul McCartney. "He'd had a bad break, his mother had died. He did go through a bit of a rough patch then. I think it shattered him a lot; maybe it made him turn to other things, like practicing his guitar and getting away from the school environment, which was very academic. But his mother's death certainly didn't have the effect of making him become noticeably difficult. I vividly remember on the day it

29

happened him coming into the class, in room thirty-two, and going to his desk, which always used to be under a window. He was still very nice, very polite, and always softly spoken: hardly the kind of person you'd expect to become a rave singer."

Also teaching at the Institute was Arthur Evans, who had left Cambridge with a Double First—the highest possible degree—in German. The tyrannical but brilliant and amusing Evans taught German to both Paul and his brother, who, somewhat to the surprise of his teachers at Joseph Williams, followed him to the Institute two years later. Evans's memories of Paul McCartney accord with those of "Dusty" Durband: "Eminently likeable, charming, pleasant . . . Always armed with very ready quips, but not impertinent. Good ability, though I wouldn't say he always put it to the best use, though I suppose that depends on whether you regard academic attainment as important. . . . He did more than enough to get by. I don't think he ever really exerted himself, but I didn't think he needed to—he was very able. Yet if he had pushed himself, he could have done very well indeed academically."

As a complete intellectual, who all the same won the trust of both McCartney boys, it seems something of a paradox that Arthur Evans should have been in charge of the Liverpool Institute scout troop. Perhaps this had something to do with the sense of absurdity, almost an intellectual development of Scouse humor, that seems to have diluted the despotic actions of J. P. Edwards, the headmaster, and pervaded much of the school's due processes.

On arriving at the Institute, the new German teacher was informed by the headmaster on his first day that as the school scoutmaster had left the previous term, he, Arthur Evans, a man who could hardly possibly have been more unsuited, was being appointed his replacement.

This reluctant scoutmaster resolved to cope with his unwanted role by the most expedient manner: fortified by unguents, potions, and balsams to counteract his acute hay fever, Arthur Evans would retire to his tent for the entire ten days of camp, responding to requests for assistance in such matters as tracking down missing boys with the words, "Go away, I don't want to know."

On one occasion in 1957, however, Arthur Evans was obliged to stir himself. Somewhat characteristically attempting to bypass their mother's death by carrying on as though nothing had happened, the McCartney brothers again went to scout camp the year after Mary passed away. This time the tents were to be pitched at Hathersage, in the Derbyshire Peak district, again some sixty miles from Liverpool, though in the opposite direction to the previous year's expedition. Camp was due to run from July 29 until August 7. On the very day that they arrived, the pastoral revelries into which Arthur Evans was gladly lapsing were brusquely interrupted by the sound of crashing wood and shrieks of pain.

A pulley system had been swiftly assembled to haul logs up a cliff for camp fires. At the suggestion of his brother, Michael McCartney tried to see if he could be transported down the cliff face with the same facility as the pile of logs. But when Michael got halfway down, Paul and the other scouts, worried about Michael's speed, attempted to induce a braking effect by tugging on one of the ropes. Unfortunately, they pulled the wrong rope and Mike McCartney plunged down the precipice, smashing into an oak tree at the base of the cliff. His left arm severely fractured in three places, Michael spent the entire scout period and two extra weeks in the Sheffield Infirmary, some ten miles away. Arthur Evans admits that he and many of his colleagues already felt great sorrow and sympathy for the two brothers because of the loss of their mother; Evans had lost his father at a similar age. "That had been the most shattering experience of my life, and one of the most influential. The suddenness of it affects one profoundly. I don't remember any outward show of grief from Paul. But you bottle it up at that age—you're very concerned with your new maturity."

It was with something of a heavy heart, then, that he contacted Jim McCartney to give him the news of this latest calamity. Their father made a considerable impression on Evans: "A very charming, very, *very* concerned man. I liked him very much. He was a very warm, generous, concerned parent. Some of the parents who would visit the camp wouldn't come and speak to me unless I went over and spoke to them first, but that certainly wasn't the case with Mr. McCartney. Certainly he didn't reproach me over Michael's accident."

Paul, meanwhile, adopted what was beginning to become a familiar role: "Paul was a *very* unflappable person. And while he was obviously concerned—I had the impression he and his brother were very, *very* close—he took the situation calmly. After coming to tell me, with a face as white as a sheet, that Mike had fallen down this gorge, he then stayed on. He certainly didn't seem to have considered going home with his father. In fact, he went into Sheffield every day to visit his brother in the hospital."

Arthur Evans's other memories of Paul at camp involve the chilly evenings that would rapidly set in in the high terrain of the Peak district. Around the camp fire, Paul would entertain the rest of the scouts with his guitar. "The instrument was an immensely cheap affair—it can't have cost most than a couple of pounds. But at least he had one. He entertained us with his guitar, his singing, and his very ready wit. And I think some of the songs he sang were of his own making. At such a young age he displayed no qualms about entertaining the whole camp—thirty or forty boys."

Apart from enjoying the exalted position of being able to display his talent in the evenings, Paul McCartney spent his time at the camp in a manner similar to that of his fellow scouts. "The main object of the exercise," recalls Arthur Evans, "seems to have been to spend the time getting yourself as black as possible from the smoke of lighting fires. They had to do their own cooking in groups known as patrols: they would get their own materials and get on with it. There would also be a good deal of outdoor pursuits and instruction, which I would leave to the senior boys, because to this day I am unable to tell one tree—or one knot, come to that—apart from another.

"I think Paul was extremely adept at tying knots, incidentally. He had a very adroit touch. But as with so many things, I don't think he would have taken the tying of knots very seriously."

Perhaps it is surprising that Paul McCartney chose to join the

Scouts at all. A regimented, almost army-like institution, scouting seems antithetical to the free spirit in Paul that had instantly empathized with rock and roll. Equally, however, it can be seen as illustrating what Jack Sweeney, his teacher in the sixth form and a friend of Arthur Evans's, saw as "the conformist rebel" in Paul McCartney, the boy whose rebelliousness was tempered by a sense of comfort that institutions gave him. That Paul and Michael went to camp as usual the year after their mother's death suggests a need to be reassured that the old structures had not all broken down.

That said, however, Arthur Evans confides, "I was never able to regard him as the Baden-Powell ideal: he was very much his own form of Boy Scout. I was not supposed to know they were smoking behind the latrines of the camps. But I always had two blind eyes to that sort of thing.

"I've no idea why he joined: there is no stereotype boy who joins the Scouts. It might have been the attraction of camps, or it could have been because his friends were in it—I think that applies more to Michael, though, who I suspect joined because of Paul. Certainly Paul was always very willing to help and participate. Some of them would skive off if there were less important chores to do. But Paul would muck in with anything at all."

When Michael's cast was removed, it was discovered that his injuries were more serious than suspected: his arm was completely useless, and it required much time and physiotherapy before it could be coaxed back to its normal functions. Thus Michael was unable to use the set of drums that his father had bought for him the previous Christmas, largely as a diversion from mourning. Soon after, Mr. McCartney gave Paul a cheap guitar, and—once Paul discovered that though he was right-handed, he played the guitar left-handed—the brothers struggled together to master their instruments. With Mike's drums lying unused, Paul—with an industriousness that he brought to all musical matters—set about learning and using them himself. Eventually this would be the drum kit for a group called the Quarrymen.

For an English adolescent there was little choice in the form taken by those social functions intended, in an era of ample chasteness, to introduce them to members of the opposite sex. The dances held by youth clubs, or even political parties, in church halls and dingy, unused hotel ballrooms, were watery affairs, with music provided by 78 rpm records of ballroom music, or a three-piece band made up of old men playing drums, sax, and piano. These "live" sounds would alternate for an hour or so at a time with those from the wind-up gramophone.

The main purpose of these events was to assist the smooth, boring transformation of British youth from uniformed school-children to equally uniformed junior adults. There was no in-between stage. Until the fifties the word *teenager* did not exist in England: it was as much an American import as the music that it accompanied—rock and roll.

By late 1955, however, Britain had experienced its first out-break of rock and roll mania, courtesy of a portly, kiss-curled figure named Bill Haley, who would have looked at home playing his guitar in one of those old men's dance band trios. But Haley's record, "Rock Around the Clock," and its various follow-ups, had a revolutionary result everywhere around the world where it was heard, even though it was only a dilution of a style of black American rhythm and blues popular since the forties. Featured in the film *The Blackboard Jungle,* a tale of high-school juvenile delin-quency, the song had a cathartic effect on the young Paul McCart-ney. "I remember watching telly and seeing Bill Haley perform the song and it was the first piece of music that ever sent a tingle up my spine."

Though few were aware of this at the time, the term "rock and roll" was actually a black colloquialism for sexual intercourse. And the man who was to become the principal perpetrator of rock and roll was to make it quite apparent that a decidedly funky attitude was an integral aspect of this new music, so widely de-rided by adults. With his ducktail haircut, sneering grin, and passion for pink and black clothing and equally subversively col-ored Cadillacs, Elvis Presley was the embodiment of the perfect antidote to the gray drabness of the fifties. He and his music represented spirit and vitality and, most of all, hope: it was the fate of this primal, improbably beautiful figure to act as the liberating archetype of his time.

And Paul McCartney was as turned on and transformed by Elvis as any of his contemporaries were. Lying expectantly in bed, listening on a radio earpiece wired up by his father to the ever boosting and fading strains of Radio Luxembourg, the overseas station whose nighttime English-language service played the new rock and roll sounds with an enthusiasm that the strictly establishment BBC would require over a decade to emulate, Paul would feel the shivers run up his spine as the first magical notes of "Heartbreak Hotel" or "Hound Dog" or "All Shook Up" would ring out. Unlike the majority of film critics, Paul also liked Presley's movies, rating highly the star's moody acting talents, so obviously influenced by figures like Montgomery Clift, Marlon Brando, and James Dean. He particularly loved Elvis's performance of "Poor Boy," which Elvis sings on the back of a wagon in *Love Me Tender.*

Laying the foundation for a pattern that was to become familiar over succeeding years, and in which Paul was himself to participate with some success, it did not take long before various British artists attempted their own interpretations of this American music. Perhaps reflecting the differences in the two nations' economies, this English version, whose do-it-yourself nature predated punk by twenty years, utilized a more basic instrumentation and so circumvented the expensive electrical equipment by now widely in use in America. "Skiffle" music (from a southern American term for similarly improvised jazz) was exemplified by the scraping of washboards and the thudding of strings attached to tea-chests and broom handles, thereby simulating the sound of a double bass, that dominated the music. Though skiffle was considered amateurish, its main proponents were often respected veterans of the thriving British jazz and folk scenes. The principal part was played by Lonnie Donegan, a Glaswegian with a stirring nasal vocal whine who had been a banjo player in the revered Chris Barber Jazz Band. Now, in his new incarnation as number-one skiffle idol, Donegan was an inspirational figure to hordes of schoolboys whose vision of their personal futures was suddenly transformed.

When Donegan played the Liverpool Empire in 1956, Paul McCartney was in the audience. An equally formative experience, however, had taken place during his school lunchtime, when he had gone to the theater to try and catch a glimpse of the star. There he saw Donegan, who was running late, scribble notes of explanation to the employers of the factory girls who were hanging around for him, remaining there long beyond the end of their "dinner hour." The commendable, and rare, consideration that Donegan showed toward his fans struck Paul as the right way for stars to behave.

As his fondness for rock and roll mushroomed, so Paul immediately took up the music's external trappings. Plastering his hair with pomade, he had quickly trained it to sweep into a Presley-like quiff and at least some semblance of a ducktail, or "DA" (an abbreviation of "duck's ass"). His clothing also underwent a metamorphosis. In his regulation school uniform, Paul maintained his pristine appearance, his new hairstyle being the only visible evidence of his new affection. Outside the Institute, however, Paul took to wearing the uniform of a Teddy Boy.

The "Ted" 's style was characterized by clothes whose inspiration came from Edwardian (hence "Teddy") dandies and from that frock-coated style of dress affected by riverboat gamblers in Hollywood Westerns. To many British adults, the term "Teddy Boy" was absolutely synonymous with juvenile delinquent. Such a fear was not completely the product of paranoia: inspired by films like *The Blackboard Jungle* and *The Girl Can't Help It*, many Teddy Boys had taken to gathering in street gangs, carrying switchblade knives and "coshes" (a weighted weapon similar to a blackjack), and—by those with a truly artistic understanding of violence—adorning the insides of their pencil-thin lapels with a collection of fishhooks, in order to rip to shreds the fingers of any dance-hall assailant who might attempt to seize them.

Among many working-class—and even middle-class—youths, a brief career as a Teddy Boy was the only desirable way of filling in the years between leaving school at fifteen and entering the army for two years' compulsory national service at the age of eighteen. (This system was abolished in November 1960, by an Act of Parliament, thus making the various members of the Beatles among the very first British male teenagers to escape conscription.)

When Paul began coming home from shopping trips to Liverpool city center with long, padded-shouldered, white-speckled sports jackets and American-styled, brightly colored shirts, Jim McCartney began to fear that it was as a young street-corner thug that Paul might work out his sorrow over his mother's death. He would pay for him to go to the barber's, and Paul would return looking exactly as he'd set off. And those pairs of black trousers that he would purchase for his son: he knew they weren't *that* tight. Now, however, they looked no different than those drainpipe things that all the Teddy Boys wore. What Jim didn't know was that the trousers *had* been wider—at least until Paul took them to a tailor, where he had the legs narrowed an inch each week.

All the same, Jim, who was struggling to be both mother and father, began to fear for the consequences of having bought Paul that guitar. And the racket he was beginning to make at all hours of the day and night strumming away on it. ". . . But what can I do?" he'd ask his next-door neighbor, Thomas Gaule. "The boys have lost their mother: they've got to have *something.*"

With a friend from the Institute, Ian James, who lived in the Dingle, a tough area of back-to-back near-slums that was the heart of Teddy Boy territory, Paul would roam the streets in his new gear. For a time in 1957, inspired by the hit song "White Sport Coat (and a Pink Carnation)," they wore identical speckled white jackets and black "drainies," and would visit the various fairground sites around the city, gleefully absorbing the way that rock and roll records never sounded better than when blared out by the high-powered, crackling speakers of the various rides. Attempting to pick up girls, with generally dismal results, was another fairground pastime.

In fact, Paul was somewhat obsessed by girls. His first girlfriend was a girl called Val, who he would see every day on the bus to school. Suprisingly for the ebullient Paul, he was so enamored of her that he didn't have the confidence to talk to her, until he heard the word that she liked him, too. After a few visits to the cinema, however, this first romance fizzled out. From then on Paul claimed to have been interested in girls as long as he could remember, and that he had first "got it" when he was fifteen. "It" was "got" at the house of the girl in question—she had been involved in that traditional opportunity for sexual experimentation, babysitting. As is the custom of young men, Paul bragged of his conquest to anyone who would listen to him at school the next day.

It was not with Ian James, however, but with another school friend, Ivan Vaughan, that on July 6, 1957, he cycled to the summer fete at Saint Peter's Church in the posh Liverpool suburb of Woolton.

If he had been given an opportunity to really get to know Ivan Vaughan, Jim McCartney would have known not to worry that the direction of Paul's interests in clothes and music would lead to his son becoming a ne'er-do-well. For despite his elaborate, tangled DA and skintight drainies, whose tightness was accentuated even more by his gangling, lanky frame, Ivan Vaughan was also a brilliant classical scholar, a boy who would one day make his mark as an academic. Vaughan was, moreover, "a complete original," in the words of Peter Sissons, an Institute classmate who was himself to later enjoy a most distinguished career as a top anchorman and penetrating interviewer for ITN News.

From a similar council house background and area of Liverpool as Paul, Sissons would often travel in to the Institute on the same bus. His recollections are clear: "Paul stood out as a bright lad, but a cheeky lad. It was much more than just the proverbial Liverpudlian wit, though. I mean, George Harrison," he said of another Institute boy in one of the classes two years behind them, "had the wit, but *not* the brain: George was in one of the lower classes when I was head boy of the Institute—I remember George giving cheek, and my hitting him over the head with a rolled-up newspaper, which the prefects were allowed to do to the cheeky lads in the yard.

"But intellectually Paul was in a completely different world. I've never talked to him about it, but I wouldn't mind betting he might be a little tinged with regret that he missed going on to further education, because he was a phenomenally bright lad. And still is: just so alert and sharp. In fact, whenever I bump into him now it's as if time *has* stood still, because he's just the same guy. He really hasn't become what I would call more *sophisticated* as a result of everything he's experienced. He's still the boy one knew."

But it was Ivan Vaughan who stood out even more to Sissons and, he claims, to the school in general. "He was the only other key figure there at the time who I would have thought would make it as some sort of creative personality. He stood out head and shoulders above everybody."

The dominating feature of Vaughan's life was "an entirely distinctive sense of humor." This, in turn, was influenced by "The Goon Show," the British radio humor program starring Peter Sellers, Spike Milligan, Harry Secombe, and Michael Bentine to which every schoolboy would avidly tune in. But Vaughan's surreal originality extended even beyond that, being, according to Sissons, "some ten or fifteen years ahead of his time."

A fatherless boy, one of the many members of the cast surrounding Paul McCartney who had lost a parent, Vaughan one day painted his name in three-foot-high letters across the front of the house while his mother was out. Another time, he arrived at school with, for no apparent reason, the dull appearance of his regulation black shoes having been altered by a thick, vivid coat of canary yellow paint. Later Vaughan employed a more subtle creativity with regard to his footwear: playing truant for days at a time, he would reappear at the Institute with an explanatory note, in his own carefully disguised handwriting, declaring his absence to have been caused by "shoes gone to the menders"—an absolute masterstroke, for what member of the staff would dare question the undreamt tales of poverty and hardship that lay behind such circumstances?

The one true stroke of japing genius that cemented Vaughan's legend, however, was played as a double-act with the boy onto whose aunt's garden Vaughan's mother's house backed. John Lennon was a true soul brother of Vaughan's in matters of artistic absurdity. Lennon, with his other close friend Pete Shotton, was a pupil at the "posher" Quarrybank Grammar School, not far from his home. The school's inflexible discipline was such, however, that it could only be endured by John by his constantly submitting it to new, more extreme tests.

One morning John Lennon arrived at Quarryback accompanied by Ivan Vaughan, who had abandoned his Liverpool Institute uniform for the day. At morning register, Vaughan was enrolled as a new student. As each class began, Lennon would catch the attention of the teacher, "Sir, new boy here today, sir!" and Vaughan would be issued the appropriate set of textbooks. This masterly experiment could probably have been satisfactorily completed without its principal characters suffering any recriminations. Such was their triumph, however, that at the end of the day, John Lennon and Ivan Vaughan were unable to resist an urge to confess.

Quarrybank's headmaster, however, was a man who had no time whatsoever for the consistently troublesome Lennon. Furious, he phoned the head of the Institute to expose Vaughan's culpability. Fortunately, in a way very typical of the Liverpool Institute, J. P. Edwards, the headmaster, was immediately able to see the humor in this monstrously insolent prank: Vaughan's only punishment was a mild reprimand.

"John Lennon was a highly original character," sums up Peter Sissons. "But in my opinion, much of the outrageousness and unpredictability he displayed later in life came from Ivan Vaughan, and not the other way round."

On that Saturday in July 1957, Ivan Vaughan and Paul McCartney cycled together, Paul on his Raleigh three-speed racing bike, to the annual summer fete at St. Peter's Church. At such events there was always the chance of picking up girls who might be drawn by the rock and roll group that was playing, the Quarrymen, a skiffle outfit led by John Lennon, in which Ivan Vaughan occasionally played the tea-chest bass.

Having witnessed the abilities of his friend McCartney—

Vaughan was one of the very few people at the Institute who referred to Paul by his surname—on the guitar at one of the open days with which the Institute would wind up each term, Vaughan had come to the conclusion he was a character of sufficient weight to meet Lennon, a decision not lightly arrived at. But he knew Paul was "a great fellow." And, as he put it, "I only ever brought along great fellows to meet John."

Peter Sissons has no doubts at all as to exactly how the balance in the relationship between the two Institute boys weighed up. Though Paul's intelligent sense of humor was beyond question, he was by far the most conventional of the pair, his Ted-like appearance notwithstanding. "Ivan was certainly the leader: people followed him around because he was such an outrageous character, such a funny guy to be with, always making quirky jokes, which were never evil or yobbish, but just downright hilarious. So people would follow him around just to be amused."

The Quarrymen were a ramshackle affair, scruffy and amateurish. But because of the dearth of live new sounds and the prospect of those dreary trios of elderly men, they were as acceptable as any of the scores of other similarly shambolic Liverpool skiffle groups. Formed by John Lennon the previous year—after he had persuaded his mother to buy him a second-hand guitar—the group essentially consisted of friends Lennon had brought together at Dovedale Primary School. Later, they had terrorized St. Peter's Sunday School together. At first, John recruited Pete Shotton to play with him, giving him the part of washboard scraper. Then the rest of the gang were brought in: Eric Griffiths on guitar, Rod Davis on banjo, Colin Hanson on drums, and Nigel Whalley and Ivan Vaughan sharing the role of bass player (eventually Len Garry replaced them both).

At first the Quarrymen's repertoire consisted of everything that Lonnie Donegan had recorded—"Rock Island Line" (Donegan's first hit), "Wabash Cannonball," and "Cumberland Gap" were particular favorites. The addition of the current Elvis Presley hit, "Blue Suede Shoes," at John's insistence, pointed the direction in which the Quarrymen were traveling. Although other rock and roll numbers were added, John rarely learned their correct words, instead inventing lyrics as he went along. His knowledge of his guitar was similarly rudimentary: performing onstage, he would attack the strings with a gusto intended to disguise his ineptitude on the instrument and his lack of understanding of it. When, in the middle of a song, a string would break, he would simply hand his guitar to the diligent Rod Davis to fix; when it came to tuning his instrument, John had not the least idea where to begin. All the same, he cut a mean figure onstage, hunched over the microphone and giving his most authentic scowl. That day, July 6, 1957, at St. Peter's Church fete, the scowl was not just theatrical.

John had spent much of the morning in the bathroom and his bedroom at 251 Menlove Avenue, changing and rechanging his clothing, and teasing and tousling his thickly greased hair until it tumbled over his eyes in the requisite loutish manner. The sight of John in his plaid shirt and skintight jeans almost gave his stern Aunt Mimi heart failure. In the frequent absence of his mother, Mimi had been largely responsible for bringing him up. Suddenly she realized that John was turning into a full-fledged Teddy Boy.

After the resulting row, John stormed out of the house to find Pete Shotton. In the tradition of Northern men on a Saturday lunchtime, the pair had given full airing to this problem of John's, as well as musing over more abstract questions of life, over several bottles of ale. Their gaits were still unsteady by the time they arrived at St. Peter's.

The appearance of the Quarrymen was a token concession to the teenage members of the church youth club, to which Lennon and his chums would make infrequent visits, rarely leaving before inciting some disturbance. For the main part, however, the fete, which was blessed by the prayers of the Reverend Maurice Pryce-Jones, was given over to such charitable fund-raising activities as bring-and-buy stalls, competitions for guessing the weights of cakes, and coconut "shies" (narrow stands on which coconuts were balanced, so that wooden balls could be thrown at them). This delicate scenario, suggestive of some gentle, pre-war, English comedy of manners, was shattered by an eruption of uncoor-dinated instrumental sound from the adjacent Scouts field. There, on a makeshift stage, the Quarrymen were thumping into their set.

As they did so, John's Aunt Mimi came striding out of the refreshment tent, a cup of tea in one hand, to see what was causing all the racket. Not only had she not known where John was headed that morning, but Mimi had never heard of the Quarrymen. As his aunt stepped hesitantly toward the group and came into the near-sighted John Lennon's view, he ad-libbed, singing "Uh-oh, Mimi's coming down the path."

These domestic dramas were observed by Paul McCartney, standing by Ivan Vaughan in the shadow of the stage. Paul, as much a perfectionist in his passion for rock and roll as he was in everything else, had immediately spotted the group's musical limitations. Even though he had little against which to measure their ability, he knew the Quarrymen were severely lacking. Yet that friend of Ivan's who was their leader certainly had something going. He looked the part, particularly the way he swayed back and forth behind the microphone, hunching his shoulders, casually glancing about him as though he was sizing up everyone in the audience. (What Paul did not know, of course, was that this performance marked the first time John had attempted to present such an image. Much of the required confidence, moreover, came from the afternoon's beer.) Most impressive of all to Paul, however, was the fact that these schoolboys had actually managed to get a group together: despite the persistent diligence with which Paul approached his instrument, he had not yet found anyone to play with on any long-term basis.

That evening the Quarrymen were scheduled to play another show at the fete, in the church hall. There, as they moved their equipment, Ivan Vaughan introduced Paul McCartney to John. Paul's outward cockiness notwithstanding, the pair obviously had little to say to each other, and Ivan Vaughan briefly wondered if he had miscalculated. But here—as later—it was not Paul's confident air and social abilities that endeared him to John, but far more fundamental, practical attributes: that zealous perfectionism, of which the cheerful garrulousness—with all its insistence on precise, absolute detail—formed only a fraction. When John complained that his histrionic stage act had knocked his guitar out of tune, Paul immediately showed him how simple the solution was, though first he needed to persuade him to forget the banjo-tuning method he had been taught by his mother, which was creating much of his confusion.

Besides showing John that he had the detailed practical knowledge of an adept, Paul also impressed him with just how hip his musical taste was. He wrote down for John the lyrics to "Twenty Flight Rock" by Eddie Cochran, considered the quintessential rock and roller by the music's true cognoscenti; then Paul compounded the effect by writing down all the words to Gene Vincent's "Be-Bop-A-Lula." Encouraged by Lennon's interest, Paul pulled up a chair and, resting one foot on it, picked up John's guitar and casually ran through a repertoire of the very choicest rock and roll songs, both popular and obscure. As he played, his natural cockiness re-emerged; unconsciously his body loosely twitched and shook as the rhythms of the various songs took over.

Seven years later, in the introduction to John's book, *In His Own Write*, Paul described this first meeting at Woolton village fete: "I was a fat schoolboy and, as he leaned an arm on my shoulder, I realized that he was drunk. We were twelve then (sic) but in spite of his sideboards we went on to become teenage pals. Aunt Mimi, who had looked after him since he was so high, used to tell me he was much cleverer than he pretended."

John Lennon was extremely impressed with Paul. In fact, for once he was relatively speechless, a state he would later attribute to the quantity of beer he had consumed. In Paul he had immediately detected somebody who *understood*. Though the Quarrymen, particularly Pete Shotton, were close friends, rock and roll did not affect their lives with the same all-consuming passion that it did John's. John had even had to endure battles of ideology with Rod Davis, who wanted the Quarrymen's material to be restricted to the purist folk end of skiffle.

John even thought that Paul looked a bit like Elvis. Still, John had been top dog in the Quarrymen up until then. If he offered Paul a place in the group, he might face the threat of a more skilled rival. In the end, however—and after it had also crossed his mind that maybe Paul was too skilled to *want* to play with them—John decided to ask Paul to join. He was obviously so good that he just couldn't afford not to have him in the group.

A week later Paul rode on his bike up through the golf course that separated his home off Mather Avenue from Menlove Avenue to Ivan Vaughan's house. On the way back across the fairways he ran into Pete Shotton. They'd been talking about him, Pete told Paul. Did he want to join the group? Okay, he said, that sounds all right.

Not long after, one of those inexplicable incidents occurred that, in retrospect, can be seen as the prescient power of the subconscious ensuring that destinies are fulfilled. At a Saturday night party in Smithdown Lane, when all concerned had consumed a skinful of booze, John Lennon laughingly turned to his blood brother, Pete Shotton, and casually crashed his washboard over his head. Shotton, who really had no musical aspirations anyway, no longer had an instrument with which he could play in the Quarrymen. Moreover, both boys had left school, the scene of their most outrageous joint schemes, that same month that Paul had come along to Woolton fete. This smashing of the washboard seems both a symbolic and very literal break with the past.

Paul's love for his guitar occupied his every waking moment. He would even dream about it at night, and as a matter of course would take it into the bathroom with him to strum as he sat on the toilet.

Once he had adjusted to playing left-handed, he quickly mastered the instrument. With his usual assiduous attention to detail, all the available Play-in-a-Day handbooks, instantly published to capitalize on the skiffle boom, had been avidly absorbed. Yet he had not joined any of the dozens of usually extraordinarily amateurish groups that were proliferating in the schools and youth clubs of Liverpool. Again, Paul had been looking for the *right* musicians to play with. He did not suffer from stage fright or any nervousness about performing in public. At school, indeed, he had already surprised "Dusty" Durband with the ardor with which he had sought a leading part in the school play at the Institute. Each year Durband would direct the school play. One year he put on George Bernard Shaw's *Saint Joan.* "Now I would never have dreamt that Paul aspired to act, or wanted keenly to be in the play. But along for auditions came all the star people who acted in various school activities and house plays, and Paul turned up and auditioned for the part of the Earl of Warwick.

"But I didn't give him a speaking part: all he got was a non-speaking role in the last act of the play, as a monk. And he turned out to be a perfect pest. It's a big scene, with a lot of characters in it, about thirty people, and you rehearse after school until maybe eight in the evening, and everyone has to wait for their parts. And Paul was an absolute nuisance with his *sotto voce* remarks, and I had to tear a strip off him for being impatient and having a good time, which was what I would have been doing had I been his age." When the play was performed, in fact, all that was visible of this plague of the rehearsals was that still youthfully angelic face, gazing with numinous awe from the cowl.

Years later, Roy Corlett, a classmate who became a successful journalist, revealed to "Dusty" Durband the full extent of Paul's misery. "Did you ever realize how upset Paul was that he didn't get the part of Warwick? He'd told me that you'd tried several people reading for it, but you'd given it to Peter Sissons."

"I would never have guessed," admits Durband, "that he was the kind of person who cared that much about acting. But he obviously did. Yet he just didn't have the talent—he was very quiet in his speech. Peter Sissons, meanwhile, had a huge booming voice, already very much the projected personality of the newscaster. But Paul was talking down in his throat, swallowing his words, as he still does very much when he's onstage."

Before he and the Quarrymen could start to tread the rock and roll boards, however, Paul went to that Scout camp at Hathersage where Michael suffered his painful accident. His brother was discharged from the hospital just in time to enjoy the holiday booked for them by their father at Butlin's Holiday Camp at Filey, in Yorkshire, some 125 miles from Liverpool on the opposite coast. Peculiarly British, and determinedly downmarket institutions, Butlin's Holiday Camps in the fifties offered such a wide selection of facilities that the McCartneys hardly needed to step outside of its precincts.

While there, Paul performed in front of an audience for the first time as a musician. Before Mike's accident, the two brothers had practiced an Everly Brothers imitation, with the duo's recent hit "Bye Bye Love" as the featured number. Paul was developing a great affection for the soft yet simultaneously strident songs of the Everlys and of Buddy Holly. At Butlin's, *The People*, a British Sunday newspaper, was holding a talent contest in the camp's Gaiety Theatre. Unbeknownst to Mike, Paul entered both of them as contestants, a scheme Mike only learned of after the show's emcee urged him to step up onto the stage. Together, the McCartney Brothers performed "Bye Bye Love" and "Long Tall Sally," but did not win the £5,000 prize.

Back home in Liverpool, Paul reacquainted himself with John Lennon. His first show with the Quarrymen was at a Conservative Club dance. Afterward, while fooling around on his guitar, he played John a song he had written himself entitled "I Lost My Little Girl." John was astonished: Paul was Ivan Vaughan's best find yet. Though he had managed to form his own group, it had not occurred to John that it was possible, even permissible, to write your own songs.

From then on, the pair spent all their time together, swapping musical knowledge. Paul showed John all the guitar chords he had learned, but as Paul played left-handed guitar, John would have to go to the mirror in his bedroom and relearn them. Their relationship, however, was not one-sided: as much as John was inspired to progress by Paul's unswerving diligence, so the younger boy was equally liberated by John's anarchic approach to music. "I went off in a completely new direction from then on. Once I got to know John, it all changed," admitted Paul.

With Jim McCartney out at work all day, John would go around on his bike to 20 Forthlin Road. There, eating fried eggs and—perhaps prophetically—smoking Typhoo tea in Jim's pipe, the pair plunged into what were at first exploratory rehearsals that later developed into songwriting sessions. As the early numbers were completed, Paul would note down their chords and lyrics on foolscap paper. At the top of the first sheet, he would proclaim, in the neat, italic handwriting of his, "Another Lennon-McCartney original."

Only a couple of weeks after he had first met Paul, John left school, having taken his GCE O levels the previous month. (Academic attainment in the General Certificate of Education [GCE], which took place each June throughout the country, smoothed the path of successful candidates to future employment and further education. After five years of secondary school, at the age of fifteen or thereabouts, the boys at the Institute would take formal, written examinations in eight or nine subjects in the Ordinary ["O"] level GCE. Two years later, in senior year, they would take Advanced ["A"] level GCEs in three or four subjects.) As he expected, he failed every one of these tests. Aunt Mimi, who had struggled to bring him up properly, was at her wits' end as to what to do with her beloved but increasingly troublesome nephew. And John Lennon was only too aware that in many people's eyes, his life was virtually over, and that he was already condemned to a career as a street-corner lout, with consequences too fearful to even imagine.

Though one might consider Lennon's creativity largely positive, the energies that seethed and thrashed within him had gone largely undirected so far. It was significant, though, that almost the only attempt to channel them had come at John's own volition, when he formed the Quarrymen. Quickly he tried to emulate the same obsessive attitude with which Paul applied himself to music. This co-opting of the younger boy's attitude, which fitted more awkwardly on the less orderly Lennon, had its inspiration in an extremely basic instinct—survival. At the last moment, fate had thrown him a lifeline: Paul McCartney.

And Paul McCartney was not the only source of salvation. During John's last year at Quarrybank a new headmaster, William Pobjoy, replaced the military-like rule of E. R. Taylor, a man who had no sympathy whatsoever with John's persistent questioning of authority and breaking of rules. To Pobjoy's credit, he had perceived a measure of the frustrated, unchanneled talent lurking at the core of John's permanent indiscipline, a perception that had been magnified when he noticed the boy's new addiction to music and the willingness with which he would proffer the free services of the Quarrymen for school dances.

In mid-fifties Britain there was one form of educational institution that did accept, and sometimes even encouraged, unorthodox and rebellious behavior—the art school. In provincial Britain, such colleges were spoken of by the man in the street in awed whispers that hinted that the goings-on in them might be on a par with those in Dracula's castle. In reality, though they were not averse to their students developing a certain lateral view of life, at least a relatively structured, disciplined education was offered. Moreover, a good portfolio of work could substitute as an entry requirement for O level passes.

As a good headmaster then, William Pobjoy contacted Aunt Mimi. At their subsequent meeting, he informed her that there might be a warranted place of refuge for John at Liverpool Art College, where he would be able to develop his very raw, but undoubtedly unique talents. And after appropriate interviews and encouraging letters of reference had been dispensed, John Lennon found himself in the middle of September 1957 set to start at Liverpool Art College, just a courtyard away from where Paul McCartney was about to begin his own O level year at the Liverpool Institute.

CHAPTER FIVE

By failing all his O levels, John Lennon had demonstrated his complete inability to size up and work within the academic system. In marked contrast, Paul McCartney was able to demonstrate his superiority even in that. Though nearly two years younger than John, Paul was only one class below. Moreover, he had taken two of his O levels a year early. This should not, however, be taken as evidence of his extraordinary intelligence; boys in the top percentiles like Paul would automatically take O levels after four, rather than five, years. And if they were the very brightest of the school's pupils, they would take all their subjects while still in the fourth form. The fact that Paul only took two of them, Spanish and Latin, shows that it had already been decided, perhaps by himself, to take the easier route of a further year over his O level GCEs.

In fact, of the two subjects he did take, Paul only passed Spanish. That satisfactory result, in a course that was very much a sweatshop, can be attributed to his female Spanish teacher, who adopted a rather curious technique with her charges. "You are all my bunnies, you are all my rabbits," she would tell them. And as these bearded, raunchy youths of fifteen and sixteen pranced and bounced about the room on all fours, perpetrating all kinds of criminal enormities behind her back, they would recite the rules and declensions of Spanish grammar. As a result of this somewhat unorthodox method, most would pass their GCE exam.

During the year of his O levels proper, the time Paul was spending on his guitar and with John Lennon and the Quarrymen began to monopolize the hours he should have spent on his studies. He utilized to its maximum his natural facility for penning essays and answering set questions on the bus on the way to school. This talent, which drew envy from his less skilled contemporaries, grew as a response to the somewhat inverted social requirements of living in public housing. Had Paul confessed to the other, less academically blessed boys in his neighborhood that he was not joining them because he had to stay in and do his homework, he'd have suffered social ostracism and, at worst, beating.

Now, however, this skill stood him in good stead: by focusing his concentration he would produce fluid, though often glib, answers. From time to time, he overplayed his hand. "Dusty" Durband recalls giving Paul a homework project to research on the works of Steven Leacock. Paul responded by giving the class an obviously off-the-cuff dissertation on the logo of Bodley Head, Leacock's publishers. (Later this was to become something of an in-joke for Paul McCartney: when asked by interviewers his favorite author, he would respond with whichever writer impressed him at the time; when asked for his favorite work by them, however, he would invariably reply, his face utterly deadpan, "The Bodley Head.")

Despite his devotion to rock and roll, Paul's progress with the Quarrymen did not always compensate for the slipping standards of his schoolwork. Moreover, some dissension among the other musicians toward the new member was evident. And most of this was initiated by Paul himself. His Northern financial canniness getting the best of him, he would complain to deaf ears that Nigel Whalley's position as manager was not sufficiently exalted for him to receive an equal share of their meager gig fees. Colin Hanton, the drummer, came in for particular criticism: his playing was never up to Paul's demanding standards. Gradually it dawned on Colin that the others only tolerated him because they needed his drum kit.

Despite Paul's criticisms of him, Whalley continued to secure bookings for the Quarrymen. St. Peter's church hall became a frequent venue, as did St. Barnabas on Penny Lane, where Paul had once sung in the church choir. They also began to play regularly at Wilson Hall in Garston, a dockside area with a tough reputation. One night at that venue, the group was horrified when an enormous Ted stepped out of the audience and onto the stage. But all he wanted was to ask Paul to do his by now reasonably renowned Little Richard impersonation.

By this time Nigel Whalley had become a trainee golf professional. At the Lee Park course where he worked, Nigel became acquainted with a player whose son, he told him, was the owner of a jazz club in the city center. Late in 1957 Nigel secured a booking there for the Quarrymen.

As soon as the group hit the stage, they burst into their usual medley of Little Richard and Elvis numbers, only to receive a written request from the club's management: it demanded that they cut out "the bloody rock." The club, in the the damp cellar of a warehouse in Mathew Street, was called The Cavern. It did not immediately welcome the return of Paul McCartney and John Lennon and their fellow musicians.

*   *   *

The Cavern was not the only new musical venue in Liverpool. In a suburb of Liverpool called Old Swan, on a road called West Oakhill Park, the cellar of a large suburban house was being painted all in black, colored light bulbs were being installed, and a small stage was being built.

The Morgue, as it was to be known, was the brainchild of the leader of another Liverpool group. As Alan Caldwell, he had led the Alan Caldwell Skiffle Group. But with skiffle on the wane, Alan became Rory Storm, eventually changing his name legally. Despite a ferocious stutter offstage, he was a live performer of formidable reputation: Rory, when playing New Brighton open-air baths with his group, the Hurricanes, would conclude their set by climbing up to the uppermost diving board, stripping off his clothes and, as the last notes pealed out down the coast, diving headfirst into the water.

When she was twelve, his sister Iris was the girlfriend of a thin, shy boy from Liverpool Institute named George Harrison. With his friend Arthur Kelly, who escorted Iris's best friend, George was a frequent visitor to the Caldwell home in West Oakhill Park, and the pair were dubbed, for reasons no one can now remember, Arthur and Murthur.

Other than Iris, a major reason for George's persistent visits to the Caldwell home was his chance to demonstrate his growing expertise on his guitar. His mother, Louise, had bought it for him at considerable sacrifice after she had noticed how drawings of such instruments filled every available space on the covers of George's notebooks. The tune that George regularly would perform for the Caldwell household was called "Those Wedding Bells Are Breaking Up That Old Gang of Mine." But it failed to have the desired effect—to gain him a place in Rory's group. "Go away, son," Rory would say, laughingly dismissing George's nervous requests, "you're much too young."

At the Institute, however, George had developed a musical camaraderie with a boy two years ahead of him—Paul McCartney. Ordinarily, such an age gap would have been prohibitive, but in matters of rock and roll it often seemed to have no importance.

Musicians of ability were so few and far between that age was not a serious consideration when forming a group. The pair had been brought up close to each other on the Speke estate and would travel together to school on the same bus. George's father was himself a bus driver for the Liverpool Corporation, and one day when Paul had been short his fare, George's mum, a warmhearted, joking woman, had given him the few pennies he needed.

George Harrison was not held in particularly high regard at Liverpool Institute. Always in one of the lower streams, George revealed himself a true Teddy Boy when he was barely into his teens. His lime-green waistcoat and folds and furls of pomaded hair were reminders to those academic staff members of how far the school had sunk: Harrison was downright *common*.

More sympathetic teachers, like Arthur Evans, overlooked George's outlandish dress and style. No doubt both were expressions of George's need to assert himself, a result of his being the youngest child in a family of three brothers and one sister. "Harrison was the greatest surprise to me of all during the Beatles' meteoric rise to fame," admits Arthur Evans. "My memory of him was of a very quiet, if not even introverted little boy who would sit in the farthest corner and never say a word, or even look up. I'm not saying he was unintelligent, but you were always aware of the presence of both Paul and Michael in the classroom. But Harrison hardly ever spoke. And I noticed that when they reached the pinnacle of their fame, he always stood about a foot behind the others. Which was in character with what appeared to be a rather retiring little boy. Obviously one doesn't know what friendships there are among schoolboys. But I was not aware that Paul and Harrison knew each other at all."

Months before he had met John Lennon, in fact, Paul had determinedly renewed the friendship with George that had lapsed somewhat after Paul had moved from Speke to Forthlin Road. When the younger boy told Paul he had a guitar manual that he couldn't figure out, Paul pedaled over to Speke one evening. Together they managed to make some sense of its instructions and, learning a couple of chords, managed to play the song "Don't You Rock Me Daddy-O." Though younger, George did have one over on Paul: already he had played onstage in a group, the Rebels, which he had formed himself, enlisting his brother Peter, Arthur Kelly, and two other boys to play one skiffle date at the Speke British Legion Club.

George's appearance certainly endeared him to Paul: it was proof positive that they shared the same rock and roll attitude. Never without the very latest Ted styles, George was far more brazen than Paul, as probably befitted a boy who had *not* escaped the aimless stretches of the tough Speke estate. Whereas Paul would hide from his father the fact that he had had his trousers narrowed, George altered his himself on his mother's sewing machine when she was out. When Harry Harrison angrily demanded that his son return the trousers to their original width, George would boldly inform him that he had thrown away the spare material.

There was, moreover, something almost breathtakingly stunning about the skill with which George was able to balance his Institute cap at the very back of his head, as though it were somehow hooked onto the elaborate sausage-roll haircut that tumbled out over his forehead from beneath its peak. By so wearing his cap, of course, George managed to turn this supposed symbol of a regulated, correct mind into an object of contemptuous ridicule. Such an image characterized his attitude toward the Institute. Though more sensitive teachers like Arthur Evans may have been content to leave George alone in his own shy world, his introversion was interpreted as a sullen aggression by the more pompous members of the Institute's staff. Something indefinable about the Institute's self-perpetrating love of its own tradition provoked within George profound distaste and discomfort. The blatant manner in which he would swagger silently about the school in his luminous waistcoats and blue suede "winkle-pickers" (pointy-toed shoes) was his own quiet attempt to debunk what he perceived as monstrous presumption.

The political leanings of his father, a union official, helped instill such an attitude in George. Paul, who was slowly developing his own sense of social rights and wrongs, was secretly impressed with George's rebellious stance, which he perceived as a

1. Stockton Wood, Paul's model primary school, a short walk from his parents' home. *(Pictorial Press)* **2.** 20 Forthlin Road, Liverpool, Paul's home from 1955–63. Here he and John Lennon would write songs together on afternoons on which Paul had "sagged off" school. *(Pictorial Press)*

1

2

1

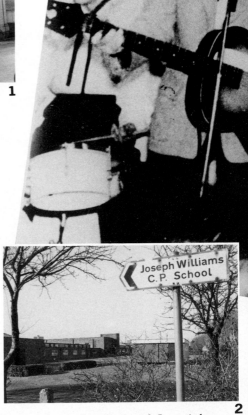

■ **1.** Liverpool Institute, situated next to the art school where John Lennon studied. Paul McCartney empathized with the liberal academic tradition of the "Innie"; unfortunately, he was distracted from his intended career of schoolteacher by a fondness for playing the guitar. *(Pictorial Press)* ■ **2.** Joseph Williams, the "overspill" school to which Paul and Mike McCartney were sent from Stockton Wood. *(Pictorial Press)* ■ **3.** Builders were busy transforming 7 Cavendish Avenue in 1965, before Paul and Jane Asher moved into the house he still owns today. Only a short walk from the Abbey Road recording studios, it was very much a London townhouse, as opposed to the stockbroker-belt mansions bought in the suburbs by the other Beatles. *(Pictorial Press)* ■ **4.** Paul, who had spent hours in the bathroom perfecting and oiling his quiff, in an early line-up of the Quarrymen. *(Pictorial Press)*

2

4

3

1. In December 1961, at Liverpool's Cavern, the Beatles, with Peter Best on drums, play back up to American artist Davey Jones. *(Pictorial Press)*
2. In 1962, with friends. *(Pictorial Press)* **3.** The bass player at one with his instrument. *(Pictorial Press)*

3

■ **1.** Jim McCartney with his already quite successful son in 1964. (*Pictorial Press*) ■ **2.** Characteristically, Paul is the only Beatle waving to the local fans as the Beatles' limousine wends its regal way to the Liverpool premiere of *A Hard Day's Night* in July 1964. (*Pictorial Press*)

1

2

■ 1. Rough boys in Hamburg. *(Pictorial Press)* **■ 2.** While still in Hamburg, the Beatles quickly learned how to complement their new neat haircuts with neat pictures. *(Pictorial Press)*

real rock and roll attitude. But his father's beliefs influenced Paul's bearing. No matter how much he modified his uniform or how many minutes of his morning milk breaks were spent in front of the washroom mirror perfecting his quiff, it was his cheery greetings and friendly smile that his teachers noticed. They resolutely refused to consider Paul a Teddy Boy, and would comment among themselves on how neat and smartly turned out he was; perfect material, they thought, for some provincial teachers training college that, from their conversations with this communicative boy, they had deduced he had set his heart on.

And so it was that that evening late in 1957, Paul took George with him down to Old Swan to the newly opened Morgue, which had been well publicized by word-of-mouth at recent dances. As the sounds of the most exclusive rock and roll and American R & B 45s that Rory Storme had been able to find jostled their way out of a record-player—whose volume was cranked up to maximum in an effort to emulate the awesome force of fairground speakers—Paul introduced George to John, who was standing sipping from one of the bottles of warm Coca-Cola that were on sale ("The Morgue: admission free: soft drinks 9d"). Though John admired the cut of George's trousers, he was hardly enthusiastic about meeting a boy so much younger than himself. "Hello," he grunted with a half-smile, then ignored him, turning to myopically eye a pair of beehived girls jiving together in a dimly lit corner.

There had been a possibility of the Quarrymen playing that night, though arrangements for playing at the Morgue were always loose. All the same, Paul had his guitar with him. When George picked it up and, with his tongue clenched tightly between his teeth, squeezed out the intro notes to "Raunchy," John became less stingy with his attention. "Can you play any more of that?" he demanded. George nodded, and picked out another verse. John was impressed, though he was careful not to show it. Certainly this kid looked good, and his playing seemed better than a lot of the guitarists around Liverpool. But someone of John's age couldn't be seen hanging around with youngsters like that.

Eventually, it was simple expediency that broke down the age

57

barrier between them. For a while, George would turn up at Quarrymen shows and hang around with Paul before and after he played. John maintained his reserve. "Play 'Raunchy' again, will you?" he would often request, however, and George would always oblige. George finally got a foot in the door one day when John and Paul's rehearsal plans got botched by Mimi and Jim McCartney, who would both be staying home. "My mum's out this afternoon; you can use our place," offered George. Suddenly they had a third place to rehearse. Despite supplying rehearsal space, George was still not a full-fledged Quarryman. But he would show up at all their dates, talking to Paul during breaks. "Look, I've learned this new chord," would invariably be his greeting.

From time to time he would be permitted to sit in for a set, usually as the replacement for a missing member. All the same, Eric Griffiths commanded the role of lead guitarist, notwithstanding the occasional solos that Paul would take, notably on "Twenty Flight Rock."

By dint of sheer persistence, however, George Harrison gradually began easing himself in as a regular member of the group that John Lennon and Paul McCartney were now jointly leading. But George's inclusion resulted in a surfeit of guitarists. In the choice between George and Eric Griffiths, there was no contest—it was quite apparent who *looked* the best. Accordingly, one afternoon Paul McCartney, John Lennon, and George Harrison gathered at 20 Forthlin Road to rehearse without Griffiths. Also with them was Colin Hanton, the Quarrymen's drummer whose kit Paul and John had decided they still required. Duplicity had been invoked by this trio, the full extent of whose ambitions was very gradually beginning to unfurl, to persuade Hanton to come over to Forthlin Road for this session—for the drummer was Eric Griffiths's closest friend in the group. In order to secure his services Nigel Whalley had been dispatched to Hanton's home, told of the plot, and sworn not to reveal its details to Griffiths.

While the four were rehearsing at the McCartney home, however, Eric Griffiths phoned. In something like a dress rehearsal for a later, brutal lineup change, none of the three guitarists would accept responsibility for the deed that had to be done. So Colin Hanton was asked to take the call and tell Eric what the score was, as John, Paul, and George tinkered on their guitars in the living room, fixing their gaze on the Chinese pagoda wallpaper. Griffiths was understandably upset, but neither John, Paul, nor George had had the calm of their thoughts disturbed by having to hear his distress: had there been any instructional handbooks written at that time for would-be rock and roll musicians, the three might have realized that this self-deluding desire to employ someone to take the responsibility of their decisions and absolve them from any accrued guilt ideally suited them.

Forthlin Road and George's home in Speke became the best rehearsal sites; at Menlove Avenue, there was often the inhibiting presence of Aunt Mimi. When practicing on his own, John frequently would be banished by Mimi to the front porch to play. And when all the boys were together they had to face the discomfort she would create over their Teddy Boy appearances. It was that Paul McCartney, Mimi was innocently—*loyally!*—certain, who was putting all these silly ideas into John's head. Much of the time, however, John and Paul would still practice without George, spurring each other on. Their production of new songs became prolific: in the first year that they knew each other, they wrote over a hundred. None of these were played on Quarrymen dates, however: they were neither convinced that the songs were good enough, nor that audiences would want to hear anything but tried and tested, familiar rock and roll numbers. Spurred on by Paul's enthusiasm for the Everly Brothers, the pair also practiced their vocal harmonies, Paul's sweet, high voice blending with John's nasal sneer to produce something that, with time, became far more than just a combination of the two.

In their songwriting, a similar balance was evident. While John would work out a rough chord structure, Paul would add the sense of sweet, lingering, somehow archetypal melody that he had inherited from his father and from his own catholic appreciation of music. If Paul's tastes differed from John's, it was only that they were broader: he was just as much a genuine rock and roller as the art-school student, as was attested to by his obsession with that absurd, ultimate rock and roller, Little Richard.

There was a fourth possible location for rehearsals: the house in which John's mother, Julia, lived with her common-law husband, Twitchy. After years of separation, Julia and John had been reunited when he was fifteen. Now they were making up for all that lost time, communicating more like brother and sister than son and mother, and loving each other deeply. The contrast between Julia and her eldest sister, Mimi, could not have been more striking. Whereas Julia was irresponsible, fun-loving, and witty, Mimi was stern, conservative, but also very fair; while Mimi made her feelings about the Quarrymen abundantly clear, Julia loved her son's group. The two sisters fought each other for John's affection, a game that John equally took part in as he manipulated one or both of them; in doing this perhaps he felt he was justified by the decision he had made, at the age of three, to live with his mother and not his wayward father, Freddie, or "Alf," as he later demeaningly referred to him.

Yet he loved his mother so much. One evening, after a rehearsal session at George's house, the endlessly encouraging Mrs. Harrison gave the three boys beans and toast for their tea. As they were sitting eating, the absence of any permanent female presence in Paul's house seemed suddenly to dawn on John. "I don't know how you can sit there and act normal with your mother dead," he said suddenly, turning on Paul. "If anything like that happened to me, I'd go off me head."

Paul simply shrugged his shoulders in reply. And fought, no doubt, to keep from falling into the yawning abyss that opened at his feet every time Mary's death was mentioned.

Was that question that John put to Paul that evening in the Harrison's Speke kitchen triggered by some unavoidable presentiment? For on July 15, 1958, Julia was killed. John had gone to stay with her and Twitchy for the weekend, but Julia still insisted on paying her customary daily visit to Mimi. As she left 251 Menlove Avenue, Julia bumped into Nigel Whalley, who had come around to see if John was in. As ever, Julia had a few new jokes ripe for the telling, and Nigel walked with her on her way to the bus stop. Waving good-bye to her son's friend, Julia made her way across the island between Menlove Avenue's traffic lanes, and Nigel continued along his side of the road.

At the sound of a squeal of brakes, Nigel looked up to see Julia's body thrown high in the air before it crashed down. She died instantly.

John didn't quite go off his head, but he came close. Now for the first time, as he cried himself to sleep at night, John had an inkling of Paul's silently borne pain. And he started to deaden his anguish with alcohol. The death brought the pair, each privy to a secret shared by few of their contemporaries, even closer; inexplicably, the woman they each loved had been taken away from them. But oddly, this helped their music: from now on, an intriguing, mysterious melancholia lay at the back of everything they wrote and played, no matter how lively and uptempo. And Paul knew that someone finally understood his own suffering and loneliness.

At Art College, a new girl named Thelma Pickles enrolled. Early in the new term she began going out with John. "John was really larger-than-life as a human being. You just felt the minute you saw him that he was different, in the way he spoke to people, and in his attitudes to them. At the same time I thought, 'This man is a genius, but he'll end up doing nothing, because he hasn't got the application.' All I could think of him being was a comedian, because he was so incredibly funny. He was talented in many directions. But at the time that I knew him, none of it was channeled. Also, as with many captivating people, there was an edge to him—in his case, an unpleasant edge."

Thelma also met Paul McCartney, who had just started in the sixth form in the adjoining Institute. "He used to come into the Art College during lunch with George, and have lunch in the canteen. It was quite okay for them to come in: the Art College was a wonderfully relaxed and flexible place. Also, the canteen doubled as the hall—it had a stage, and we'd sit on the edge of that as we ate the beans and toast that we used to buy for nine old pence.

"Paul was quite young then, though, and quite quiet—and George was even more so. And they were both overshadowed by John's personality."

As John's girlfriend, however, Thelma was permitted to accompany the Quarrymen to rehearsals, particularly those that took place at Aunt Mimi's. There, on more familiar territory, a different Paul McCartney would emerge. "Paul definitely seemed to me to be the motivator. John could just as easily have gone over to the golf course across the road and gone for a walk, or gone to town. That's not to say he wasn't interested: he was, but I think that if he'd found something more interesting to do at that stage, he could well have deviated away from the group. Dedicated seems too grand a word to describe Paul's attitude, but at least music seemed to be his consuming interest."

At least it surpassed his interest in his schoolwork. Paul had only been able to add three O-level passes to the one he had achieved the previous year. Though his mercurial charm had allowed him to wing it in the classroom, when it came to the examiners, Paul found he couldn't fare any better than any other unprepared student. Significantly, in fact, the subjects he had passed—English language, mathematics, and art—were those for which prepatory study was virtually impossible. That English and math had the highest failure rates spotlights Paul's natural ability, of course. Without passing those subjects it was impossible to get into a university. But by failing to compliment those prestige passes with an array of other successes, Paul had effectively written futher education out of his immediate future.

His four O levels were just enough to allow him to scrape into the sixth form for the final two-year A-level course. The three subjects he chose were art, geography, and English literature, the latter taught by his old mentor "Dusty" Durband. Much later, Paul would speak highly of Durband: "At school we had a great hip English master and instead of keeping us to the drag stuff like

Return of the Native, he would let us read Tennessee Williams, and *Lady Chatterley's Lover,* and *The Miller's Tale."*

All the same, the slipping standards of Paul McCartney's work were quite apparent to "Dusty" Durband, as they were to the school's headmaster. "Now," said Durband, "Paul had been head boy of his class for year after year after year. So when he got into the sixth form, the normal thing for someone like that would have been to become a prefect. At the Institute, prefects were exalted people: they had academic gowns to wear, various privileges, and their own, really quite beautiful, oak-paneled room. But Paul never became a prefect. So he would have been one of the very few in his class—there would be about eight or nine boys doing A-level English—who didn't get to wear a gown. Obviously that was because he was giving all his attention to his guitar, and very little of it to school.

"He was slightly different at the Institute in that he didn't become academic. The 'normal' boy there was someone who'd gone on to Oxford or Cambridge, and he dropped out of that, he wouldn't compete to become an Oxbridge type of person."

Jack Sweeney, a modern-languages teacher who had been a contemporary of Arthur Evans's at Cambridge, was Paul's formmaster in the sixth form. Sweeney, who had himself been educated at the Institute, was of Irish origin. Accordingly, allied to an unerring perception, he possessed a deep-seated sense of humor that consisted largely of an endless stream of feeble puns and cracks, which Paul greatly appreciated.

It is quite clear to Jack Sweeney that Paul McCartney would not have wanted to be a prefect: "I don't think he was blackballed by the powers-that-be. But prefects had to stand around in lunch hours and break, and Paul wouldn't have been around. I'm sure he would have relished being a prefect, as long as it was purely honorary. He was never a prefect, not because he was damned by the authorities as a dissident, but because it was a huge sixth form of about two hundred fifty boys, and the competition was intense.

"Now George Harrison would not have wanted to be a prefect, because he was *agin* everything. But Paul was very pro the establishment. I think George may have felt lost in this academic environment—he wasn't as clever as Paul. But Paul never felt lost: he was very much able, through his own native wit and abilities, to cope with his situation."

Jack Sweeney stresses the almost relentless manner in which Paul McCartney conformed to the Institute's standards and attitudes. This conformity was rare, for the rebelliousness of rock and roll was just one symptom of a new mood sweeping through all of popular culture and the arts. Closer to the academic clime of the Institute was that of literature, and in England in the late fifties this was the time of John Osborne's Angry Young Men and Colin Wilson's *The Outsider*.

Yet Bill Kenwright, an Institute contemporary of Paul's who is today a millionaire theatrical impresario, told Jack Sweeney how, "Paul McCartney lived up the road from us, and we used to go in on the bus together. Now when we meet we always chat about the school. We loved it. The Institute has this incredible family feeling about it."

Jack Sweeney is sure such a feeling must have been important for Paul McCartney. "Because I think he was always insecure. And there was this cozy, family feeling about the school: the refusal to nag, the ineffectual discipline. And yet it got far more effective results than the schools that are run like police states, like John Lennon experienced."

Jack Sweeney is not alone in noting the insecurity and sensitivity behind Paul McCartney's breezy facade. Alan Durband saw it also, and traces its first appearance to around the time of Mary McCartney's death. But perhaps it was also the sense of inadequacy he felt as a boy from a housing project in this academic environment. Whatever his background, a schoolboy trespassing into the adjacent Art College would have been unlikely to put forward a forceful persona. Even without being overshadowed by John Lennon, Paul would have been low-key; he was, after all, in alien territory.

Yet most lunchtimes, with his mac buttoned up to the neck to hide his school tie, he would assiduously traipse through the corridors and courtyard that separated the Institute from the Art

College and meet his musical confrere. Sometimes they would have lunch in the cafeteria. Other times, if John was still flush with the money that Mimi gave him in his first year, and which in his second year came from financial aid, they might adjourn, often accompanied by Ivan Vaughan, to Ye Cracke, a pub one street away from the Institute whose timbered beams and beer garden supplied it with the requisite "atmosphere" for a "student" pub.

Men in the North of England frequently drink vast quantities of beer. Some of this is the result of machismo: Real Men Can Take Their Ale. Yet the more specific explanation of the drinking that goes on in cities like Liverpool is that there is simply nowhere else for people to meet other than in pubs. Whether this was because it was convenient for the British ruling class to have its workers obliterated beyond thought during non-working hours is a question for sociologists. Nonetheless there is a social atmosphere in Northern pubs, which seem dedicated to a thorough erasing of the senses, that contrasts sharply with that of such establishments in the London area.

After Julia's death, Paul frequently found himself greeted in the Art College by a tense and anxious John Lennon. "C'mon, let's get out of here," John would mutter out of the corner of his mouth. "Let's go down the Cracke." And Paul silently would accompany him, the embers of his own pain rekindled by his friend's suffering.

Paul, however, hadn't a head for drink, something he had luckily learned at an early age. In fact, neither did John, but he drank all the same. By the end of the lunch hour he was often well on his way to being drunk, something Paul was prepared to tolerate only because he understood the reason. It meant, however, that valuable rehearsal time was wasted. Paul would often return to school for the afternoon's lessons, rather than sneaking into an unused room in the Art College with John, or jumping on an 86 bus to Forthlin Road. Still, he was absent enough to inspire Jack Sweeney's ironic explanation. "The school was his town club. It was convenient, because it was so central, and there was John next door at the Art College. I sometimes think he came to school as often as he did not through assiduity, but because it was convenient.

"It is no exaggeration that Paul is said to have been held in very high regard at the Institute. He *was*—his sheer charm ensured that. You might have thought that the charm was a self-defense mechanism. But it wasn't: it was absolutely natural, quite extraordinary, and quite irresistible. There is, of course, the legendary Irish charm: I don't know how strong that Irish strain is in the McCartneys, but that could well be an explanation for it.

"And I don't think Paul ever got into disfavor at the school. I would take the register [or roll call] in the mornings, and tell them off if they were bunking off or if they were late. And that was the only thing 'wrong' that Paul really did—and we knew perfectly well that he was sagging off. But nobody really bothered about it once they'd got into the sixth form. He sort of came and went as he pleased. But he was at school more than he wasn't. Compared to modern truancy, he was probably a model pupil: these days his attendance would be considered so exemplary that he would be made head boy. He would have enjoyed the glamour of that position.

"Paul is a very complex person. People feel that it was John who was the complex Beatle. But in the first place, Paul had this extraordinary dualism: at any given moment he could be so easygoing and so casual, yet there was also this toughness: he would hold the class entranced. He was a born leader, so gregarious, so popular.

"And he had this extraordinary faith in his own star. Yet at the same time he had an ironic detachment from what he was doing. In fact, I think the most important thing I have to say about the whole man is that he had that quality: he was able to view it all dispassionately. I think it takes a remarkable man who can do just that. I bumped into him in the city center when the Beatles were enjoying their first success, and I said, 'What's all this about this sudden fame?' And he laughed and replied, 'It's a giggle, isn't it? An absolute giggle.' He was laughing at his own success. And I think this is something that comes from his sheer intelligence, for he was very, very bright. Irony is an elusive gift, and quite rare, particularly when it is so self-deprecating.

"But he could also be as sardonic as John Lennon. I remember this from when he was holding forth in class: he could deliver the sardonic, the *devastating*, comment even at that age. But because he's such a decent bloke, he wouldn't cultivate this, he wouldn't make a thing of it, as John Lennon would. Lennon *loved* hurting people and stirring them up. Paul could do all of that, too. Everything that John said, he could have said. But he didn't.

"And this idea that he was just *nice*. . . . He was *very* complex: yes, he could be so nice, but he was also the most astute of them all—the toughest and the shrewdest, right from the start. There is this absurd oversimplification that it was John, the creative, complicated bloke, and Paul, the easygoing extrovert. No such thing. Paul is both. And a clever man to be able to wear two hats."

On entering the sixth form, all boys were handed sheets of paper on which they wrote down the number and subjects of their GCE O-level passes, their interests, and the career they had chosen. As befits a boy with a keen understanding of what was expected of him, Paul McCartney made no mention whatsoever of his musical interests. This was, after all, an age when guitars were considered unmentionable, and perhaps this information might be drawn upon by teachers writing references. So, using a technique he would develop far more fully later on, Paul simply kept well away from this potentially tricky area, thereby ensuring that it didn't exist. The one school activity he lists is as safe and boring as you could get—the geographical association. And his out-of-school hobbies are listed, in that meticulously formed handwriting, as "Swimming," "Church Youth Club," and—the only surprise—"Modern and Ancient Architecture." The suspicion that this last interest may be something of a mendacious attempt to present a safe, tame picture of James Paul McCartney falls away when we consider the future possible careers that he lists. The obvious one is there: "Teaching—University or Training College." But underneath in parentheses, almost as though an afterthought, he has appended the more ambitious

"(Architect?)"—not perhaps a surprising choice for a boy studying A-level art.

But the other side of Paul McCartney, whose Gemini nature is so evident in all he does, is unable to be suppressed when he provides the final piece of information. The pleasant, rather dull boy that information suggests disappears altogether when asked to list his father's occupation. Though he has subsequently crossed it out most thoroughly in an effort to obliterate what the other side of him has written, Paul McCartney has described Jim's job as "Lead guitarist with Rory 'Shakin' Blackwell." Underneath remains his father's real employment: "Or Cotton Salesman."

"You see there all the ambitions of the academic," claims Jack Sweeney, "all the ambitions of somebody who in fact was following the academic tradition of the Institute. Perhaps those traditions had impinged in some way. And if his fans had heard about it, they probably wouldn't believe it at all."

Yet Paul McCartney was never one of those avid sixth-form culture vultures who would be seen around the school corridors and in the streets and on buses clutching well-read copies of Kafka or Sartre or T. S. Eliot. Instead he helped define his identity by lugging his guitar around with him everywhere: there wasn't time for reading too much else other than his set exam texts. However, photographs of him taken at about this time by his brother show Paul avidly perusing "heavyweight" Sunday newspapers like *The Observer*, wearing a "serious" expression. You can imagine him as one of those young, fresh teachers straight from training college whose appearance and attitude suggest to the elder pupils that they are their peers, but who very quickly decide that the way to maintain their authority is to erect subtle but immovable barriers.

Jack Sweeney feels that, because of the total lack of academic tradition in his background, it was a bold ambition for Paul McCartney to desire to be a teacher. Yet it was also limited and safe, almost too obvious a choice for a boy wishing to better himself; it hardly matched the loftier ambitions he was already beginning to show, even in such matters as his attitude toward the Quarrymen. It does not seem totally believable.

In fact, the suggestion—added apparently almost as an afterthought—that he might also be considering becoming an architect, rings much truer. Not only was architecture a profession with a promise of great financial rewards, but, at a time when Victorian England was beginning to be torn to pieces and replaced with buildings that were considered very much of the twentieth century, the very word *architect* had a resoundingly modern resonance.

Even so, Jack Sweeney remains convinced he would have been a succesful teacher: "He would have been a very imaginative schoolteacher, because he was a born communicator. There was about him this intellectual curiosity: in fact, a curiosity about all things."

Alan Durband, whose intelligence and energy so fired Paul McCartney, is not so certain of his former pupil's intellectual powers. "There were people far more intellectually clever than Paul," he insists, "and I don't think that even if he had pushed himself he would have made it to Oxford or Cambridge: I think teachers' training college was the rank order—but he wouldn't have just gone out and been a clerk."

Durband remembers that after a lesson, Paul wouldn't just pick up his books and walk out, but would linger, discussing theories and possibilities about the plots and characters in their texts. "He wasn't a background but a foreground person. But I suppose he had that slightly flip manner of a non-dedicated person. He wasn't studious, just . . . normal."

Paul's A levels had to be worked in as best they could around the far more involving business of practicing his instrument and rehearsing with John, George, and Colin Hanton, and playing dates as and when they could get them.

In the second year of the sixth form, Alan Durband would make his A-level candidates spend their lessons answering essay questions similar to those in the exam. At the end of the second term, he reviewed their progress in tackling the various set texts: D. H. Lawrence's *Sons and Lovers*, Milton's *Paradise Lost*, Chaucer, a pair of Shakespeare's plays. "I told Paul that he would pass only if he worked. He was middle of the class rather than at the top, but he was by no means a dead ringer to fail."

When he took the exam, in July 1960, Paul McCartney did pass his A-level English literature, though with a low grade. He failed geography, a subject he had not even succeeded in at O level. And as for art, his third subject, he was only awarded the O-level pass that was given like a consolation prize to candidates who didn't achieve sufficiently high marks for an A-level pass but whose work had shown merit. This result, which effectively ended his architect ambitions, could seem rather like a case of damning with faint praise, though that's not truly accurate. For Paul McCartney's artistic abilities were considerable; much of his strength in later years—the natural way in which he could successfully turn his hand to most aspects of the arts—came from the fact that Paul McCartney is as much an artist as John Lennon (who, for what it's worth, didn't even have that O-level pass). But at the Institute, as Arthur Evans explains, "some subjects, largely because they were non-academic, were just not treated seriously: art and music were given very short shrift."

Jack Sweeney expands further: "Paul would have got his A-level art, except for the fact that he had an utterly delightful but entirely ineffectual teacher who was really quite hopeless, and never got anybody through their exam. In fact, for him not to just fail under such a teacher was an extraordinary feat."

If he had done his exam fifteen years later, in a more liberal artistic climate, Paul McCartney might have successfully submitted his own existence as his final-year project—that he was a conceptual artist and was himself a piece of art. Except for wearing his school uniform, he felt at home during those lunchtime expeditions to the Art College. Paul and John had a common, unspoken understanding based on their both being artists; their Teddy Boy clothes were worn with a natural style that transcended street fashion. By now, in fact, perhaps because he had something to prove that John didn't, Paul was designing their group's posters, embellishing with love and pride the letters of the names under which they were now trading their music, the "Quarrymen" having been succeeded for a short time by "Johnny and the Moondogs." Still, their progress was painfully slow. "Each year seemed like five years," Paul remembered years later.

Jim McCartney had been skeptical about Paul's involvement in the group. It was the particular style of music, with all of its connotations of juvenile delinquency, that worried him more than the fact that Paul might choose a career as a musician. Jim McCartney seems to have gleaned no great insights from the derision that had been heaped upon his own musical tastes years before by *his* father, and would deliver equally sardonic assessments of rock and roll to both his sons. Yet secretly, Jim knew he couldn't be prouder if Paul did become a musician, for it stirred up within him all the thrills he'd been forced to forget when he gave up Jim Mac's Jazz Band.

And he realized that it was becoming increasingly likely that this might be Paul's destiny. After at first supplying cautious criticism, Jim McCartney came home one night at 5:30 and heard the three guitarists playing strong new chords. He still couldn't understand why they didn't want to play numbers like "Stairway to Paradise" and "When the Saints Go Marching In"; he could have taught them such good arrangements. From time to time, Jim would even sit in with his son and his friends, playing the piano almost as easily as he had twenty years before.

As time went by, when John Lennon visited 20 Forthlin Road, more and more often he would be accompanied by an attractive blond girl who appeared to be modeling herself—at John's explicit request, in fact—after Brigitte Bardot. Her name was Cynthia Powell, and she was a fellow art student. "We would never fail to receive a warm welcome from Jim," Cynthia remembered. "The warmth I experienced whenever I entered the modest home of this talented family was wonderful. Jim was a father in a million. The cheerful way he coped with a situation that many a man would have run away from was admirable."

Jim, Cynthia recalled, would frequently greet them with a tea towel in one hand and a saucepan in the other, his sleeves neatly rolled up and an apron tied around his waist. "In the kitchen we would be confronted with chaos, a wonderful homely chaos." As they had been spoiled by Mary's splendid cooking, Jim sometimes had trouble satisfying his sons' finicky tastes. John Lennon and George Harrison, however, would wolf down anything that was put in front of them, even the McCartney boys' leftovers. After a while, Jim stopped pretending that the food he often gave them was anything other than leftovers. Years later, George would turn up on the doorstep, requesting some of Jim McCartney's world-beating custard.

Tom Gaule was the McCartneys' next-door neighbor. He had moved into 18 Forthlin Road when the street was first built, two years before the McCartneys. The rent, then £2¾ a week (or about five dollars), was not cheap for a council house but not sufficiently pricey to prevent nearby homeowners from protesting that their property was being devalued by the influx of working-class people.

Tom Gaule remembered Mary's first year at the house, how she and Jim both would leave the house at 8:30 in the morning, and the sudden, nameless sense of hurt that her death brought a year later. At first Jim arranged for the Gaules to give his sons their afternoon meal when they came in from school, settling up for these feasts of egg and chips and other schoolboy favorites at the end of each month. On Tuesdays and Thursdays Auntie Jin and Aunt Milly would turn up and cook the boys their tea, lighting the fire in winter and cleaning the house before they arrived.

When it came to rehearsing music at 20 Forthlin Road, Mike McCartney remembers how Paul would instruct him to hit the drums as Paul walked down the street away from their house: if he couldn't hear it a hundred yards away, the pair deemed it insufficiently offensive. These assessments, however, did not include Tom Gaule. He recalls Paul coming back from school early in the afternoon, accompanied by John Lennon, and the cater-wauling and yowls that would start up shortly afterward, booming through the thin dividing wall into the Gaules' home. "It was a terrific row to our ears in those days—absolutely horrible: I like classical stuff, to be honest."

Their neighbor confirms that, despite his own musical bent, Jim McCartney was not greatly in favor of the sounds either. Although he occasionally sat in on those sessions, he would voice his true feelings to Tom. " 'Oh, this noise!' he used to complain. But he didn't discourage it.

"Quite frankly, if Paul's mother had been alive, there would have been no Beatles as far as Paul was concerned. She'd never have stood for that row. The lady was a real stickler, very much a You-do-as-I-say kind of person. She was the dominant factor next door—there was no nonsense with Mrs. McCartney. She'd never have allowed it, all that argy-bargy. Jim offered to buy her a washing machine once, but she wouldn't have one, because she thought it was somehow immoral. So you can imagine what she'd have thought to that row.

"She brought them up very well: When I first heard Paul talking in that 'wacker' accent, I thought, 'Good God: that's not Paul!' "

Like many of their contemporaries, Paul McCartney, John Lennon, and George Harrison had taken to frequenting one of the new coffee bars that had sprung up in Liverpool. Such establishments were inextricably locked into the new rock and roll culture, particularly since Britain's first rock and roll star, the tame Tommy Steele, had been discovered singing in the the 2 I's coffee bar in London's Soho.

The Jacaranda, in Liverpool's Slater Street, had been started on a family loan of £100 to its proprietor, Allan Williams, a bearded character of Welsh origin. Williams, who was for a time to play a central part in the cast of characters around McCartney, Lennon, and Harrison, was a pugnacious figure whose hustling spirit was lent color by a certain artistic sensibility that rarely developed beyond marshaling the aim of his eye for the main chance.

The "Jac" was situated at the end of a terrace row of shops on the edge of the city center, not far from the Institute and the Art College. Its ground floor contained the coffee bar itself, fitted out in the requisite pseudo–Italian-style plastic leather and plastic marble. Past the hissing and gurgling Gaggia espresso machine was a corridor leading to a steep, narrow flight of stairs that led into a tiny basement room. There, on any evening, to the alien sound of the finely tuned oil drums played by the West Indian steel band of Lord Woodbine, the packed joint would appear to literally heave, as though being jolted by distant earthquake tremors.

73

Despite, or probably because of, the all-pervading atmosphere of sleaze that emerged from behind the Jacaranda's facade of respectability, the coffee bar was favored by teenagers of relatively "respectable" backgrounds, with the Art College students as much a source of customers as the trainee nurses from the nearby Royal Infirmary. The presence of these girls was often at least as much a draw for the teenage males as the antics in the basement.

Sitting with Paul, John, and the ever-silent George, and sipping the coffee that cost five pence or chewing the toast that could be purchased for four pence a slice (an extra penny if it had jam on it), would often be Stuart Sutcliffe, one of John's Art College friends. This friendship had started in the autumn term of 1959, the first one of the new college year, when for much of the time John was bombed on booze, grieving over the death of Julia.

While John was considered by most of his tutors to be the very worst sort of student that the college could have accepted, Sutcliffe was seen as one of its foremost talents. As befitted such a slight, brooding figure (who obviously had spent much time studying the style and mannerisms of James Dean), Sutcliffe refused to work on his practical projects in the Art College. He would work at home instead, he declared, in the tiny basement studio he rented. There he would be visited by Arthur Ballard, his tutor, who regarded Sutcliffe as the most talented student he'd ever come across. Yet at the same time, almost uniquely among his contemporaries on the college staff, he also perceived the worth in John Lennon's absurd cartoons, and went out of his way to gain some insight into John's deliberately difficult behavior. Later, he would admit to another of his students, Bill Harry, that it was partially because he knew of Sutcliffe's and Lennon's friendship that he looked more closely at John's work. He had such respect for Sutcliffe that he knew he wouldn't have chosen to spend his time with someone who had not also got plenty going for himself.

It was this Bill Harry, in fact, who had introduced John to Stuart. The college's first commercial design student, Bill was a prolific reader with a particular fondness for America's new Beat writers and poets like Allen Ginsberg, Lawrence Ferlinghetti, Gregory Corso, and Jack Kerouac, an interest he shared with

Sutcliffe. He was also a keen writer himself. Above all, he was a fanatic about rock and roll, and, perhaps a reflection of his own humble origins, likely to be as ardent a supporter of any local talent as he was of big-time recording stars.

The Quarrymen had had a sporadic career throughout the first nine months of 1959, playing dates at venues like the Wilson Hall and Finch Lane bus depots. On such nights, talent contests would be held, and Paul later remembered how they were invariably beaten by a woman who played the spoons.

With the advent of producer Jack Good's "Oh Boy!" TV show, Britain's first true rock and roll television program, the Quarrymen's act improved. Now they could actually see where the musicians were placing their fingers on their instruments. After carefully studying Cliff Richard's backing group, the Shadows, play the introduction to his hit "Move It," one of the first authentic English rock and roll songs, Paul leapt on his bike and, with his guitar strapped on his back, tore over the golf course to John's house. "I've got it!" he shouted as he opened the front door.

On August 29, 1959, still playing with Ken Brown on rhythm and various drummers, the Quarrymen were the first act to play on opening night of the Casbah, a club whose setup closely resembled the Morgue, the basement teenage night spot that Rory Storm and his sister had had in Old Swan. Run by Mona Best, a sharp-eyed woman of considerable garrulousness and vitality in her middle thirties, the Casbah was based in the cellar of her house —some of which was rented out to paying guests—in Heyman's Green, a lush, leafy road in the village-like suburb of West Derby.

Though an even more unlikely setting for a rock and roll club than that of the Morgue, the Casbah had had a similarly low-key conception. Mona's eldest son, Pete Best, a bright pupil at Liverpool Collegiate, had begun to clear out the vast cellar underneath their house so as to have somewhere to hang out with his friends. Gradually, the idea evolved into something far grander. Ken Brown, from time to time joined by George Harrison, was also playing in a West Derby group, the Les Stewart Quartet, who gigged mainly at workingmen's clubs. Ken and George helped decorate the basement for the first night, for which Ken had promised the Les Stewart Quartet would play. But Les Stewart, annoyed that Ken Brown had missed rehearsal time with his group, refused to perform. George, who was with him during this angry scene, promptly offered to turn up with Paul and John.

On the opening night, the Quarrymen played with Colin Hanton on drums and received an ecstatic reception from a crowd of almost three hundred; Mike McCartney vomited after inadvertently drinking hair lacquer from a bottle marked lemonade in the Bests's private quarters; and Pete Best, who had been considering how best to start a career in show business, resolved to take up the drums.

Over the next two months, the Quarrymen played at the Casbah on numerous occasions. The club, which charged one shilling admission, was a success, and a bouncer was hired to keep out the worst Teds. Then one night Ken Brown was sick, and Mona Best suggested that instead of playing, he should sit upstairs and chat with her ailing mother. Out of fairness, Mona Best gave Ken the same fifteen shillings that the others received. This raised the hackles of Paul, John, and George. Why hadn't the extra money been split between them? The resulting row led to Ken Brown walking out on the other three Quarrymen. Moreover, he got together with Pete Best and his new drum kit and together they formed a new group, the Blackjacks, which took over at the Casbah as resident band.

These Casbah shows were the last ones by the group known as the Quarrymen.

On November 15, 1959, Paul McCartney, John Lennon, and George Harrison auditioned at the Liverpool Empire for a national TV talent contest, "Carroll Levis Discoveries." Playing as Johnny and the Moondogs, they made it through to the next heat, to be held in Manchester, thirty miles away. Whether because of his own nerves or his scrupulous attention to detail, Paul was increasingly critical of Colin Hanton's drumming. On the bus ride to Manchester Paul discovered he hadn't enough money for his return fare. Hearing of his plight, a man getting off the bus handed him a two-shilling piece as he passed by his seat. "I love you!" Paul called out after him.

But that two bob was the most he would make from the Carroll Levis show. The show's winners were chosen by the amount of applause they drew at the end of the evening. Because Johnny and the Moondogs couldn't afford hotel rooms, they had to run for the last train home to Liverpool and so were unable to wait for those crucial bursts of clapping at the end of the program.

By now the three guitarists were playing under a variety of different names. Once they were the Rainbows and all turned up at a party in different colored shirts. Sometimes Paul and John would play together as the Nerk Twins. Tom Gaule watched them set off together to hitchhike to Reading, near London, to stay in the pub run by Paul's Uncle Mike. "I remember seeing the pair of them walking along Forthlin Road, carrying rucksacks and with their guitars in bloody great plastic bags. They just started hitchhiking from the end of the road."

In the eyes of the great British public the stereotypical rock and roller was a subnormal member of society who by some quirk of fate had been snatched from the unvaryingly dead-end future of that lowest underclass from which he must have emerged. As they were all over the world, rock and rollers were in England the butt of crass attempts at humor by second-rate comedians and newspaper commentators.

In fact, George Harrison seemed already to be fulfilling the aimless future hinted at by his weekend and holiday job of butcher's boy; in the summer of 1959, he had left the Institute with no qualifications and been taken on at Blacklers' department store as a trainee electrician. The job he had applied for had been as a window dresser, but as that had been taken, George settled for what was available. Later, when it came to wiring up the group's limited equipment in the least lethal way, George's knowledge was to stand him in good stead.

To many of the Liverpool groups, the Quarrymen, or Johnny and the Moondogs, or whatever they were calling themselves that week, were considered standoffish, distant, and conceited. They were also considered as not very good—"not worth a carrot," in the words of Johnny Hutch, the drummer with the rated Cass and the Casanovas. In a Sunday afternoon jive session, they had supported Hutch's group and been almost laughed offstage for their scruffy appearances and Paul McCartney's high, girlish vocals.

Cass and the Casanovas, in fact, were one of the very few groups who frequented the Jacaranda, in which the inseparable trio of John, Paul, and George could so often be found sitting hunched over a table, sipping not very good espresso coffee and smoking ciggies. Invariably they would be accompanied by Stuart Sutcliffe. The intellectual tone of John and Stu's conversation stimulated Paul, who needed some form of bookish nutrition in lieu of his skipped lessons and the rushed homework. To outsiders, of course, Paul would never confess to still being in school and would attempt to pass himself off as a student at the university.

Rory Storm and the Hurricanes and Gerry Marsden were other musical habitués of the Jac, whose every word Paul and John would surreptitiously attempt to absorb. But the quasi-intellectual atmosphere of the coffee bar kept away many of the local groups. This notwithstanding the cheery atmosphere created by Allan Williams, whose bubbly ebullience and good nature made him popular with his customers. In contrast, his Chinese-born wife, Beryl, was less well-liked. Roy Corlett, a contemporary of Paul's at the Institute, remembers that she "would stand with a scowl on her face, almost disapproving of the fact that Allan spoke to the customers, because her view quite clearly was that she only wanted to get their money."

Joining John, Paul, George, and Stuart in the Jac would often be Bill Harry. Bill's first meeting with Paul had been in the Art College. "Stuart was just starting to play music with John, and they got Paul round from the Institute to rehearse in the 'life room' at the Art College: that was on the top floor, a gigantic room with skylights where they did their modeling. Anyway, John got them together, and they'd be rehearsing in a corner of the life room. To some extent, skiffle was still struggling along, and I remember being in one corner of the life room, playing kazoo with a skiffle group, while they were in another corner, behind the screens, rehearsing."

The material they practiced was of an extraordinarily eclectic nature and gave little hint of the strong rhythm and blues direction that they would soon follow. Included were standards like "Ain't She Sweet," "You Were Meant for Me," "Home," "Moonglow," and "You Are My Sunshine." Though such songs were very much a reflection of Paul's musical background, their presence also debunks the purist, revisionist theory of rock and roll history that states that—certainly in Britain—only absolute fanatics, the lunatic fringe, would listen to one narrow musical style. "Paul, in particular, never felt that if he liked something then he should pretend he didn't," says Iris Caldwell, Rory Storm's sister. "He wouldn't say he liked something if he didn't, or put some sort of music down just because it wasn't what was supposed to be 'in' at the time."

Interspersed among these songs were numbers that Paul had written with John. Some of these were instrumentals, like "Looking Glass," "Catswalk," and "Winston's Walk." Others, with vocals ("composed with the modern audience in mind," as Paul once wrote to a local journalist) had titles like "Thinking of Linking," "Years Roll Along," and "Keep Looking That Way," as well as one of John's titled "The One after 909," and a tune of Paul's called "Love Me Do."

"Paul would come and participate in all the Art College events," says Bill Harry. "For instance, we would have Panto Day every year in which everyone from the Art College and university would collect for charity around the city. Paul, I remember, was always the most pleasant to talk to—very nice and easy to chat to, and he gave off such a pleasant aura all the time. You see, he was less intense that either Stuart or John—with those two you always felt you had to be on your toes. And with George you'd get virtually nothing going on between you. I think George was just extremely shy: he kept in the background so much in those days that he was almost like the Invisible Man. But it was always a nice experience being with Paul.

79

"He was always very helpful to people, he was always like that. You see, his father was a gentleman, the old style of gentleman: so pleasant and very well mannered, and considerate of other people. And he brought Paul and Mike up to be the same way."

Frequently Bill Harry would find Paul in the Jacaranda with a girlfriend, a blond with a pretty, pixielike face, named Dorothy Rhone. Dorothy, or Dot as she was known, "spoke almost in a whisper, blushed frequently, and idolized Paul," according to Cynthia Lennon. She worked in a drugstore in north Liverpool, and the strictness of her parents made it difficult for her to spend as much time with her boyfriend as Cynthia did with John.

Though he was aware of their musical inclinations, Allan Williams, who was also a music promoter, was not aware that Lennon, McCartney, Harrison, and Sutcliffe formally constituted a group. Of them all, he was most impressed by Stuart, knowing of his recent artistic success. At Liverpool's renowned Walker Art Gallery, in the John Moores Exhibition that takes place every two years, a painting of Stuart's had been selected to go on display. Moreover, the work had been bought by the man after whom the exhibition was named, John Moores himself, a man of vast fortune and the city's principal patron of the arts. With the £65 that his painting brought him, Stuart had promptly gone out and purchased a bass guitar.

Though Williams did not know of the sale, he did know of Stuart's immense creative ability. Accordingly, when at the end of 1959, in the kind of move that characterized his imitative abilities, Allan Williams decided to ape London's successful Chelsea Arts Ball by promoting a Liverpool Arts Ball, he enlisted the assistance of Stuart Sutcliffe and his cronies to help paint the requisite floats.

Stuart, assisted by John, Paul, and George, made some striking floats, the most outstanding of which was shaped like a giant guitar. By now Allan Williams was aware of the seriousness of their musical intent. But his comment was one that could be heard echoed by any of the city's more seasoned group members: "I think you would have made better stage designers than musicians." Ever aware of the need to grab every penny, Paul turned the compliment into an attempt at wage negotiation. "They're so bloody good, you ought to pay us a bit extra," he said, trying it out. Later, Paul told Williams that Stuart had been most upset when it came time for the ritual of breaking up the floats.

That Allan Williams should only have a partial awareness that the four were actually a group, and who shortly after agreed to paint the Jacaranda lavatory, was not too surprising. "People in groups didn't mix: they found out who the other musicians were by trial and error," says Bill Harry. "There were hardly any phones. People became managers purely because they had a phone, and maybe a van to drive [the groups] around. Groups would usually travel to gigs by corporation [public] bus."

Early in the spring of 1960, Eddie Cochran and the far more chaotic Gene Vincent, whose crippled leg, bulging eyes, and sweat-drenched face made him closely resemble the rock-and-roll-performer-as-torture-victim, performed at the Liverpool Empire. John, Paul, and George managed to each buy a ticket. And so did Allan Williams, who smelled money. He persuaded the promoter, the all-powerful Larry Parnes, to let him put on another Cochran–Vincent show in Liverpool, at the end of their scheduled tour. And accordingly he booked the 6,000-capacity boxing stadium for April 19.

On April 17, Eddie Cochran was killed when the car carrying him, Gene Vincent, and songwriter Sharon Sheeley, hit a tree on the way back from their date in Bristol. Though Vincent had been injured, his already battered body was deemed fit enough to undergo the Liverpool show. To augment the bill, Allan Williams drew on his only source—local Liverpool groups. John, Paul, and George watched jealously as Rory Storm and the Hurricanes, Gerry and the Pacemakers, Cass and the Casanovas, and Bob Evans and His Five Shillings shared the bill with the legendary Gene Vincent.

After the show, back at the Jacaranda, the three overheard Williams and Larry Parnes discussing the possibility of using other local groups. "What about taking us on?" asked John Lennon, though he had to confess that they didn't have a drummer.

"Why don't you use Tommy Moore?" suggested Cass of Cass and the Casanovas, referring to a skilled jazz player of the ripe old age of twenty-five.

With Moore laying down the backbeat, the musicians began rehearsing in the basement of the Jacaranda. They also decided that with this rebirth they should begin performing under a new name. Always having had a fondness for the name of the Crickets, who supported Buddy Holly (a vast influence on Paul), Stuart suggested the "Beetles." John, with his indefatigable adoration of word play, promptly spelled it "Beatles." Then the word *Silver* was added at the beginning, originating from Long John Silver.

The next time Paul McCartney saw Roy Corlett in the Jac, he rushed over to him. "Roy, Roy! You work on a paper, don't you? Can you give us some publicity?"

"What for?" asked Corlett suspiciously.

"For our group. We've got a drummer and everything now."

"What's the angle?" demanded the hardened newsman from *The South Liverpool Gazette.* "What's the story?"

Stumped by such specifics, Paul's enthusiasm waned momentarily, and the pair chatted briefly.

"Anyway," said Corlett, "tell me what you're going to call yourselves."

"The Silver Beatles," proudly announced Paul.

"God! With a name like that you'll never get anywhere!" Corlett brusquely chided him, and wheeled away.

This was not Paul's first effort to curry favor with the press. Earlier in the year, when they were not only drummerless but nameless too, he had written to a Mr. Low, a journalist they had met in a pub. He added a year onto his age, and—as was becoming his wont, or even his fantasy—claimed to be studying literature at the local university. (From an early age Paul had a shrewd understanding of those subtleties that confer social status in Britain.) In the letter he similarly kowtowed to the far greater social acceptability of jazz, a much safer, middle-class music: ". . . as the boys have an above average instrumental ability they achieve surprisingly varied effects. Their basic beat is off-beat, but this has recently tended to be accompanied by a faint on-beat; thus the overall sound is rather reminiscent of the four in the bar of traditional jazz. This could possibly be put down to the influence of Mr. McCartney, who led one of the top local jazz bands (Jim Mac's Jazz Band) in the 1920s."

Throughout the United Kingdom groups were forming and splitting and re-forming and somehow trying to make it all work. None, however, were as influenced by what was happening in the United States as those in Liverpool, Britain's closest port to America. Everyone in Liverpool knew someone who worked on the transatlantic merchant ships or liners—"Cunard Yanks," as they used to call those lucky Scousers who regularly would find themselves in New York. And it was those Cunard Yanks who brought back to Liverpool the hard R & B sounds that were never released in the U.K., the sort of songs that when performed by Merseyside's top R & B exponent, Kingsize Taylor, had John, Paul, and George standing as close to the stage as they could, scribbling down the lyrics he belted out.

In other parts of Britain, even in neighboring cities, Liverpool's name inspired dread—it was a fearful place, they said. Vice and violence were its best-known features, a reputation that would have given heart murmurs to the likes of Jim McCartney or Aunt Mimi living in the city's just-as-typical, cozy, village-like suburbs.

To lads from the slums of Dingle like Ronald Wycherley, however, a rough, tough past, present, and future seemed all that fate could guarantee. In fact, thanks to the intervention of a sharp girlfriend who had seen the worth in the songs he had been writing, Ronald Wycherley escaped Liverpool, and under the stage name of Billy Fury, had become Britain's best and most believable rock and roll star. By turns smoldering and shy, the reputedly "difficult" Fury was like a cross between Elvis Presley and Johnnie Ray; not even the expensive sharkskin suits he took to wearing could disguise the fact that he was The Real Thing, that his sulky, undernourished demeanor was identical to that of the young, switchblade-carrying Teds you'd find hanging around, scratching their initials in the listening booths of record stores or striking James Dean–like poses in the doorways of coffee bars.

Shortly before his death in 1982 Fury, in reality a shy, gentle man who took to running a wildlife sanctuary, described to me the life from which he'd escaped. Loaded with money, as many working-class teenagers were in those affluent times, he lived with his parents until he left Liverpool: "All I had to do with my money was buy clothes and records, and go to dances on a Saturday night. Maybe a few bottles of Bristol Cream sherry on a Saturday.

"There wasn't really all that much to do in those days. We were street-corner kids. We were too young to go to the pubs properly. But if we stood on a street corner, a copper would come along and tell us to move along. So you'd go down the road and then come back to the corner. And then he'd probably come back again, and give you a whack with his stick. It was pretty rough. If a few Teds got together at a dance, the police would have to stick their nose in—they'd never seen those kind of gatherings before, unless it was for some kind of gang fight.

"Before rock and roll started, I'd been into country and western music, because I couldn't get anything out of the popular music of the time. Actually, in Liverpool everybody used to play country and western—Hank Williams or whatever. Anything with some real lyrics about a bit of trouble or a bit of heartbreak."

Billy Fury was part of the Larry Parnes stable. It was Parnes, the promoter of the Cochran–Vincent tour, who had renamed him ("It happened a few days after I'd started on my first tour, supporting Marty Wilde. Larry Parnes rang me up and said, 'You're in *The Daily Mirror.*' So I went and got a copy, and inside it was a picture of me, and underneath it said 'Billy Fury.' Thanks!"). Parnes had also subtly interfered with his curriculum vitae so that mundane, uninspiring former employment such as having been a deckhand on the Mersey ferries was re-created as the far more glamorous "merchant seaman." Parnes was Mr. Big in British pop: his "stable," all of whom were rechristened with near-camp surnames intended to suggest the nature of their sexual performance, included Britain's first rock and roller, Tommy Steele, as well as Marty Wilde, Duffy Power, and Vince Eager.

The week after the Vincent boxing stadium show, it was

learned that the mighty Parnes was returning to Liverpool at the beginning of May. Moreover, the great man would be accompanied by Billy Fury himself, who, loyally, was seeking a permanent backing group from the various rock and roll outfits in his home city.

Naturally, Allan Williams involved himself in this scheme. And, as they were one of the acts that had slipped under his managerial wing, so did the Silver Beatles. Suddenly there was a chance to break away altogether from the confines of playing at suburban dances and parties for—sometimes literally—peanuts. Accordingly, on May 5, 1960, the Silver Beatles auditioned before Parnes and Billy Fury. Tommy Moore, however, couldn't make the date. So Johnny Hutch, the drummer with Cass and the Casanovas, reluctantly sat in with this unrated bunch.

Though he didn't know their material, Hutch proved no hindrance, for he was probably the most renowned player on Merseyside: if anything, his skills enhanced their performance. What immediately struck Larry Parnes, who was somewhat taken by the spirited playing of the guitarists, was that the bass player, Stuart Sutcliffe, was totally inept. In fact, he even asked the Silver Beatles to perform a number without the bass player, for Fury was quite taken with the group. To their credit, they refused. Out of the corner of his eye, however, Paul McCartney cast his gaze over Sutcliffe's thin frame and shook his head; he knew, too, that Stuart was not up to scratch, though he was fond of him. But even the mild awe he felt for Stuart's talents as a painter couldn't interfere with what Paul knew was his true purpose: ensuring that the Silver Beatles were as perfect as they could possibly be. Not even the nagging, confusing mutterings of jealousy that occasionally welled up inside him about this new, close friend of John's could distract him from that.

"I don't think that Paul got on too well with Stuart Sutcliffe," Bill Harry says, "because I think he felt very much that Stuart was riding on the back of John, that he had been brought into the group because he was John's friend, and I don't think Paul really rated him as a musician—which he wasn't. He was a painter, not a musician. I don't think Paul liked the idea of that at all. And I also don't think he liked the idea that John and Stuart were always together."

Although the Silver Beatles had failed the audition to back Billy Fury, they soon received an offer from Parnes to back one of his lesser luminaries, Johnny Gentle, on a tour of Scotland. Sutcliffe was not included on the contract, for Parnes didn't see why they needed to take along a non-musician. So, at John's decision, the other Silver Beatles, including Tommy Moore, had to each give up part of their pay so that Stuart could earn an equal wage, a settlement that stuck very much in the craw of the financially "careful" Paul McCartney.

But even John Lennon seems to have been aware of the uncomfortably triangular nature of the relationship between himself, Paul, and Stuart. For, in addition to forever verbally bullying the hapless Moore, Lennon constantly chided Sutcliffe mercilessly for his miserable musicianship, as though he were attempting to show Paul that he also understood the problem and desired to punish Sutcliffe for having entered their lives.

For Paul, who had diligently plugged away at his music and the group for so long for such little reward, the tour was an opportunity that couldn't be missed. Even the fact that his A-level exams began three weeks after the tour would end must not be allowed to interfere with what was the first real opportunity he'd yet had. Ivan Vaughan, however, sternly counseled against the decision Paul had made to hardly do any studying at all for exams on which his whole future could depend.

But Paul had already decided on what his whole future was to be based. One night early in May, when Jim McCartney returned from the Corn Exchange, he was met by his eldest son.

"Dad, Dad. We've been given two weeks off school so we can rest up before our A levels and do a little bit of revision. They always do that in the sixth form, didn't you know? And guess what? Our group's been asked to do a tour of Scotland at exactly the same time. I reckon it's just what I need to take my mind off the exams, don't you?"

Jim McCartney was not at all convinced that this was just

what Paul needed. But the musician in him warmed to the idea. And when—at Paul's instructions—Mike McCartney also badgered his father about what a golden opportunity Paul would miss if he didn't go, Jim agreed with a readiness that made him feel guilty.

If any glory came Paul's way as a result of the tour, however, the McCartney family would gain no fame. Perhaps because he was affected by the spectre of Larry Parnes hanging over his future, Paul felt a need to find a suitable stage name, eventually settling on Paul Ramon, which he felt to be most glamorous, "sort of Valentino-ish." Three of the others followed: there was Carl Harrison, Johnny Silver, and Stu de Stijl. And Tommy Moore.

The tour took them to the most northerly outposts of Britain, to tiny ballrooms in one-horse towns like Inverness and Nairn. "I've been asked for my autograph," Paul wrote to his dad on a postcard.

The drab circumstances in which the group played and lived were hardly a taste of the big time, and their pay for the whole tour was only £18 each (about forty-five dollars). Yet it lifted their spirits immeasurably, and provided them with something they now had to better.

Yet Paul persisted with the tale that he was going to teachers' training college, even though he felt more and more that he was deluding himself. Indeed, he'd gone as far as applying and being given a place at one, in Hereford. Upon the completion of his A-level course, as far as "Dusty" Durband knew, Paul would be starting in Hereford the following September. In fact, Paul didn't even need to pass his A levels to get into the college: such was the shortage of teachers in Britain at that time that his meagre O-level passes were sufficient. But a stint at teachers' training college indubitably had a sense of the second-rate about it. Considering the lofty ambitions of the eldest McCartney boy and the fact that he had been passing himself off as a university student, such a career would have seemed very much like a downward turn in his life.

And musically he was on an upswing, even if only because Allan Williams had now started securing the Silver Beatles Saturday night bookings at such murderous venues as the Grosvenor Ballroom, "across the water" in Seacombe, and the Neston Institute, which they played for the first time on June 2, 1960. At that date, as part of the fulfillment of the Ted obligation to start a fight if he hadn't gotten a girl by the end of the night, a sixteen-year-old boy was booted to death.

As the prettiest Beatle—they dropped the "Silver" before that first the Neston Institute date—Paul was at a considerable disadvantage. Every time a girl would gush about how "gorgeous" he was, he earned even more rancor from those Teds who had been unable to find a partner for the evening. The bouncers, meanwhile, who were at least as much a threat as the paying customers, loathed him on principle. It often took all of Paul's indominatable charm and fast-growing street smarts to kept him in one piece.

Less glamorous work, though not without its own specialist charm, was also offered the Beatles by Allan Williams. The latest enterprise of the man who was now their manager was a strip club. And, driven as much by an itch to get up on any stage at all as by their persistent lack of cash, the Beatles on a number of occasions obligingly provided backup music for Janice the Stripper.

Such a familiarity with low-life types was to provide good training for a rather more major project that Allan Williams was to offer them. Through a sequence of circumstances he had become acquainted with Bruno Koschmider, the owner of a club in Hamburg, a German port with a reputation not dissimilar to that of Liverpool's. His club, the Kaiserkeller, was situated within the city's blue-light district, the Reeperbahn, and was open most of the night, providing a release for the stolid German citizens who not only work hard, but play—and drink—hard, too. Koschmider had decided that his club required prodigious amounts of live rock and roll music. In the whole of Germany, however, there was no ready source of such sounds.

Playing on the similarity between their two cities, Williams had persuaded Koschmider that Liverpool had the very best rock and roll groups, outside of America. Earlier in the year, he had dispatched the highly rated Derry and the Seniors to the Kaiserkeller for a season that had proved an outstanding success. His profits up, Koschmider demanded more groups from Williams.

One day on the way home from school with his brother Mike, Paul casually mentioned that he and the rest of the Beatles had been offered a season in Hamburg. Surprisingly to Mike, however, Paul appeared to have little enthusiasm for something that the younger McCartney boy could see was a potentially splendid opportunity. Later Mike realized this was a feint; with his characteristic cunning Paul had implanted in his brother the seeds of the same great enthusiasm that he secretly felt, so that Michael could prove a dauntless ally in the real task that lay ahead: persuading Jim McCartney to allow Paul to venture off to Germany.

Ever a believer in the formal and correct way of going about things, Paul also arranged for a visit to 20 Forthlin Road by Allan Williams to supplement his and his brother's pleas to Jim. True to his chaotic form, Williams referred to Paul as "John" throughout his conversation with Jim, but at least managed to impress his father with the details and probity of the arrangements.

Eventually, Jim went along with Paul's plans. To Tom Gaule he confided the real reasons why he let Paul go to Germany. "He's being offered as much money as I make a week: how can I tell him he can't go?"

The departure for Germany was set for a month after Paul took his A levels. Paul's form-master, Jack Sweeney, issued a stern warning to Paul when he revealed the details of the trip. "Remember," he admonished, "you won't be able to rely on charm all your life: get some qualifications." "Dusty" Durband was equally troubled. "Go to teachers' training college," was his advice. "We can't all be a Tommy Steele, you know."

CHAPTER SIX

This Liverpool group's entry into Hamburg was not necessarily auspicious; there was yet another of what could have been read as the same kind of ill omen that seemed to mysteriously stymie so many of Allan Williams's projects. Taking the wheel of their battered cream-and-green Austin van for the drive from the city's outskirts to the Kaiserkeller, Williams almost immediately bashed into a family car; earlier, Lord Woodbine, his co-driver, had inadvertently lodged their vehicle's wheels in a set of streetcar tracks, almost causing the entire party to be wiped out by a speeding streetcar.

Already Paul had been dashing off postcards to his dad and brother; he had encouraged the band to pose for pictures to mark their progress across Europe. A photograph of the van's passengers at the Arnhem War Memorial in Holland was notable, however, for the absence of John Lennon. Wary of losing the seat he had claimed as his, John had chosen to remain in the van, practicing on the harmonica he had stolen from a Dutch store.

Paul, for his part, had to be content running his fingers over the cheap but brand-new guitar and amplifier he had brought with him and gazing with weary but all-absorbing eyes at the monotonously flat Dutch scenery. George at least had an instrument on which to play along with John's breathy harmonica riffing: he would beat out a rhythm on the empty biscuit tin he was clutching.

As the van crossed the German border and trundled along modern autobahns, it was constantly rocked by the speed of passing Mercedes and BMWs, evidence to the Scousers of the German postwar economic miracle, which in a decade and a half had transformed a battle-ravaged country into the most affluent nation in Europe.

Stuart Sutcliffe, also tucked into the rear "creative" section of the vehicle, away from the "administrative" department of Allan Williams, his wife Beryl, and Lord Woodbine, drew rough sketches of their travels, oblivious to the fate that awaited him. From time to time, Paul would glance over at the bass player, wondering vaguely at his exact purpose, and knowing he had to come to terms with Stu's closeness to John.

Also on board was a new member. Tucked away in one corner or wedged morosely on a bench seat between two of the other Beatles, sat their new drummer Pete Best, whose perpetual silence lacked even the flavoring of dry wit that rendered palatable George's sparse speech. Realizing that, as ever, they were without a drummer at a crucial time, the Beatles had wracked their brains for a suitable candidate to fill the drum seat. At the last moment Paul had remembered that at the Casbah, where they were once again playing, Pete Best had prominently displayed the drum kit he had been using in the Blackjacks until the group had folded when Ken Brown left Liverpool. Accordingly, Paul had phoned him up. " 'Ere, Pete, 'owdja fancy comin' to 'Amburg with us as our drummer for a couple of months?" Pete Best, who had left school five weeks before with the intention of somehow making a career in show business, hardly felt he had a choice to make.

The world the Beatles found in Hamburg was far removed from the leafy streets of suburban south Liverpool. The Indra Club, into which Bruno Koschmider had booked them, was situated on the Grosse Freiheit, off the notorious Reeperbahn in the St. Pauli district, an area famous for the variety of sexual pleasures local prostitutes offered. To say the least, it was a raunchy neighborhood, run by shady characters on the fringes of the underworld who did not hesitate to resort to violence. It made Liverpool's supposed vice and violence seem tame.

The Indra, where the Beatles were booked to play for four and a half hours each weeknight and six hours a night on weekends, had been a strip club: seedy, shabby, and tatty. The five musicians were lodged across the road, in a room behind the screen of the Bambi Cinema, a flea-pit that attempted to draw customers by showing ancient gangster movies and Westerns— the sound of screen gunfire during the first showing was what frequently acted as the Beatles' alarm clock. Their washing facilities were the sinks of the mens' toilets.

But dealing with the harsh, hard-core realities of life in this toughest part of the German port was as crucial in the development of the Beatles as human beings as were those long, long sets for the development of their music. That grueling time they spent onstage, meanwhile, was like an endless paid rehearsal before an audience. With no preconceptions about rock and roll bands, the Reeperbahn audiences would accept anything, providing a reasonable standard of musicianship was met. Innocents though the Beatles were in the art of audience manipulation, the group soon discovered that various numbers went down far better than others.

And these more popular songs, a potent mixture of hard R & B numbers and popular standards, gradually began to dominate the repertoire and to focus the band's direction.

"From our earliest days in Liverpool," John said later, "George and I on the one hand and Paul on the other had different musical tastes. Paul preferred 'pop type' music and we preferred what is now called 'underground.' This may have led to arguments, particularly between Paul and George, but the contrast in our tastes, I am sure, did more good than harm, musically speaking, and contributed to our success."

Moreover, Bruno Koschmider's continual exhortations to "mak [make] show, mak show" placed what was beginning to emerge as a proven "set" of songs in a theatrical context. Partially to fill up the time, but also because they would enter that genuine trancelike state experienced by musicians when they are playing truly in concert together, the bluesy songs the Beatles played became extended, featuring five and six separate guitar solos, and often a reversion to the impromptu, skat vocals that John Lennon had featured out of necessity in the early Quarrymen.

They learned well the art of stagemanship, with Paul and George rushing to and fro about the stage in crisscross dashes, in dynamic contrast to the deliberate menace created by John's immovable stance at the microphone. Tricks were developed: to overcome the difficulty of John, Paul, and George often failing to start their vocal harmonies at the same time, they would rush spiritedly from the rear of the stage to their microphones at such moments in a song, creating an illusion of split-second timing.

No longer restrained by the knowledge that their individual performances were being judged by friends and acquaintances, as in Liverpool, the various members—particularly Paul and John when taking lead vocals—were able to throw themselves with total abandon into the onstage personae they each individually were developing.

But it was the least able musician, Stuart Sutcliffe, who devoted the most time to the development of his visual image. He met a pair of German art students, Klaus Voorman and his girlfriend, Astrid Kirchherr, and became close friends with both of them, soon taking Klaus's place as Astrid's lover.

It was Astrid who one day washed the grease out of Stuart's swept-back hair, brushed it forward, and trimmed it into a short fringe. This look, which of course was to become known in subsequent years as the "Beatle cut," was already popular among the most hip male dressers. It was known in London, where it was sported by members of a coterie of stylesetters who termed themselves "modernists," as the "French cut," after the country in which it was believed to have originated. Among certain art-student types, in particular, it was already popular, and it was on friends of Astrid's—who herself had a similar short style—that Stuart was modeling himself. His close art-school pal, John Lennon, however, sneered at Stuart's haircut when he first saw it, and was almost the last member of the group to submit his carefully cultivated DA to be cropped. Pete Best never succumbed to the scissors, perhaps his one fatal error.

Paul McCartney, always in tune with—or just ahead of—the latest styles, followed Stuart's lead almost immediately, his baby-faced "cute" features rendered even more so by the fringe that now framed them.

This was the only matter in regard to the group, however, in which Paul permitted himself to be influenced by Stuart. More and more, the musical perfectionist and driving force within the Beatles was becoming as concerned as Larry Parnes had been about Stuart's almost complete lack of ability, which Stuart tried to disguise by playing with his back to the audience. Having forced himself to cope with the dilution of the intensity of friendship between himself and John that Stuart's arrival had caused, Paul McCartney now found himself troubled by the way in which Stuart's all-encompassing romance with Astrid took away time he desperately needed to spend practicing on his instrument.

Astrid, meanwhile, had taken her unofficial role of Beatles' art director one step further. At her suggestion, the five group members had spent part of their wages on leather jackets and trousers. Now, with the Beatles looking like Marlon Brando in *The Wild*

One, their image firmly stated that they were hipsters, one step ahead of the other outfits from Liverpool with whom Hamburgers were becoming familiar.

Of all the groups playing in Hamburg, the Beatles were the most highly regarded. Such a position was in stark contrast to the complaint by Derry, of Derry and the Seniors, to Allan Williams that the Beatles were so inept they would let the side down and spoil it for everyone else if they were sent to Hamburg. A month after they had arrived in the German port, Rory Storm and the Hurricanes followed the Beatles there; originally, they had been the group Allan Williams had selected to go, but they had been prevented by the season they were booked to play at one of the Butlin's Holiday Camps.

Early on a damp Sunday evening, Storm's group got out of their van in the Reeperbahn, near Grosse Freiheit. The evening's revelries were yet to commence, and the district seemed deserted. Coming from further up the street, however, the Merseyside musicians could make out what sounded like familiar music. Drawing closer, they heard "Roll Over Beethoven," and a very good version of the Chuck Berry song at that, coming from the open doors of the Indra. Johnny Guitar, the group's lead guitarist, remembers the amazement with which the four musicians peered through the doorway, past the tatty maroon velvet curtaining that was a joking effort at soundproofing. "It was the Beatles! And I'll never forget the sound, because it was so *fantastic!* So different, so much better than we'd heard them doing in Liverpool."

Astrid Kirchherr didn't only tell the Beatles how to look, she also influenced their thinking in a formative way. In her bedroom, decorated in silver and black, Astrid, who was twenty-one, would show the young musicians shelves of esoteric literature, of a type rarely encountered in provincial English cities. Here the Beatles first saw in substantial quantity volumes of arcane mysticism. Her works of de Sade shocked John Lennon who, displaying the narrow-minded conservatism of a typical British Northener, was startled that a woman would read such stuff. John showed his conservatism in other ways: when Paul would play Astrid's

Sibelius or Stravinsky LPs, John would scornfully demand that he replace them with Buddy Holly.

Later, the Beatles were to discover that the toilet attendant at Koschmider's Kaiserkeller Club, to which they were soon moved, kept a jar of Preludin under her table, doling them out in exchange for deutschmarks. In the usual manner of amphetamines, the pills drained their users of a desire for food—hence their use as slimming aids—but created a dryness in the mouth that the foaming flagons of German light beer would alleviate, while the alcohol blended with the speed to create mild hallucinations.

Beer was available in quantities. On Koschmider's instructions a daily ration of beer was doled out to all the musicians. The Beatles rarely had to pay to supplement this, for as is the custom in such German nightspots, in the middle of a number Paul or John would find one of the sweating waiters placing a tray of mugs down on the front of the stage, a sign of an audience member's appreciation. As the Beatles continued to blossom, the trays were sometimes replaced by crates. Considering the nature of certain of the donors, the Beatles generally felt it unwise not to drink every last drop.

Despite the high calorie content of the beer, it fought a losing battle against the Preludin. By the end of the month the clothes the Beatles had brought with them from Liverpool hung loosely on their now slender frames. For the first time, and despite all his assurances to his father that he would not neglect his diet, Paul McCartney lost the baby fat that had plagued him. Now that his cheeks were hollowed out, however, they only served to accentuate the cupid's bow of his mouth and his doe eyes. Girls found him cuter than ever.

And of girls there were plenty. Nobody could fail to be stirred by the area's sharp scent of sexuality, especially young men away from home for the first time. The Beatles were never short of female company, finding girls in the audience or being offered freebies by the area's countless hookers, many of whom were rather taken by these young innocents abroad, so different from their usual paying customers.

However, Horst Fascher, a former boxer who led a team of bouncers for Bruno Koschmider, remembers that Paul was not as partial to one-night stands as John Lennon and George Harrison. "He tended much more to *go out* with girls: they would become his girlfriend for ten days or a fortnight."

No doubt this was to the good of his health: their constitutions already weakened by an almost vitamin-free diet, of which cornflakes and milk—a particular favorite of Paul's—was the staple, the most promiscuous Beatles soon contracted various venereal diseases and viruses, from which they were only completely cured on their return to Liverpool.

Staggering back to their rooms behind the cinema screen at five in the morning, the Beatles would fall into a dead sleep until at least lunchtime the next day. When, bleary-eyed and often with vicious hangovers, they woke, they would make their way down to the English Seamen's Mission, overlooking the docks. There, over cups of tea and bowls of cornflakes, they would slowly awaken.

After becoming acquainted with Astrid, however, their afternoons were often spent wandering the city, in search of suitably gritty photographic locations. Astrid Kirchherr had studied photography and was working as a photographer's assistant; hers was the first serious attempt to capture with a camera the group's visual image, which she had helped create. In fairgrounds and parks around Hamburg she shot endless sets of pictures whose main quality was that same hauntingly melancholic yet soothing and inspiring mood that so much of their music expressed. "Nobody could take our picture as well as Astrid did," Paul said later.

Which was a difficult admission. For between Paul and Astrid's boyfriend, Stuart, to whom she soon became engaged, there was always an ineluctable tension. Partially it existed because of the relationship between Stuart, John, and Paul, though Stuart and Astrid's love affair had done much to ease the awkwardness of that situation. Now the tension was largely caused by Paul's frustration at Stuart's musical ineptness, an ineptness that the hours of performing—from which all the other Beatles were immeasurably benefiting—seemed to do little to diminish. Paul McCartney came to consider this as a perfidious dereliction of duty, and would loudly criticize Stuart, as he sat behind him onstage playing piano during Stuart's one solo spot, a vocal performance of Elvis Presley's "Love Me Tender." Somehow Stuart managed to persuade Astrid, and perhaps even himself, that this barracking was due to a loathing that Paul had for the way in which the slow ballad interrupted the rocking pace of the set. Yet Stuart was fully aware of Paul's propensity for sentimental, crooning songs. "You could tell Paul really hated him," said Astrid.

But Paul was by far the most popular of the Beatles, the girls adoring his neatness and cleanliness. He was, Astrid remembered with unmistakable irony, "always smiling and being diplomatic." But if this natural facility for presenting a good face remained unstinted, his abilities and talents were improving in quantum leaps, the onstage piano at the Kaiserkeller offering an opportunity to further demonstrate his versatility as he pounded out songs from the Ray Charles and Jerry Lee Lewis songbooks.

"I was always coming across Paul backstage, practicing the guitar or singing snatches of songs I'd never heard before," says Horst Fascher. "The others would be running around chasing girls or getting drunk, but Paul did that much less: he seemed to be grabbing every opportunity to improve his music."

Throughout the Beatles' stay in Hamburg, Allan Williams had constantly received requests from Bruno Koschmider to extend their engagement. Though the group was receiving nothing like the £100 a week they had been promised—more like £15, Paul later estimated—Koschmider himself was pulling it in from the 500-strong audience, who most nights would fill the booths, shaped like wooden boats sawn in half, in the Kaiserkeller.

Koschmider, it seemed, would have liked nothing better than for the Beatles to become his permanent resident group. Yet eventually his fiercely territorial feelings about his act, an attitude common to Hamburg club owners, could not tolerate an incident that Koschmider considered the epitome of disloyalty.

The Beatles had become good friends with another expatriate

English rocker, Tony Sheridan, who was the resident act up the road at the Top Ten Club. From time to time, various members of the group would join Sheridan onstage. At the beginning of December 1960, however, one of Koschmider's henchmen happened to venture into the Top Ten, at a time when all the Beatles were onstage supporting Sheridan. Bruno Koschmider immediately fired the Beatles.

This by no means meant that the group would have to quit Hamburg. For Peter Eckhorn, the Top Ten's owner, offered the group more money to come and play for him. At the same time, however, the *Polizei* somehow came to check on George Harrison's passport and, learning that he was only seventeen—under the eighteen-year-old limit required to be in a club after midnight —immediately deported the guitarist.

The rest of the group, though, were ready to take up the engagement offered at the Top Ten, and moved into the attic above the club. Returning with Pete Best to their squalid digs behind the cinema screen to pick up the rest of their belongings, Paul jokingly set fire to a condom. Some mouldy wall-drapes also caught fire, though the flames were quickly extinguished. As a result, Paul and Pete Best were arrested and held for several hours at the Reeperbahn police station on suspicion of arson. Eventually the pair were released. But they were obliged to follow George back to England when it was discovered they had no work papers. They flew back on the next available flight. John and Stu had no choice but to follow shortly after.

Notwithstanding the ignominious circumstances of his departure from Germany, it was a typically cheery Paul McCartney to whom his brother answered the door. As Paul sat down on the sofa in the front room, unpacking his bags and presenting Mike with a blue "plazy" (plastic) mac and showing him his new electric razor, his blue short-sleeved velvet shirt, and the Spanish guitar he had bought, Mike could not help but notice that the ankles showing above Paul's pointy-toed shoes were "as thin and white as Dad's pipe-cleaners."

When the Beatles eventually trekked down to Slater Street to contact Allan Williams in the Jacaranda, he reminded them of an event that they could now only dimly recall through the mists of time, beer, and Preludin. Before Williams had left Hamburg to return to Liverpool, he had arranged for the group to go into a tiny recording studio, at the back of the Hamburg railway station. For whatever reasons of his own, Williams had come to the conclusion that the Beatles themselves were not sufficiently strong vocalists to sing the songs at this momentous event. So five tracks, including "Summertime" and "Fever," were recorded, with the vocals performed by Lou "Wally" Walters, the bass player with Rory Storm and the Hurricanes. Again, for reasons of his own, Williams didn't invite Pete Best to drum on the session. Instead, he invited along "Wally" Walters's rhythm-section partner, drummer Ringo Starr.

CHAPTER SEVEN

Also waiting for Paul back in Liverpool was the General Certificate of Education for the one A level he had passed, in English literature.

Daily, Jim McCartney would remind his eldest son that it was time for him to put his educational qualifications to use and get a proper job; perhaps, he would suggest, Paul could pay a visit to the Institute and have a talk with Alan Durband, to see if his favorite teacher could pull any strings to help him get into training college the next year. "Yeah, Dad, maybe I should," Paul would absentmindedly reply.

A few days after Paul had arrived back in England, he strolled down to the local Labour Exchange and took a job at £7 a week delivering parcels from a truck for the Speedy Prompt Delivery Company. Though he was motivated by his father's influence, it was not by the vague admonitions to seek worthwhile employment, but by that sense of the work ethic that had inspired Paul's almost obsessive practicing of his instrument and the perfectionistic zeal with which he approached songwriting.

Besides, Jim's advice was falling on deaf ears. John Lennon, who even as Paul jauntily jumped on and off the Speedy Prompt Delivery truck, was lying in bed on Menlove Avenue, a position he would occupy almost until Christmas. He had informed his songwriting partner as soon as he returned to Liverpool of the offer of Peter Eckhorn of the Top Ten Club. They planned to wait until George turned eighteen, next March, then go back to Hamburg.

As they soon discovered, news of the Beatles' Hamburg triumph had filtered back to Liverpool. A rapid reappraisal of the group had taken place, and they found themselves elevated from virtual no-hopers to something of a cult mystery whose next live shows in their hometown were eagerly awaited. The first, just before Christmas at Pete Best's Casbah, which was to again become a regular booking for the group, was relatively low-key.

On December 27, 1960, however, they played to their first substantial audience since arriving back on Merseyside, at Litherland Town Hall. So ecstatic was the audience response that Brian Kelly, the promoter, felt like kicking himself. As the crowd surged forward to the stage, leaving the dance floor behind empty, he thought, "I could have got twice as many people in here."

Billed as "Direct from Hamburg" and wearing the black leathers they had acquired there, the Beatles were, many members of the audience assumed, German. Until John, that is, exhorted them, in solid Scouse, to "Get your knickers down." At Litherland Town Hall the Beatles also encountered a man who was to become a loyal ally, one Bob Wooler, a local disc jockey and promoter who was acting as emcee that night for Brian Kelly.

Wooler, who was then twenty-seven, had recently given up his job as a railway clerk to become the full-time emcee at a Beat club opened by Allan Williams earlier in the month. Based loosely on the Hamburg venues, it was also named the Top Ten. True to Williams's luck, however, the uninsured premises burned down under suspicious circumstances six days after it opened.

The otherwise jobless Wooler persisted, however, with his promotions. And it was in January 1961, at the Hambleton Hall in Huyton, subtitled by Wooler's unerring talent for the rock and roll *mot juste* as the Hive of Jive, that the Beatles were seen for the first time by Sam Leach. A self-effacing, ebullient optimist, Leach was forever unearthing new venues for local groups to play, and was one of the few local promoters passionately in love with the music of rock and roll rather than the money it could add to his bank account.

"It really was completely magical," he said, remembering first seeing the Beatles. "They came on, these five figures in black leather, to the opening bars of *The William Tell Overture*, which Bob Wooler had found for them. And they were *wild*. Their first number, I remember, was Little Richard's 'Tutti Frutti,' with Paul on lead vocals. Paul, in particular, used to bomb around stage like a jackknife, like Brenda Lee used to do: he got an awful lot of feeling from the kids, and was really *fantastic!*"

John Lennon took the lead on the next number, "Slow Down." "I can still feel those numbers vibrating through me," says Leach. "It was absolutely knock-out: I couldn't believe the dynamism and the charisma."

At the end of the set Sam Leach charged into the Beatles' dressing room and introduced himself. "You're going to be as big as Elvis," he gushed.

"Another nutter, Paul." John nodded sardonically in Leach's direction.

"A nutter with bookings, though," Paul reminded John.

John McNally of the Searchers, another Liverpool group that later was to enjoy great worldwide success, confirms that, after the

Beatles had been to Hamburg, Beatles' songs in their stage shows would often last for up to twenty minutes, with several guitar solos.

Sam Leach concurs. "The world never saw the Beatles as we saw them in Liverpool," he insists. And it was the symbiosis between Paul and John that was the core of this dynamism: "They were good mates, they'd help each other, and they never tried to upstage each other. While one was at the front of the stage, the other would do the backing, and vice versa. But whoever was doing the lead singing would put so much into it, that it was as though he was saying to the other, 'Go on, follow that!' That was the rivalry they created—they pushed each other on. But it was a very healthy rivalry.

"The funny thing is, you'd think somehow George would get left behind. But he didn't, and he developed his own style. Paul was a bit bouncy, and John was sneery, but George came across as a bit shy, and the girls really liked that. But I think Paul definitely had an edge on the fans: no doubt about that—I'd say he probably had about sixty percent of them.

"The thing is, John is made out as the real rock singer, but Paul certainly was a rocker—more so than John in many ways, because he did more movements onstage. John stood there like a big Ted, just giving it all out with his voice: there was no body language at all, though he'd hand out a lot of verbals to the audience. Paul would never do that: he really *was* the diplomatic goody-goody who would never say anything out of place, and was always clean-cut and very anxious to please."

The first place Sam Leach booked the Beatles was at his own Casanova Club on Temple Street. Then he put them on at a new venue he had opened, again a town center club rather than one of the halls on the fringes of the city. It was called the Iron Door Club, on the same street as the Casanova Club, and on March 11, 1961, Sam Leach promoted there the first of many twelve-hour-long Beat sessions, this particular event going under the none-too-inspired title of "Rock Around the Clock."

The session was headlined by the Beatles, who were obliged to cut back their set to an hour, the same length of time allotted to each of the twelve groups who were playing; they included King-size Taylor and the Dominoes, Rory Storm and the Hurricanes, Gerry and the Pacemakers, the Big Three, and the Searchers.

The walls were awash with condensation: the Beatles, who since Hamburg had been using American equipment wired differently to British gear, were forced to stand on their amplifier covers to avoid electrocution. "The heat was shocking," quipped Paul afterward.

Parallel to Temple Street was Mathew Street. Here, ten days later, the Beatles returned to a venue they had not played since Nigel Whalley secured them a booking when its musical policy was strictly jazz—The Cavern. By this time, however, it was apparent that the popularity of traditional jazz was on the wane. Pragmatically, the owner, Ray McFall, had begun lunchtime rock and roll sessions, catering to city center office workers. As one of Merseyside's greatest Beatles fans, Bob Wooler had been hired as the emcee of these sets, and he persuaded McFall to try out the group. Though their pay was minimal—not usually more than £1.25 a session—the Beatles were to play a total of 292 shows at The Cavern over the next two and a half years. And The Cavern —a sweaty, uncomfortable cellar dive—became the Liverpool equivalent of the arduous training ground that the Indra and Kaiserkeller had been in Hamburg.

Before the group could thoroughly benefit from their local fame from regularly playing The Cavern, another season was spent in Hamburg.

Pete Best, whose drum kit was still at the Top Ten, had confirmed the booking, telephoning Peter Eckhorn in Hamburg. Eckhorn offered £40 a week, plus rail tickets. As they had set up the dates without Allan Williams's involvement, the group decided to withhold his commission. Yet, demonstrating that character deficiency that is so often an integral aspect of the desperately ambitious artist, they neglected to inform Williams of their decision, allowing him to secure work permits for this visit.

Despite their improved financial deal, the Beatles' hours of employment at the Top Ten were at least as draining as those at Bruno Koschmider's clubs. Alternating with Tony Sheridan's group, they performed from seven in the evening until two or three in the morning.

Confident of a rousing reception, both Paul and John had invited along their girlfriends. Cynthia Powell was lodged, as befitted the lover of Stuart Sutcliffe's friend, at Astrid Kirchherr's mother's; Dorothy "Dot" Rhone, meanwhile, went to stay with Paul on a barge in the harbor, loaned them by Rosa, the Top Ten's lavatory attendant and Preludin supplier. "Dot was an extremely quiet girl, but also extremely nice," says Horst Fascher, who had left Koschmider to work for Eckhorn. "They kept very much to themselves, and I always had the impression Paul didn't really want Dot to come down to the club very much. Perhaps this was because he saw that Cynthia had a lot of trouble there, with guys trying to pick her up."

Perhaps, moreover, Paul did not care for Dot's image of himself to be in any way reduced by the relentless bickering between himself and Stuart Sutcliffe that now daily formed a small but significant feature of the Beatles' Top Ten set. Eventually this clash of temperaments exploded in the only way it could, in an onstage fistfight between the two. Emboldened into an avenging fury by his grievous sense of having been wronged, the slighter Stuart was beginning to prove more than Paul's match when the two were at last pulled apart. The Top Ten audience, by now ready for any wacky antics from its favorite group, applauded loudly.

This unseemly fracas, however, forced Stuart into a self-admission: that his heart was not in playing rock and roll music, but in painting. At the urging of several of Astrid's friends, he had discovered he could obtain a place at Hamburg State Art College, where he would study under Edouardo Paolozzi, for long an inspirational figure for the Liverpudlian.

Even before the Beatles left Liverpool for Hamburg, Sam Leach had perceived that Stuart's days were numbered. "It wasn't that Paul was jealous of his job: Paul was ambitious and wanted a better group, and Stuart was in the way. Money-wise as well it was better to have four rather than five in the group—especially when Stuart couldn't play to save his life. It wasn't that Paul was jealous by any means, because his place was assured—Stuart wasn't any kind of threat. And, anyway, there was never any jealousy in the Beatles—it was always competitiveness. Stuart *did* get in the way: nice fellow, but as a musician, a non-event."

Stuart never formally left the Beatles, but gradually drifted away, loaning Paul his Hofner President bass. Before this Hamburg trip was over, Paul had acquired a Hofner bass of his own, a new model, shaped like a violin, that was to become an integral aspect of Paul's Beatle image.

As they had done when Nigel Whalley had been obliged to adopt the role of hitman to sack Eric Griffiths, the other Beatles now used Stuart to distance them from the consequences of another underhanded act: Stuart was appointed to write the letter to Allan Williams in which the Liverpool entrepreneur, whose assistance in furthering their career had been beyond question, was told he would not receive his commission. Conveniently for the group, Williams's contracts with them had been destroyed in the blaze at his Top Ten Club.

Their consciences untroubled by thus invoking the aid of Stuart, whose bass-playing role Paul McCartney now assumed for himself, the Beatles were free to take yet another of the seemingly infinite, upward steps in their career. On their previous visit to Hamburg, at the instigation of the miserably mistreated Allan Williams, they had gone into a recording studio for the first time. This visit they again recorded, and the result of the session was the release of a moderately successful disc.

But it wasn't under their own name that they recorded—it was as the Beat Brothers. And the featured vocalist was again not one of the Beatles. Instead, they formed the backing group for Tony Sheridan. Sheridan had been noticed playing at the Top Ten by Bert Kaempfert, a leading German orchestra leader and producer for Polydor Records. The two songs he produced for the singer were versions of standards: "My Bonnie Lies Over the Ocean" and "When the Saints Go Marching In." Kaempfert also recorded the Beat Brothers on two songs without Sheridan: "Ain't She Sweet," a live favorite on which John sang lead, and "Cry for a Shadow," an instrumental composed by George as a parody of the melodious guitar-based hits then being enjoyed by Cliff Richard's backing group, the Shadows. Though the Beatles also played Kaempfert several songs that Paul and John had written, the bandleader was unimpressed.

In June 1961, the month that "My Bonnie" was released in Germany, the Beatles returned to Liverpool. Though they quickly resumed their lunchtime sessions at The Cavern, they also played a date at Sam Leach's Iron Door Club. At that show Leach's assistant Terry McCann claims he took admission money from a local businessman, Brian Epstein, who stood in the shadows intently watching the group and avidly clapping after each number. If correct, this sighting of Epstein at a Beatles gig is a good four months before legend has it that he first saw them there.

Everywhere that Paul was seen around Liverpool, he would be with Dot Rhone, their arms intertwined around each other. "We used to call her Paul's 'crutch,'" said Sam Leach, laughing. "He always seemed to be leaning on her. She hardly said a word, never really talked much. But neither did Paul, in fact. When he was finished for the night, he'd be off—and away. He didn't go to all the parties that were on."

Early in the summer, the Beatles' career received a further boost. Bill Harry, who for so long had diligently jotted down details and anecdotes about the burgeoning Liverpool "beat" scene, had decided to utilize to the full his embryonic journalistic talents. On July 6, 1961, Merseyside music fans who ventured forth to their local newsstands to obtain a copy of *New Musical Express*, or the more self-consciously elitist, jazz-orientated *Melody Maker*, discovered that these nationally circulated weekly publications had a local rival, *Mersey Beat*, edited by Harry.

Moreover, as befitted a paper run by a close friend of the Beatles, one of the three columns on the front page was entirely given over to "A Short Diversion on the Dubious Origins of Beatles—translated from the John Lennon." In this typical example of Lennon's absurdist writing, he refers to Paul, as he frequently did, as Paul "McArtrey, son of Jim McArtrey."

Some confusion must have resulted. For in the paper's second issue, on the newsstands two weeks later, a picture caption of the Beatles in Hamburg, accompanying the main front-page story, "Beatle's (sic) Sign Recording Contract" (the details of their sessions with Tony Sheridan), Harry has Paul's surname down as "MacArthy." And in the gossip column on the same page, "Mersey Roundabout," there is a brief (and, for the time, controversial) item containing a further misspelling: "Howie of 'Derry and the Seniors' says that Paul MacArtrey of The Beatles is a better singer than Cliff Richard." It may be wondered whether Lennon's original misspelling was not an unconscious effort to dilute somehow the force of his musically more accomplished songwriting partner. Whatever, the misspelling lingered for months.

Harry's constant trumpeting of the Beatles as Merseyside's finest and most popular group went far in turning it into reality. In fact, Harry admits that at the time *Mersey Beat* existed only in "dummy form," Cass and the Casanovas and Rory Storm and the Hurricanes were bigger crowd pullers.

"People complained," the editor admits, "that I was giving too much space to the Beatles—they were regarded as just another group. Around that time Pete Best was the most popular one—mean and moody, like Jeff Chandler. But I always thought Paul had such great looks. In those days he was still very much baby-faced, but all the girls thought he was really cute, too.

"But he and John had been writing all the numbers. By 1960 they'd done between eighty to one hundred songs: a lot of the songs that became the hits in the sixties they'd already written long before. Initially they were unsure of introducing them to the local audiences, because I don't think they believed their material was all that good."

Whatever their own assessments of the songs they had written, John and Paul plugged ceaselessly away at their writing, the usual location for these arduous sessions still being Paul's house, in the afternoons when Jim McCartney was at work. Sometimes, indeed, as though he knew what he would be disturbing at home,

Jim would stop in at *Mersey Beat*, at its tiny offices in Renshaw Street, on his way home from the Cotton Exchange.

"He really was a great fellow," Harry says. "And he was very proud of what was starting to happen with Paul. I don't think he had any regrets that he hadn't made it as a full-time musician— he enjoyed his music, but knew the limitations of it. Paul's father was more concerned with his job and his work. He worked all his life and his was that ethic of his generation and class from the early part of the century for whom work was the major part of their lives. People from that era felt that most of their lives consisted of working, with very few hours for leisure, but that you should make the most of those few hours. And you had to be good at your work, and honest and conscientious. Mentally, he was a full-time worker."

Though Paul, John, and George had politely ignored Jim's suggestions on material, Jim had clearly influenced Paul's taste. "I'm sure it was his father's influence," says Harry, "that was behind Paul always liking ballads and soft songs and numbers from musicals."

Even in these early days of the Beatles' Cavern sessions, one of Paul's showcase numbers was "Till There Was You" from *The Music Man*. (Mike McCartney later described it as "a most unusual, Dad-orientated, melodic song in the middle of all the rock and roll screamers.")

"But Paul also loved Little Richard numbers. He was a really great rocker: Paul was *the* rocker, really. John had that unique voice, which meant that it came out that he was the man with the rock-and-roll soul. But really Paul was a *great* rock and roll singer. They were both really into rock and roll."

Not only was Paul talented as a songwriter of diverse influences, he was at this time, Bill Harry believes, almost as potentially strong a prose writer as John Lennon. "John always provided lots of material for *Mersey Beat*. He was really keen: he'd come into the office with bundles of poems and stories—he wanted to see his work published, he wanted his stuff in print all the time." However, it was Paul, single-minded in his relentless quest for publicity for the Beatles, who would supply Bill Harry with the most detailed information about the group's progress. "Paul had literary talent, too. When he and John went to Paris, he wrote to me from there, in a very similar style to John. It was very humorous, tongue-in-cheek, and rather good—a great sense of humor. All the stuff he wrote for me in *Mersey Beat* had a good sense of humor."

The trip to Paris, in the first two weeks of October 1961, was a deserved holiday for Paul and John after a summer of almost nonstop work in the exhausting, near-tropical conditions of The Cavern. The scent of urine from the overflowing toilet and the stench of rotting fruit from nearby warehouses were also integral aspects of the "atomsphere" of the club, where the Beatles played evening and all-night sessions almost as often as they played to office workers.

Following songwriting sessions or full group rehearsals at Forthlin Road, the musicians would lug their guitars and amplifiers onto Liverpool Corporation buses and travel down to the city center. Further rehearsals would follow, with Mike McCartney, cutting school, frequently documenting the hours with his Kohn camera. Some of his pictures show that not only did the leather-clad John, Paul, and George at various times revert to their former swept-back hairstyles, but that Mike McCartney was an exceptionally talented photographer; at the time, he was contemplating following his years at Liverpool Institute with a stint at the Art College. A typical set list of the time, in Paul's handwriting, shows the strong R & B orientation of their show: songs like "Hippy Hippy Shake," "A Shot of Rhythm and Blues," "Please Mr. Postman," "Baby It's You," "Money" (Mike Evans, a member of Liverpool's Clayton Squares group and author of *The Art of the Beatles,* says "If you want to know what the Beatles really sounded like at The Cavern, play 'Money' on *With the Beatles* with the volume cranked up to maximum; magnificent"), "Roll Over Beethoven," and "Long Tall Sally." Slotted in among these powerful, primal songs are, however, two originals, "Love Me Do" and "P.S. I Love You."

It was sets like these that inspired Bob Wooler, whose authoritative yet emotional voice introduced the group at each of their

Cavern performances, to write that year in *Mersey Beat:* "The Beatles are truly a phenomenon. I don't think anything like them will happen again."

One of these lunchtime shows, on November 9, intrigued a local businessman, Brian Epstein, when he ventured down into The Cavern. Epstein, who ran the NEMS record store, an off-shoot of his family's furniture shops, wrote a record review column in *Mersey Beat.* On October 28, a customer, Raymond Jones, had asked for a copy of "My Bonnie" by Tony Sheridan and the Beatles, a record that was a complete mystery to the dapper, former student of the Royal Academy of Dramatic Art. Later in the day two girls had also attempted to buy a copy. It was his conscientious efforts to make the NEMS record store the most comprehensively stocked in the Northwest that led Epstein, until recently something of a family disappointment, to The Cavern.

After the show he approached George, who introduced him to the rest of the group: "This man would like to hear our disc." Paul, Epstein noted, "looked pleased." And the bass player asked Bob Wooler to play the song. Although Epstein thought the single "good, but nothing very special," he decided—for no particular reason he could think of at the time—to set up a "meeting" with the Beatles, just over three weeks from then, on December 3, at his Whitechapel offices. "Just for a chat," he said.

CHAPTER EIGHT

Boredom came easily to John Lennon. Neither in his art nor in affairs of the heart was constancy his most notable characteristic. Busting, bulging, with a potent, sensuous energy, his spur was often instinct alone, an unformulated, deeply primal need to express his unconscious.

"I mainly watch Lennon. He's like a caged animal," Mike McCartney writes of the Beatles' performances at The Cavern, adding whimsically, "Not that I've got anything against my brother, but he's just a brother (you know, the one who picks his nose and won't come off the toilet 'cos he's playing his guitar or reading those nudy books)."

But the strangely etiolated, furious figure of John Lennon was mollified and calmed by the jaunty, ritualistic cheeriness of Paul McCartney. Paul's perfectionism, his belief that every detail must be just so, tempered John's mad urges. If the Beatles were John's band—he had, after all, started the Quarrymen—it was Paul who was the group's administrator, organizing both practical details and their music.

There was something strong, resilient, and durable about Paul, and he acted as an anchor for John's indiscipline and barnstorming impatience, and as an antidote to his angry air of badly secreted pain. "The Beatles were very democratic," says Sam Leach. "But I used to deal with Paul most. John would put on this big Ted act, but he wasn't really a Ted at all. I know he could be really sarcastic, but personally I never had a single bad word out of him all the time I knew him. In fact, John was a bit shy—that's why women used to dominate him."

Paul seemed far more confident, more certain of his abilities. "He'd had a good education, and he knew how to handle people, how to get by. He was always trying to get round you, 'Come on, give us a bit more money.' Almost grabbing you, having a bit of a laugh."

Paradoxically, John's female side was more pronounced than Paul's: behind the pugnacious stance and pinched, prehensile lips was a figure of infinite softness and fragility, capable of boundless love, not only for others but also for himself.

The day after their first meeting with Brian Epstein, the Beatles were scheduled to appear in yet another of Sam Leach's schemes. Leach, in fact, had ambitions to manage the group. As part of the "My Bonnie" session, they had signed a contract with German Polydor that expired at the end of the year; then, the ever-visionary Leach hoped, he would record the Beatles performing "Twist and Shout" and "Stand by Me" for a label he wanted to set up himself.

On November 10, 1961, the group headlined "Operation Big

Beat," the first of a large-scale series of shows that Sam Leach promoted "across the water" at New Brighton's Tower Ballroom. Once one of the tallest towers in Europe, and, perched on the edge of the sea, a landmark for shipping, the venue had fallen upon bad times before Leach courageously decided to revive it. To an extent, it was a risky venture, for there was no guarantee that Liverpudlians would cross the Mersey.

"If there's fog on the night, or it just doesn't pay, we'll play for nothing," Paul promised Sam Leach.

"And for the Beatles to say that was a real gesture," the promoter insists, adding, "Personally, I've never believed Paul to be as tight with his money as people make him out to be."

In fact, the night of November 10 *was* dense with damp, thick fog. And Leach was understandably worried. Moreover, by the time the Beatles came onstage at 7:30—they were booked to both begin and finish the evening—only a handful of people had arrived. His fears of financial disaster growing by the second, the promoter dispiritedly made his way across the ballroom's vast floor to the box office. "And outside there was a queue two hundred yards long," he remembers, still ecstatic.

By 8:00 P.M. the place was packed, a phenomenon for Liverpool, where people don't like to leave the pubs until they shut at eleven. And when the Beatles returned to the stage for their 1:00 A.M. slot, there were 4,500 people jammed together in the Tower Ballroom.

"That night," says Leach, "was when Beatlemania began."

And that same night the group's career could have been finished once and for all. Late in the evening, not long before they were due to go onstage, John and Paul were in the ballroom bar, having a drink with Sam Leach and Brian Epstein, to whom the Beatles had mentioned the New Brighton show the previous day.

Suddenly, a gang of Teds sent a table flying through the air toward them. It missed Paul McCartney's head by a whisker before smashing the mirror behind the bar into smithereens. John and Leach stood their ground, putting up their fists, although the promoter was feverishly looking around for his highly efficient bouncers. He breathed a deep sigh of relief when they arrived seconds later. Paul, however, had moved a good way toward the exit. "He didn't leave, though—I think if he'd had to have helped he'd have gone in. His attitude seemed to be, 'If I'm not needed —*great!*' But he would have gone in. But as soon as the bouncers arrived Paul was right in front of them, bouncing backwards and forwards on the balls of his feet. 'Alright then, let's have you—I'm ready!' John and I stood there, looking in awe at this act he was putting on. I said, 'It's all right Paul, I saw your knees knocking there!'"

Brian Epstein, meanwhile, had scurried off and vanished. "Brian was very chicken."

The Beatles were no strangers to this type of violence, meted out by Teds jealous of the attention their girlfriends were showing them. Leach would always keep a special eye on Paul, who he insists was the girls' favorite and not, as legend has it and Bill Harry says, Pete Best. "After all, Pete was at the back of the stage —you couldn't see him that well. If you were going to pick on anybody, it would be Paul, because he was baby-faced and young, and you could see he would be easily frightened."

On one occasion in Joe's, an all-night snack bar, John and Paul were rendered almost speechless with terror. One Eddie Palmer, whose descriptive sobriquet was "The Toxteth Terror" ("Not a bad feller, but a bit of a nutter") approached the table where they sat, hunched over mugs of tea; then he posed the quintessentially Liverpudlian puzzler, "You can sing, but can you fight?" Luckily, before they were required to offer Eddie an answer, one of Leach's bouncers stepped in.

The meeting with Brian Epstein, on a Wednesday afternoon early in December, did not seem necessarily hopeful for the well-spoken businessman. The Beatles, who arrived late, as was their wont, were lukewarm about the offer of management that he made. Besides, to take their minds off the need to make a decision, there was another intriguing Sam Leach plan. Still with his own managerial eye on the group, he had decided that the four musicians needed a London agent, if possible the omnipotent Tito Burns, to take them under his wing. To Londoners, however,

Liverpool was only a name, a name with a decidedly unsalubrious ring at that. There was no possible prospect of such an eminent figure, or even of any of his lackeys, traveling the two hundred miles north from the capital to see them.

Accordingly, Leach decided this was certainly a situation for the mountain to go to Mohammed. Or, anyway, nearly to Mohammed. For whatever unlikely reasons, the promoter chose as the location for the Beatles' first assault on England's southern territories the army town of Aldershot, some thirty-five miles to the west of London. After a freezing nine-hour drive, the team arrived in Aldershot late on a Saturday afternoon, complete with photographer to record the triumph. But Leach was soon dismayed to discover that his always erratic fortunes were following their familiarly unpredictable form. Purchasing a copy of the local newspaper, but not bothering to first peruse it, he handed it to the group with a satisfied, "What about that for publicity?"

John Lennon glanced through the pages. "What bloody publicity?" came his curt retort.

In line with its policy of not accepting payment by check from first-time advertisers, the paper had not run his advertisement announcing his show at the town's Queens Hall.

After scouring the local pubs and coffee bars, the luckless crew managed to attract an audience that numbered eighteen people. Moreover, as the hall's record player had broken down, the Beatles were obliged to play to this eighteen-strong audience for three and a half hours, with only a fifteen-minute break. George, sullenly defiant as ever, was considerably unhappy. And, as ever, the controls on his sense of the absurd set at maximum, Paul rallied the troops, cheerily cracking, "There's no business like show business."

A redeeming feature of this somewhat unsuccessful foray to "break" the south was the night spent in London on the way back. Here, at the Blue Gardenia Club, run by Cass of Casanovas fame, the group jammed on stage for a few numbers—the Beatles' London debut.

At their next meeting with Brian Epstein, he again expressed his desire to manage them. "Yes," replied John brusquely, after a moment's silence. The more cautious Paul wondered whether it would affect the sort of music they played; he was assured it would not. Still withholding his final decision, Paul contacted Sam Leach, told him that "this millionaire wants to manage us," and asked him to check Epstein out.

Leach met him in the Kardomah coffee bar, above the NEMS shop Epstein ran. "It was obvious he was a gentleman, and he had plenty of money. I told Paul, 'He seems keen, and he's genuine.' I could tell he was more interested in them as a group than just as a way of making money. It wasn't just that he had his eye on John: I thought he was a real fan of the band—he was so enthusiastic."

A stumbling block was Paul's father. With typical Northern anti-Semitism—an unusual but unsurprising character flaw—Jim was most concerned that his eldest son should be associated with a "Jew boy." After a meeting with Brian, Jim's fears were quelled, however; he was charmed by the obvious sincerity of a man with whom Paul was quickly discovering he had more in common than he had realized.

The 4,500-strong audience at "Operation Big Beat" watched one of the last performances the Beatles gave as a raw R & B group. The "rough trade" aspect of the group—the leather jackets and smoking and swearing onstage—had admittedly been part of their attraction for Brian Epstein. Yet his understanding of both theater and of record marketing was sufficiently extensive for him to know that such an appearance was too threatening for mass market consumption. The leathers were, moreover, faintly dated. Though still only a minority cult, London's modernists—"mods" —were pioneering a neat, almost fastidiously precise look, often influenced by French, Italian, and even American fashions. High-buttoned suits, button-down collared shirts, and elastic-sided boots were the dominant style. Already the Beatles' fringed, feminine haircuts took them part of the way toward such an image. Brian decided to complete it, with sharp, velvet-collared suits ordered from the local branch of a tailoring chain.

To complement their new, tidy appearances, Brian insisted

1. Paul with Mini car in 1964. *(Pictorial Press)* **2.** In October 1963, at ATV's Birmingham studios, Paul psyches up for a recording of the weekly "Thank Your Lucky Stars" show with a refreshing cup of tea. *(Pictorial Press)*

2

1. Wacky antics in the dressing-room at ATV Studios in Birmingham, where the Beatles are recording the weekly "Thank Your Lucky Stars" in October 1963. *(Pictorial Press)* **2.** Ed Sullivan hands out advice to Paul, ever ready to learn, during rehearsals for his show. *(Pictorial Press)* **3.** Eighty million Americans get their first sight of Paul in musical action in the Beatles' performance on "The Ed Sullivan Show" in February 1964. *(Pictorial Press)*

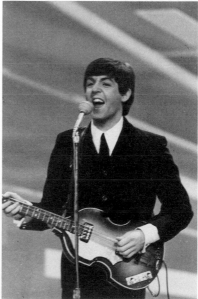

3

1. Before appearing on "The Ed Sullivan Show" in February 1964, Paul tunes his famous Hofner bass. *(Pictorial Press)* **2.** Onstage with the Beatles. *(David Redfern/Retna Ltd.)* **3.** Casual to a degree of perfection, the Beatles' diplomat prepares himself for yet another endearingly wacky one-line answer to reporters' questions at the group's New York press conference in February 1964. *(Pictorial Press)*

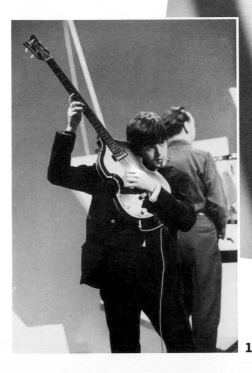

2

3

2

■ **1.** The Beatles arrive at San Francisco airport on August 18, 1964, in the midst of their first full-scale U.S. tour. *(AP/Wide World Photos)* ■ **2.** In Washington D.C., February 1964. How much of his baby-fat would Paul have sweated off if the Beatles had played longer sets? *(Pictorial Press)*

1

■**1.** Paul in a scene from *Help*. (*AP/Wide World Photos*) ■**2.** Paul and George in *Help* in 1965. (*AP/Wide World Photos*)

their music and stage shows must have a similarly elegant simplicity. The songs were tightened up and restructured; smoking on-stage was absolutely forbidden. All this appealed very much to Paul; Brian's insistence on precise attention to detail very much paralleled his own.

"Paul would always go along with what Brian said in those days," says Sam Leach. "In fact, I have to say that he was a bit of a suck-up: that's the only criticism I've got of him—he tended to agree with Brian too much. And John didn't. And that would lead to a bit of friction, when you'd get John and Paul taking sides, and sometimes John would get a bit of a mood on."

John Lennon, however, was already having his fair share of problems with Brian. Early in 1962, the two of them, along with Paul and Sam Leach, went out for an evening's drinking. This was the only occasion that Leach ever saw Paul drunk: "Usually he was just too well-behaved to get blind drunk. But on this occasion he was pissed by midnight, and we just put him in a taxi and sent him home."

Then the three of them made their way to Leach's home, where they sat around the kitchen table, drinking some more. "And Brian is saying to John, 'Let's go to Amsterdam for the weekend.' And I'm saying, 'Go on: you'll enjoy yourself—have a laugh.' Dead innocent. Suddenly I get a kick under the table. I think, 'What the fuck's that for?' Then I tell them again they should go, and get another kick. So I go for a wee, and John follows me and tells me to shut up. 'Don't you know he's a queer!' Oh dear, sorry."

Nor was Brian having any more luck in his efforts to interest record companies in the group. His first priority was to secure the Beatles a record contract, but after two auditions Decca Records had turned them down, preferring to sign the local Brian Poole and the Tremeloes. Pye, Phillips, Columbia, and HMV would not even listen to him. The Beatles, who had finally signed a contract with him at the end of January, did not berate "Eppy" for his lack of success, but instead offered him support and encouragement.

A local photographer, Les Chadwick, was hired by Brian to provide publicity stills of the group; he was only too aware that in the world of rock and roll, appearances counted for as much as the music. At the end of February, Chadwick arranged for the Beatles to meet him in the Dingle studio he shared with Peter Kaye, an even more prominent local photographer. The appointment was made for eleven in the morning, but it was three hours later when the Beatles eventually turned up, driven by Paul in the racing green Ford Classic he had bought from his saving of gig earnings. "Paul had made the effort to save up for a car," says Chadwick, "because he was a little more down-to-earth than the others: a car to Paul was a little bit of security and a slight status symbol. And when he got it he took the others around in it. He had, or perhaps *needed*, just a little more stability than the other lads."

The pictures that eventually emerged from this and a subsequent session were a variant on the gritty location shots that Astrid had taken in Hamburg—bomb sites, a burnt-out car, and the pier head were all used as backgrounds. Epstein was pleased with the results, though less so when Chadwick had thousands of copies printed up with the name Beatles spelled as *Beetles*.

All the same, Chadwick rode out this minor disaster, and continued to work with the group. In different situations from those Sam Leach observed, the photographer saw a different relationship between Paul and Brian Epstein.

"Paul was a bright lad—in his own way the brightest of the lot. And I don't think he fell as easily for this vision of El Dorado that Brian was giving them glimpses of. The others were all going, 'Yes, yes, let's have it.' But I got the impression he was wondering if it was all possible, if they weren't going to come down to earth with a bad bump. Paul always seemed to me to be the one that had one foot on dry land. He never lost his grip on reality, he was never swept away by it, in the way that the others would allow themselves to be picked up by it and go along with it because it was a laugh.

"John would go along with anything new and different, even then. He would create situations that Paul would go along with; Paul didn't create situations, but equally it wouldn't matter if John lost it all. But Paul was more of a thinker; he could see the other side, and was always trying to envisage what would happen if the whole thing fell apart. In a way, it's a shame he couldn't just enjoy it all for what it was. But caution got the better of him."

On Saturday, March 17, 1962, Sam Leach threw a party at his future mother-in-law's house, to announce his engagement. Earlier in the week, however, Paul had reminded the promoter that he had the Beatles booked to play that night; where would they be performing? he asked.

Renting an available hall in Knotty Ash, a Liverpool suburb, Leach put the group on the same bill with Rory Storm and the Hurricanes. The last-minute gig only drew two hundred people. However, Rory Storm proved a sensation, turning in one of his wildest-ever performances.

"We're not going on!" Paul declared to Leach in an unusual display of unprofessionalism. "They'll just laugh at us—we've got no chance with this."

"You're the Beatles, aren't you? Go up there and prove it!" came the reply.

The resulting show, Leach claims, was one of the finest he ever saw the Beatles give. "They even topped Rory!"

Leaving the hall in Leach's van, however, the entire complement—the Beatles, Rory Storm and the Hurricanes, and Leach—were almost wiped out when a speeding ten-ton truck, into whose path they'd pulled, slammed on its brakes and stopped less than a foot from their vehicle.

At the party, Paul, with Dorothy Rhone, was his usual well-behaved self. In stark contrast, John Lennon was made to go and stand in the garden for half an hour by Leach's future mother-in-law. This schoolmistress-like punishment was for a schoolboy-like crime: John had been rolling eggs down a girl's bird's-nest hairstyle, laughing uproariously as they smashed on the kitchen floor, the yolk and egg whites spreading in a drift of thick slime across the linoleum.

In one corner of the room, both shocked and amused by the appalling behavior of his favorite Beatle, stood the nervous figure of Brian Epstein. Sam Leach's fiancée's sister, Vera, found him giving her what she thought was quite a line of chat. She rather fancied him, and was amazed to later discover he was gay.

Paul, says Leach, seemed similarly unaware of the true nature of Brian's sexuality. "I think Paul was like me, a bit innocent about what it was all about. People in Liverpool didn't know what a homosexual was in those days. I don't think Paul really cottoned on to it at all in those days. And later, when he did, he's the type that would just be very diplomatic about it."

If no London record companies seemed interested, at least the Beatles' reputation as an outstanding live act continued to grow, not only in the English Northwest, but also in Hamburg.

In the middle of April the group was set to open at an even larger St. Pauli venue, the new Star Club. On April 10, the day they were set to fly out—Brian insisted on this most prestigious form of travel—to the German port, Millie Sutcliffe, Stuart's mother, received a telegram from Astrid Kirchherr: Stuart was dead. The recurrent, crippling headaches he had suffered, caused originally by a boot in the head from a Teddy Boy when the Beatles played Litherland Town Hall, had been symptoms of a brain expanding beyond its space. And so the Beatles were joined on the flight by their former bassist's distraught mother.

As ever, Paul was completely unhinged by yet another sudden death. Guilty because of the constant bickering and fights that had gone on between him and Stuart, Paul attempted to comfort Stuart's mother. As always at such times of bereavement he managed to say the wrong thing. "My mother died when I was fourteen, and I'd forgotten all about her in six months," he lied, pointlessly.

Hamburg's craziness and the Beatles' usual exhausting schedule conspired to provide an escape from the grief felt by all the group. A huge venue, the Star Club featured not only the Beatles, Kingsize Taylor and the Dominoes, and the Big Three, but also major American acts like Ray Charles and one of Paul's earliest idols, Little Richard. At last Paul was able to perfect his long acclaimed Little Richard impersonation, with instruction from none other than the master himself.

As John Lennon offered to supply the American singer with "one up the bum," Paul attempted to ignore such heresy and learn as much of Little Richard's technique as he was able. "Paul was the closest to me," Little Richard says. "Paul is like my blood brother. I believe if I was hungry, Paul would feed me. We're that tight. Paul is a humanitarian."

As summer approached, the Beatles, as they had done the previous year, began to take trips to the nearby beaches. One day Paul asked Horst Fascher, who had moved to the Star Club, whether he could help him rent a car, to travel to a more distant Baltic beach. As Paul had not had a driving license sufficiently long enough to satisfy any of the car rental firms, Fascher arranged to hire a car from a butcher called Heinz, who owned all the delicatessens in St. Pauli. The car that arrived at the Star Club was a gleaming new four-door Fiat 2100, for which Horst Fascher acted as guarantor.

The Beatles were due onstage that night at nine o'clock. Yet it was to Fascher's considerably growing concern that they didn't show up for their spot; another group was obliged to play in their place. An hour later Paul charged into the club: the car was stranded on the autobahn twenty-five kilometers outside of Hamburg—he had neglected to check the oil in the engine, and it had seized up. The repair bill presented to Fascher came to over eight hundred marks. "Paul said he would pay me back, but he never did. He always claimed he needed to buy strings for his bass or other things. To this day he still owes me the money."

Perhaps Paul assumed that he would not be coming back to Hamburg, and he could run out on his debt. For before they returned to England in June, the Beatles received a promising message from Brian. Their manager had sent a telegram to *Mersey Beat* on May 9 with details of an offer: HAVE SECURED CONTRACT FOR BEATLES TO RECORDED [sic] FOR EMI ON PARLAPHONE [sic] LABEL 1ST RECORDING DATE SET FOR JUNE 6TH BRIAN EPSTEIN.

CHAPTER NINE

Nearing desperation, Brian Epstein had taken the train down to London for one last stab at the record companies. Learning that A&R men tended to be more impressed with demo songs on a disc rather than on a tape, Brian, such an avid believer in the merits of impeccable presentation, went to the HMV store on Oxford Street, where there was a facility for turning such tapes into records.

The engineer who cut the acetate was impressed with what he heard, and contacted Syd Coleman, of EMI's publishing company, Ardmore and Beechwood, located in the same building. On the spot, Coleman offered to publish two Lennon and McCartney songs on the record, "Love of the Loved" and "Hey Little Girl," and telephoned a friend, George Martin, Parlophone Records' head of A&R, whose role included the production of the acts on his label.

The A&R man was tempted to ask Brian where Liverpool was when Epstein came to visit him in EMI's brand-new offices in Manchester Square; such a thought was prompted by the surprise that Brian feigned when Martin admitted he had never heard of the Beatles.

Martin did think the songs he heard contained a certain quality; that there was more than one person singing appealed to him, as soon it would to the whole world. Listening to the songs sung by Paul, he turned to Brian and remarked, "He has the most commercial voice of the lot." (Later, in his autobiography *A Cellarful of Noise*, Brian showed himself to be of the same opinion. "This is probably still true, though each Beatle has an equal amount to contribute to the total disc content.")

When the Beatles drove down to London on June 6, to the solid, white detached house in Abbey Road that contains the EMI studios, the group was under the impression that the recording test was purely a formality.

They were unaware that routinely one of the studios would be booked for three days for such tests, and that they were one of six possible signings auditioning on that day. Such innocence was demonstrably to their benefit, for the four musicians evinced no nervousness. It was their engaging personalities that sold them to Martin as much as their music. Up until now, Parlophone had been very much an "oddities" label, with Martin signing and producing several large-selling comedy records, including those by the Goons; impressed by this, the Beatles quizzed Martin at some length about his experiences with the comedy troupe.

Unusually, George Harrison spoke the most. And, as usual, Pete Best said not one word. When it came to the Beatles actually playing their music, moreover, Martin thought that Pete's drumming was not sufficiently "regular." The engineer on the session, Norman Smith, considered it "a pain in the ass," particularly because of the state of Paul's equipment. Before they could begin playing, Smith first had to call out the studio's "technical bods" to conduct an instant overhaul of the bass player's amplifier. Then it was discovered that Paul's speaker was shot, and a studio speaker had to be taken out of the echo chamber for him to use. "I think he thought we were being ultra fussy and stupid. But I thought their music was pretty dreadful on that day. I wasn't very keen at all.

"But despite his initial sound being abominable, I thought the only one who could really play was Paul; John just stood there knocking out the chords, George's solos were not that impressive, and any average drummer could have done just as well."

Winding up this hardly awe-inspiring demonstration of their musical prowess, the Beatles turned on their charm. "I don't suppose George Martin or I got a word in for about twenty minutes," says the engineer. "It was mickey-taking and banter—Liverpudlian humor. They left George and I in a state of almost exhaustion. He looked at me and said 'Cor, dear me: what do you think?' By this time tears were pouring down my face, and my stomach ached from laughing. I said, 'Well, Parlophone has always been known as a comedy label, so you'd better sign them!'"

Six weeks passed before George Martin made a formal offer. And even when he had given them the deal, the producer was wondering which member he should elevate as the Tommy Steele or Cliff Richard figure, thus reducing the others' status to backing musicians.

"My original feeling was that Paul had a sweeter voice, John's had more character, and George was generally not so good. I was thinking, on balance, that I should make Paul the leader."

On reflection, Martin decided against this, as it would alter the nature of the group, a decision confirmed by a revelatory visit to The Cavern to see the Beatles perform live. He was stunned by what he saw: in contrast to the rock-and-roll-by-numbers of Steele and Richard, this alumnus of London's prestigious Guildhall School of Music suddenly understood what Beat groups were about.

* * *

Since their visit to Hamburg together, when Dot Rhone and Cynthia Powell had become close friends, the two girls had shared a flat near Liverpool city center. One evening, while the group waited anxiously for news from Parlophone, Dot and Cynthia were spending the night at home. Not expecting any visitors, Dot coordinated the rollers she had in her hair with a tatty old sweater and a pair of her mother's bloomers. To Dot's horror, Paul arrived. Together, the two of them disappeared into her room. Minutes later there came the sound of footsteps racing down the staircase, followed by the slamming of the front door. The uncontrollable sobs that came from Dot's room told the whole story.

"With the adulation of their fans came such a varied choice of submissive dolly-bird groupies willing to do anything for them," says Cynthia, "a temptation Paul found hard to resist. After all, he was a hot-blooded young rocker with a world full of beautiful women just waiting to be discovered by him. He was too young to settle down; he wanted desperately to be footloose and fancy-free, and I suppose he let Dot down very gently under the circumstances. The trouble was that Dot honestly believed at the time that it was because of the way she looked on that fateful night."

Shortly afterward, Paul started dating Iris Caldwell, the sister of Rory Storm. "It wasn't exactly a love affair. In those days you didn't have love affairs; he'd pay for the pictures one week, I'd pay the next."

Paul became very attached to Iris's mother. Mrs. Caldwell was never averse to staying up chatting and joking with the musicians her son would bring around after gigs. The Caldwells were a warm, loving family, bound together by a sense of humor that reached even beyond that which could be reasonably expected from Merseyside. Even when Iris and Paul stopped going out together, he continued to visit the house, having come to look on Mrs. Caldwell as something of a substitute mother.

"Our house was an escape for him," says Iris. "My mother was so easy to get along with. So he'd escape back to our place and eat cheese sandwiches and drink tea, talking all night. He'd idolized his own mother. It was like losing a limb when she died, and he'd had to rebuild himself.

"He felt he had a responsibility to his mother's memory, to say to her 'I'm still me.' He had to show her he was a survivor. He couldn't let his mum or dad or brother see him going to pieces. He had to block her death out as a matter of self-preservation. It had been a bad age for him to lose her, because it's a transition period: suddenly you are given responsibility, you realize there's more to life than you thought and that the world is not a very nice place. But you still need the reassurance of those parental figures in the background.

"He hadn't been able to put any pressure on his dad—in fact, his dad, for all his exuberance, was leaning on him. So Paul had had to prove that he was strong.

"I never heard him say a bad word about anyone. I know how much he liked Stuart. But what Paul had got was ambition; he wouldn't have approved of Stuart going off with a girl and troubling their potential. Who wants to settle down with Astrid when there's a world to conquer? I don't know of Paul ever stepping on anyone. The only person he was ruthless with was himself. Even in the Pete Best situation, it was because Ringo was a better drummer.

"He was terribly distressed by Stuart's death—it was another ending of the life of someone near in spirit to him. Why should he have to prove he's very upset? You live with yourself."

Paul's frequent presence in the Caldwell household did not result in any great rivalry between himself and Rory Storm. "The difference between Paul and my brother was his total dedication, which all the Beatles had: they lived it, they deserved everything they got. And Paul and John were very talented boys.

"Paul was so determined, with a total belief in himself to an extent that some would think he was self-centered and in love with himself. But he wasn't—it was just that he wasn't ordinary, and knew that he wasn't. He wasn't thinking, 'I'm getting ten pounds a week for being in a band—better than working.'

"He wouldn't run with the crowd. If he liked a record or a

group you weren't supposed to like, he'd say so. If he wouldn't join in for a whipround [when everyone chips in for a drink] in the pub, or go off pulling birds [picking up girls] all the time, maybe it was because he had other things to do instead; he had to get on with it. He was very correct, and liked people around him to be correct. He never swore, he never told a dirty joke. Paul was the whole driving force in the group, he was the clever one. And he was all right, Paul, he worked for everything he got."

There had been nothing unduly notable that year about the annual summer season played at one of Butlin's Holiday Camps by Rory Storm and the Hurricanes.

In 1962 their three-month engagement was at Skegness, on the east coast. Yorkshire millworkers from Wakefield had attempted to dismember Lancashire millworkers from Wigan; the dance hall had been wrecked on several Friday nights as happy vacationers celebrated their final night at the camp; Rory Storm had been obliged to cross a railway line on the narrow ledge of a bridge to escape a gang of Teds bent on murder; Johnny Guitar, a non-swimmer, had twice been thrown in his stage clothes into the swimming pool by similarly Edwardian-garbed gentlemen.

In short, everything was as it should be. Only the elderly Indian elephant that had suffered a heart attack, keeled over into the swimming pool, and drowned had disturbed this sense of harmony. The camp management was baffled as to how to remove the dead animal's bloated carcass from the deep end of the pool, where it was obliged to float for three days before a crane could be hired to remove it.

In late August, however, a more momentous event occurred. Dawn was just breaking one morning when Johnny Guitar, who had moved with Ringo Starr into a "caravan" (trailer) on a nearby site after the pair were expelled from their Butlin's chalet for entertaining girls, was awakened by a ferocious hammering on the door. Standing outside and shivering in the North Sea breeze were Paul McCartney and John Lennon. They had driven over from Liverpool in Paul's car. "I wondered what the bloody hell they wanted—something was obviously wrong. Then Paul said that they wanted Ringo to join them. I thought, 'Bloody hell: I'd better go and get Rory.' "

Rory Storm, however, was fatalistic: he knew his group couldn't match the offer the Beatles were making, a record contract *and* £25 a week.

"You've got to do what's best for yourself, Ringo," advised Johnny Guitar.

Ringo left the next day. "He still owes me the rent on the caravan—£3.50," says Johnny Guitar.

Ringo Starr, the last member to join the group, was the only Beatle from the notorious city center slumland of the Dingle, through which Paul used to pass on the bus on his way to the Institute from the leafier pastures of Allerton. Born on July 7, 1940, Richard Starkey came from a deprived background and a broken home, and had spent many of his schooldays in the hospital: an ideal set of miserable circumstances for the evolution of a genuine street-corner Teddy Boy, the sort that John Lennon so desperately strove to be.

Ringo had first taken up the drums in 1956, forming a skiffle group at the engineering firm where he worked as a joiner's apprentice; The Eddie Clayton Skiffle Group, as they were called, played the same circuit as the original version of the Quarrymen. In 1959 he joined the Ravin' Texans, who later became Rory Storm and the Hurricanes. It was with Storm's group that he changed his name to the gunslinger-like Ringo Starr, his new Christian name being suggested by the rings with which he adorned the fingers of both hands.

On his twenty-five dollar drum kit he developed a laconic, almost naive style, roughshod playing that evinced a lugubrious charm similar to that of the drummer himself. And Ringo's droll humor dovetailed perfectly with that of the other Beatles when he met them in Hamburg.

At this stage, however, Ringo Starr knew nothing of the machinations that had taken place to sack Pete Best. Earlier in the month, Mona Best, Pete's mother, had noted Paul's unease when, at a group meeting at her house, her son had declared his intention of buying a car. "You'd be better off saving your money," Paul had suggested mysteriously.

On August 15, Pete Best was called to Brian's office. Brian was not happy about the sacking; he liked Pete and had wanted to appease both sides by keeping him for live shows while heeding George Martin's suggestion and using a session drummer in the studio. The other Beatles were adamant, however: Pete had never really fitted in, and his drumming was simply not of sufficient quality.

So, as ever, Paul, John, and George distanced themselves from the unpleasantness by giving the job of hitman to someone else. Pete even remembers Paul telephoning Brian as their manager was giving Best the bad news, to inquire whether the deed had been done.

A furor broke out among Pete's fans when the story broke on Merseyside. At a Cavern date the Beatles and Brian had to run a gauntlet of insults, fists, and kicks as they arrived at the club. When the Beatles presented themselves to George Martin at Abbey Road Studios on September 11 for the recording of their first single, George Harrison still sported a black eye from the incident.

The songs selected were "Love Me Do" and "P.S. I Love You." Paul had mainly written both songs, though John contributed the middle-eight of the first title and had helped with the lyrics on the second.

It was not an easy session, says Norman Smith, who was soon dubbed "Normal" Smith by the group. (In the early seventies, as "Hurricane" Smith, he was to have his own run of hit songs.) "They were very much in awe of the studio. Also, they didn't realize the disparity between what they could play on the studio floor and how it would come out sounding in the control room. They refused to wear headphones, I remember. In fact, subsequently they hardly ever wore them."

For reasons of his own, Martin handed the session over to his assistant, Ron Richards, who had great difficulty getting the right drumming from Ringo. Eventually, Andy White, a session drummer, was brought in for the task. At this time George Martin reappeared to take charge and to oversee the song's editing. "It took a long time," says Smith. "Quite honestly, by the time it came out I was pretty sick of it—I didn't think it would do anything."

Before the single was released, Paul had become reacquainted in Liverpool with Thelma Pickles, whom he hadn't seen since she and John had split up, back in the days of the Quarrymen. For Thelma, who now went out with Paul for a time, the change in her new boyfriend was impressive. "He'd developed from the young schoolboy he'd been into someone very much his own person."

A not-infrequent subject of conversation was Dot Rhone. "From the way he talked about her, he still obviously cared about her. I don't think he thought it was finally over. I think he thought it was one of those things where you have problems and then you go back together. It all seemed a bit of a question mark, as far as I could see. I wasn't in any way a replacement for Dot."

One day, soon after they'd met up again, Paul and Thelma drove into Liverpool city center together, to Wilson's Bookshop on Church Alley. There Paul bought some ballpoint pens and several packets of typing paper. "It was to answer his fan mail with; at that stage he took the trouble to answer every letter."

Afterward they went for a drink in a coffee bar on Church Street. Thelma, no particular fan of rock and roll and so far oblivious to the Beat music in her own city, was bewildered when the woman at the cash register asked for Paul's autograph. "I thought this was staggering—she was no teenybopper either. I said, 'What's that all about?,' and he replied, 'Oh, it's just this Beatles business.' I was not clued in at all as to what was happening at that stage.

"But he was very charming about it, slightly embarrassed, in fact. But he also obviously enjoyed it. I remember him practicing his autograph, and he always wrote 'James Paul McCartney,' which was amusing."

On several occasions Paul would pick up Thelma and they'd go down to Beatles' Cavern dates. "The first thing that struck me when he turned up for me was that he appeared to have his swimming things with him—a towel and a change of clothes. 'You get really sweaty down there—you need them for afterwards,' he explained. And when we got down there I saw what he meant, because it was absolutely dripping.

"But you couldn't be seen to be with him. It was kind of, 'Don't stay too close.' I was never sure whether it was that women would be rude to me, or they didn't want to be seen with women, because it would affect the fans. I think it was a combination of a few things.

"They were certainly very big down there. People were screaming. I found the whole thing very strange. When we walked to the car afterwards, groups of girls would follow and they'd be really rude to me. I found it very odd that girls would behave like that. I must have been very naive."

Thelma felt that Paul also was somewhat mystified by women behaving in such a way. He seemed to feel that it was peculiar, she says, that when they played out of town girls would openly ask to go to bed with them. "He'd come and see me when he got back from places like Nottingham, or wherever, quite late. He'd show me the notes that girls would pass to him onstage. Some of them were absolutely *vile*. I'm no prude, but these were filthy, absolutely pornographic, with nothing left to the imagination. He found it odd that girls would do this. Quite amusing, but also a bit horrid.

"Paul would never actively treat women like shit. I don't think it was in his nature to treat anyone like shit. But John would —he wouldn't hesitate. Even though John was incredibly sensitive, he was terrified of exposing himself. Paul was a much more sensitive human being, in the true sense of the word, because he was caring and thoughtful, and wouldn't do things without thinking."

Later in life John was to confess his jealousy at Paul's ability to have a brief relationship with a woman, and then pass onto another. Yet Paul was able to move on from them with no ill will on either side. Paul, in fact, was often more comfortable with women than with men, a legacy from both his mother and the bosomy aunts who became Mary McCartney's substitute. His songwriting partner need not have felt envy, for perhaps it was this aspect of Paul that drew out the feminine, creative side in John. It also may have accounted for the ease with which he and Brian empathized, or, rather, the ease with which Brian allowed Paul to subtly but ceaselessly dominate him.

On October 1, 1962, The Beatles signed a second contract with Brian Epstein, to run for five years.

Shortly before the "Love Me Do" session, there was further evidence that their efforts at last were beginning to pay dividends. Thanks to the enthusiasm of a local fan, who had written to the national weekly music paper *Record Mirror* with the complaint that the press were ignoring a "fab" group from Liverpool, Brian's Whitechapel offices were visited by one of the paper's reporters, Jimmy Watson, and its staff photographer, Dezo Hoffmann.

It was Hoffmann who had received this letter, and it had taken him three months to persuade his editor to come up with the money for their train fares. An expatriate Czech, Hoffmann had worked as a film cameraman in the Spanish Civil War, where he had been interned in a concentration camp. Benefiting from the experience he had acquired taking moving pictures, after the war Hoffmann became a leading show-business photographer; it was central to his style that he rarely took studio shots, preferring action situations in which he would shoot roll after roll of film. Even in the studio he would constantly cajole his subjects into more and greater movement.

Of this, of course, the Beatles were utterly unaware as Hoffmann hovered in the background in Brian's Whitechapel office and Watson took down the relevant background information. For his own part, the photographer was faintly disappointed that the quartet hardly were living up to their claimed reputation. Nervous at this grand occasion, they were as humble "as little sheeps" during the actual interview.

Talking with Hoffmann prior to what they assumed would be the picture session, however, they instantly became animated when they heard the impressive roll call of stars with whom the photographer had worked over the years: Elvis Presley, Frank

Sinatra, Cliff Richard. The effect was similar to that George Martin had had on them when he told them he had worked with the Goons. And their subsequently revealed personalities entranced Hoffmann as much as they had the record producer.

As a result, Dezo Hoffmann didn't join Jimmy Watson when he left for Lime Street station to catch a London-bound train. Instead he stayed behind, intending to scout suitable locations in the city with the Beatles the next day; he ended up sticking around for another three days.

For the next three years Dezo Hoffmann worked with the Beatles more than any other photographer and was responsible for most of the iconlike shots that indelibly stamped their image on the world. "I created that clean-cut image. When they found out I'd been taking pop pictures since 1953 I became a sort of father confessor to them, and would advise them on how other bands behaved. For my part, they made me feel like I was seventeen again—that was the appeal for me."

On that first of many subsequent visits to Liverpool that Hoffmann made, most of the pictures were taken at 20 Forthlin Road. "Paul was certainly the most unusual, underestimated Beatle. Each of the four of them had a certain creativity that differed from what the other three had. Paul's particular strength," he says in words that would have warmed "Dusty" Durband's heart, "was that he was essentially a teacher."

His vision of perfection obviously sorely troubled by the photographer's at times severe Slovakian accent and considerably broken English, Paul took it upon himself to remedy this, going to extreme pains to try and drill the correct pronunciation of the letter *W* into the photographer's brain. This, however, proved a rare failure for Paul McCartney. "It was impossible because I had learned the ABC in the Slovakian way, and I just couldn't pronounce it. But Paul tried so hard to correct me every time a *W* came up in my speech. He would never let it go by. In fact, even though he meant it well, it did eventually get on my nerves. But the funny thing is that as a result of Paul's language classes I realize I now have a slight Liverpudlian accent."

An even greater attraction for Hoffmann than the McCartney

language laboratory was the fact that not only were the Beatles even at this stage already a musical phenomenon, but in Hoffmann's eyes they were also a "photographic phenomenon," because of the combination of their four unique faces. "To photograph the Beatles together was difficult, because they all have such different facial bone structures. But because I worked with them so much, I already knew which angle to do each of them from, and who to put each of them next to, so you can disguise these difficulties.

"John had very much a primitive face. To me, Paul's is like the prototype of an angelic face. George is also angelic in a way, but he had big ears—I always had to camouflage them. Paul had the best face—that's why he was most popular with girls for so long. Also because of this he was naturally the easiest to photograph."

This angelic quality was not necessarily always reflected in Paul's behavior. At least, however, Hoffmann noted that though in terms of verbal wit he could give as good as he got, Paul's replies lacked the caustic edge of John's words: "There was never really any bitterness in Paul." Yet it seemed to the photographer that the vicious vitriol John would pour on often undeserving victims was quite evidently to Paul's pleasure. "In a way Paul wallowed in it, because John always played up to his requirements. It's a useful thing to have somebody like that, who's capable of putting down people you don't like."

During those first three days in Liverpool Hoffmann noticed that Frankie Howerd, a master of the peculiarly English art of "camp" comedy, was appearing in Manchester, at Mr. Smith's nightclub. Of all the Beatles, it was only Paul who expressed a wish to tag along with him to a performance. Moreover, Paul was thrilled and impressed that Hoffmann carried sufficient weight to be able to usher him backstage to meet the celebrated comedian. Once the professional obligation of photographing the pair together had been fulfilled (*"Should* I be photographed with him?" Howard muttered furtively as the photographer inserted a fresh roll of film in his camera. "You'll be doing yourself a favor for the future," came Hoffmann's prescient reply), Paul, typically, turned the occasion to his advantage by picking the comic's brains as to how best to armor himself against the strains of stardom.

As far as Dezo Hoffmann could tell, these pressures, when they arrived, were far more intimidating for Paul McCartney than his public persona permitted him to show. A difficulty with which Paul always grappled, he detected, was a shyness that he had worked hard to eradicate but that nevertheless rose almost irrepressibly. "He was never sure of himself," says Hoffmann, echoing Jack Sweeney, Paul's form-master in his sixth year at Liverpool Institute. "He *pretended* to be—it was all pretense. That's why he was able to give such fabulous interviews later, because he covered up his inadequacies the only way he could— by joking, by pretending to jump ahead of anybody who asked him a difficult or intimate question. He would give serious interviews when he was on his own, but when he was answering questions with the others, Paul was unable to really reveal himself at all—though admittedly they'd all be joking at such times anyway."

CHAPTER TEN

The Beatles were a quartet of young men so driven and re-vealing of their place and time that it was impossible for them not to have become the pop prophets that they did.

Even before the first strains of John's harmonica riff—the main reason, really, for the appeal of "Love Me Do"—had traversed the airwaves, the atmosphere seemed charged. Somewhere, it was felt, a new set of heroes was being mustered, set to bring salvation and correct Britain's inadequacy as a source of original rock and roll. The country's traditional, perversely proud xenophobia (which was reinforced by the country's declining position as a world power) ensured that almost everyone, apart from the newly invented "teenagers," was impervious to the sweeping cultural changes made possible by Elvis Presley, who, being an American, was an object worthy of contempt from the resolutely London-oriented media pundits.

Yet already change was afoot; it was nothing but advantageous for the Beatles that the South's contemptuous consideration of the North, an area considered to begin approximately thirty miles outside London, had been softened up by the new popularity of "kitchen-sink" realism in literature. Writers such as Stan Barstow, Alan Sillitoe, and John Braine portrayed a depressing, industrial world of unwanted pregnancies, nine-to-five dullness, and bleak futures that was lapped up by the British, reaching a spectacularly broader audience when works like *Saturday Night and Sunday Morning* and *A Kind of Loving* were translated into film. Perhaps such a popularity was a purging of national guilt at being, as Prime Minister Harold MacMillan had portentously proclaimed, the English society that had "never had it so good."

A new mood was clearly in the air. Satire, which had had esoteric exposure in London's Establishment Club and the newly launched *Private Eye* magazine, had lately become part of the national conversational currency with the launch of "That Was the Week That Was," a Saturday night TV show hosted by a young man named David Frost with a swept-forward haircut and a fashion sense that suggested at least some understanding of modernism.

In the shape of James Bond, a new fictional and cinematic hero—sexy and droll and inhabiting a specious but glamorous world of status-symbol brand names—had emerged. His existence was far removed from the stereotyped Brit-world of Biggles and Bulldog Drummond.

All that was required was someone, or some people, capable of fusing these oven-ready ingredients. And why should it not be through music, that most abstract and accessible of all art forms? As yet, however, this was some way off.

One day an acquaintance of Paul's bumped into him in Liverpool city center. He hadn't, he complained, had anything to eat all day; after all, someone, he joked in a Liverpool accent that seemed to be growing broader by the day, had had to pay for those ten thousand copies of "Love Me Do" that Brian had ordered for his shop.

Notwithstanding such effort, the progress of "Love Me Do" was depressingly slow. Released on October 5, it took over two months to reach the *Record Mirror*'s charts, where it remained for only two weeks, peaking at number seventeen.

All the same, this record, nothing more than a rough outline of the Beatles' possibilities, served as a useful introduction to the national pop process. Norman Jopling, who not long after was to become the first person to write about the Rolling Stones, recalls Paul, accompanied by an as ever furiously blushing Brian Epstein, walking into the *Record Mirror* offices to badger the editor into doing another feature on his group.

After they had lip-synched to the song on their first TV appearance, Granada TV's "People and Places" program, transmitted from Manchester to the North only, Paul phoned Iris Caldwell's mother from the studio, asking if she'd seen their performance and brief interview. "I thought you seemed a bit drippy," she forthrightly told him. "You didn't come across as having any personality—you've got to push yourself out a lot more."

Mike McCartney was equally critical. "Why did you talk like that on TV?" he demanded of his brother when he finally got home at two the next morning. "It sounded like George gone wrong . . . *you* don't talk like that."

"I know," replied Paul, "*you* know that, but *they* don't know that. . . . It's part of the image."

Shrewdly, Brian Epstein and Paul, who lived in each others' pockets in terms of conceiving the appropriate image for the Beatles (it was Paul who had drawn up the sketches for the design of their velvet-collared, mohair suits), had perceived that there was room for capitalizing on the public's new fondness for Northern drama. There is something, after all, indubitably sexy about the lilting sound of Scouse.

On the shoulders of Paul McCartney, whose mother had striven with the assiduousness of an elocutionist to remove every trace of the accent from his speech, must fall much of the blame for a contemporary British social problem: the "professional" Northerners, who proliferate in London in the worlds of show business, advertising, and the media, and whose accents grow broader with every year that they remain in the capital away from their hometowns. Indeed, the Beatles' accents were to thicken with every mile that they took from Liverpool.

Had it not been for a pair of fourteen-day engagements in Hamburg, booked before George Martin had offered the Beatles a contract, it is possible that "Love Me Do" would have fared better on the British charts. At a time that was crucial for a blanket promotion of the single, however, the group was obliged to return to the Star Club on November 1 and then again on December 18, the week "Love Me Do" entered the charts.

Just days after their return from the first of these two German trips, however, the Beatles were once again in Abbey Road Studio, recording "Please Please Me." Martin insisted the tempo be speeded up before he allowed it to take preference over his own choice, "How Do You Do It," a composition by a songwriter named Mitch Murray, which later became a hit for Gerry and the Pacemakers.

"Please Please Me" had also secured the Beatles a lucrative song publishing deal with Dick James Music. Struck by the song's "ingenious construction," James had offered Brian a deal on the spot that gave John and Paul their own publishing company, Northern Songs. Established in the days when sales of sheet music far outweighed those of records, music publishers by the 1960s were primarily concerned with collecting from around the world the sums of money owed to those artists whose song copyrights they controlled: such monies came from "covers" of songs and from payment for radio and TV plays. For so servicing the material of any artist who signed with them, however, music publishing companies generally extracted a sizable percentage. Moreover, such an agreement would persist for the length of the life of the copyright, which could in some cases be as long as forty years. By having their own company, John Lennon and Paul McCartney kept the copyrights of their own songs, and avoided handing over a share of their income.

Before "Please Please Me" was released, the Beatles passed a miserable Christmas away from home, braving the deep snow and biting winds in Hamburg. On their first night of this last season at the Star Club, Brian, already with a skinful of drink, was discovered to have vanished. At four in the morning the group, who had become increasingly worried as they searched for their manager, discovered him slumped in a corner of a Reeperbahn beer-keller, unconscious. John sensitively celebrated finding Brian by pouring a glass of beer over his head.

Christmas Day was spent at a party, with fish and horseradish sauce for their Christmas dinner. The next day a party at the Pacific Club was thrown by Manfred Weissleder, the Star Club's owner. Sharing in the roast turkey were Tony Sheridan, Kingsize Taylor and the Dominoes, and Johnny and the Hurricanes, the American instrumental group who, somewhat to the Beatles' irritation, was topping the bill over them at the Star Club.

Back in Britain the weather was no better, as the country experienced its harshest winter in a hundred years. Rather to the Beatles' amazement, however, they were able to witness Britain's arctic wastes through the windows of a coach carrying not only themselves around the country but also Helen Shapiro, Danny Williams, and Kenny Lynch, three British singers. Brian had managed to persuade Arthur Howes, the leading British promoter, to let "the boys" open the show on this middleweight package tour.

Helen Shapiro, the headliner, and who at sixteen was thought to be rather over the hill, remembers Paul trundling hesitantly up the center aisle of the tour coach and offering her a song, "Misery," that he thought she might consider recording. Like Thelma Pickles, she also recalls Paul diligently practicing his autograph.

"Please Please Me," a song that was to set the standards for

British pop for the rest of the decade, had been in the stores for three weeks when the tour began during the first week of February 1963. Its progress up the charts already was sufficiently rapid for George Martin to have phoned Brian, insisting an LP must be made to capitalize on the success. February 11, a "day off" from touring, was booked at Abbey Road Studios.

Setting a pattern that would last for the rest of their career together, a large candy jar of cough lozenges was placed on the piano, at the group's request, and next to it two fresh packs of Peter Stuyvesant cigarettes ("This didn't quite make sense," says Norman Smith).

The LP was finished at 10:00 P.M., twelve hours after they'd begun, with no more than four takes being made of any of the thirteen songs. Using a two-track machine, the recording was entirely live, with none of the vocals overdubbed. In something of a radical departure from established convention, "Normal" set the group up in the studio exactly in the positions they would occupy onstage, the better to get that live feel that had Martin so spellbound at The Cavern. "They thought it was normal practice," says "Normal." "They did exactly as I told them. They were always extremely good, no bother at all."

As George Martin intuitively understood exactly what needed to be brought out of the Beatles' music, so they equally were able to channel all the unreleased musical creativity that the producer had never been able to use with his comedy records. Previously Elvis Presley (with Sam Phillips) and Buddy Holly (with Norman Petty) had locked themselves away in studios for literally months before they arrived at the unique sounds with which they revolutionized music; the Beatles and George Martin took only a few hours.

Even though the principal singers were dipping regularly into the lozenge jar, by the time it came to the last song, "Twist and Shout," only one take was possible, "because Lennon could barely speak." The coarse vocal performance of one of the greatest rock and roll recordings is attributed to the fact that the singer's vocal chords were almost in shreds, and he was literally having to scream himself hoarse to make himself heard.

146

Notwithstanding that tour de force on the LP, it was, says "Normal," "nearly always Paul who was the MD, the musical director, as early as this. Obviously John would have quite a lot to say, but overall it was always Paul who was the guv'nor. Which is fair, because he was the natural musician, and even at this stage, the natural producer. On this session he was trying to figure out everything we were doing with the controls."

Two weeks later, "Please Please Me" was at number one. And on March 7 the LP of the same name was released, rapidly emulating the single's success by topping the album charts. In an age when LPs named for a hit single consisted of the hit plus less interesting filler tracks, *Please Please Me* was revolutionary, not only for its spine-tingling quality—the crucial measure of all great rock and roll—but also for giving value for money. This was crucial: for not only did the Beatles display unprecedented—for pop musicians—wit, intelligence, and naturalness, but the LP's value-for-money showed that they were genuinely honest, that they were ethically sound, though no one in those days thought in such convoluted terms. Whereas the earlier British pop stars had been distant, the Beatles were not thought of as rather remote boys-next-door but, instead, as One of Us. They had, in words also unknown at that time, street credibility.

CHAPTER ELEVEN

A pace was being established that would not be interrupted until late summer 1966, when the Beatles stopped touring.

April 12, 1963, saw the release of their third single, "From Me to You." A slighter work than "Please Please Me," and seemingly something of a holding operation, it nevertheless was soon at number one.

Four days before it went into the shops Cynthia Lennon, whose marriage to John in August 1962 had been kept a close secret, gave birth to a son, Julian. John's relationship with his wife and son, a stormy affair not assisted by John's seeming inability to be faithful, was closely observed by Paul. It was in stark opposition to the simple, honorable view of marriage and family he had been given at home before his mother died. Still pained by the failure of his relationship with Dot, he sadly absorbed the details of the Lennons' marriage and feared that he might fare no better.

Not that this stopped Paul from taking advantage of his many opportunities to go to bed with a ceaseless supply of beautiful girls. The Beatles' performance on May 9 at London's Royal Albert Hall, a prestigious event, seemed to have potential as a hunting ground for more of the same. A BBC Light Programme "live" broadcast, the bill also featured Del Shannon, Susan Maugham, and Shane Fenton.

For whatever reasons, Paul's practiced charm failed him on this occasion, as it did the other Beatles. They left the Royal Albert Hall together, earlier than planned, as a squabble with Del Shannon's manager had left the American, who soon recorded a cover of "From Me to You," ending the show.

Drinking coffee and eating sandwiches in the lounge of the Royal Court Hotel in Sloane Square, where they were staying, they were approached by Jane Asher, an auburn-haired, green-eyed actress and regular panelist on BBC-TV's "Juke Box Jury." An extremely pretty girl, Jane, who was only seventeen, was highly intelligent and carried herself with a combination of dignity and innocence.

Radio Times magazine had asked her, as a "celebrity writer," to interview the Beatles and write an article about them. The group, however, already had decided to visit the nearby flat of a *New Musical Express* journalist, Chris Hutchins, with Shane Fenton—who later married Iris Caldwell and even later revived his career as Alvin Stardust. Leaving a tired Ringo to catch up on his sleep, the five of them drove along the King's Road in Fenton's American car to Hutchins's home. All the while, George Harrison was the only one of the car's occupants talking to Jane.

In the flat, over a bottle of Scotch, the three Beatles swapped roles with Jane and interviewed her instead. Gradually, however, John and George found they were being left out of the conversation; it was not that Paul was assuming his habitual role of PR man but that an almost visible, protective cocoon was being drawn about Jane Asher and himself, excluding the others.

At Fenton's suggestion, the party was set to visit a West End club. Paul, however, declined to go, asking if he and Jane could remain together in the flat to complete their "interview." When the four men returned, two hours later, the pair were found still sitting in exactly the same positions on the floor, still deep in conversation, talking now about, of all subjects, favorite foods.

Significantly, Jane's beauty was composed of an innocence that flowed from within her, a quality that entranced Paul, rather than from any sense of overt sexuality. She was so unlike those girls who would throw "horrid" pornographic notes at him on-stage. Perhaps most important, she was still a virgin, a crucial factor in the selection of any serious girlfriend for a young man with traditionally Northern, working-class double standards like Paul's.

The character of Jane Asher, had, like Paul's, been formed strong from the start: born on April 5, 1946, she played a deaf mute in the film *Mandy* at the age of five, but had avoided the pitfalls of precociousness to which so many child stars fall prey. When she was twelve she appeared on the stage for the first time, as Alice in *Alice in Wonderland;* she picked up critical praise for her role in the film *The Greengage Summer;* she had been, at fourteen, the youngest actress to play Wendy in a London production of *Peter Pan;* and she had had a major part in Walt Disney's *The Prince and the Pauper*.

Her father was Dr. Richard Asher, a noted psychiatrist specializing in blood and mental diseases at London's Middlesex Hospital. He also enjoyed a second career as a writer and witty broadcaster. Margaret Asher, her mother, was a teacher of music; she had taught the oboe to George Martin at the Guildhall School of Music. Jane had a younger sister, Clare, and an elder brother, Peter. A tight family unit, they lived in a five-story terrace house in Wimpole Street, close to the heart of the West End.

Soon after they met, Jane traveled up to Liverpool with Paul to meet his father. Jim McCartney took to her at once, admiring

151

this extroverted girl who did not need an overblown ego to bolster her beauty. He was also secretly impressed with her cultured accent, a speaking voice he knew Mary would have thought quite lovely, and so different from that which Paul now affected.

Jane's introduction to the entire McCartney clan came at Paul's twenty-first birthday party, only six weeks after she had first met him. The event, held in the garden of Aunt Jinnie's house in Huyton, was overshadowed by an incident that two days later resulted in blanket press coverage. John Lennon, who had recently been taken to Spain on holiday by Brian in an undisguised attempt at seduction, beat Cavern disc jockey Bob Wooler black and blue when that most loyal ally of the Beatles made a snide remark about John's sexuality. Moreover, this was not the only outbreak of violence with which the blindly drunken Lennon disrupted the equilibrium that was the understood ambience of any McCartney family social occasion. Bill Harry remembers, later in the evening, after Wooler had been driven to the hospital for treatment, how John Lennon interrupted a conversation that Billy J. Kramer and a member of the Fourmost were having with a girl by grabbing the unfortunate female by the breasts. The response of both men was to jump on the Beatle. "I remember Cynthia rushing up to them in tears, begging them to get a cab for John and send him home, which they did."

Such aggressive behavior was an egregious shattering of those rules of conduct accepted by the entire McCartney family. Paul was distinctly unamused, remembers Roger McGough, a member of the Scaffold satirical group, which also included John Gorman and Mike McCartney. "The thing about the family, and the father particularly, was that there was a very strong code of behavior. 'You're welcome here, so long as you behave in the right way.' This emphasis was extremely strong, and sometimes almost too much to take. But, understandably, John Lennon was never very welcome afterwards anywhere that Jim was. And Paul soundly disapproved."

There was hardly time for Paul to sit around mentally chastising John, however. In mid-July the Beatles had gone to Abbey Road again, to record their second LP. Its release was preceded, however, by the single that is the archetype of all that the Beatles' music stood for. Fittingly, "She Loves You" was one of the true joint compositions between John and Paul, written on a tour bus traveling through Yorkshire earlier in the year. Not only was the "yeah yeah yeah" chorus one of the most addictive, instantly appealing hooks that popular music had ever known, but it also represented an affirmation of a positive new age in which the gray negativity of Great Britain was to be utterly overturned. It was an instant number one.

Before a British concert tour scheduled to begin in October, Paul and Ringo flew to Greece together on holiday. On his return, Paul, so secretly desperate for the security of a close-knit family with both a father and a mother, suddenly discovered himself blessed with exactly that. When, lingering with Jane, he missed the last train back to Liverpool, where he was still living at 20 Forthlin Road, Margaret Asher suggested he stay the night at Wimpole Street. Then, eminently practical, Jane's mother decided that it would be better for Paul if he regarded their home as his permanent London residence; after all, it would save on all those hotel bills, wouldn't it? And so Paul moved into the house's top floor, which had two rooms and a bathroom: Peter Asher had the larger L-shaped room, and Paul had the smaller room with its large brown wardrobe and old, rarely used bed. In the two rooms on the floor below lived Jane and her sister, conveniently separated by a further flight of stairs from their parents.

At the end of the summer, Brian Sommerville, a former naval petty officer turned journalist, was appointed publicity manager to the Beatles by Brian Epstein. His function was to work solely on the Beatles' PR, while Tony Barrow hustled press on other NEMS (NEMS was the Epstein family business) acts like Gerry and the Pacemakers, the Fourmost, and Billy J. Kramer.

Sommerville, today a lawyer, is, to say the least, forthright in his opinion of his former employer. "Brian Epstein," he says, "was charming, pleasant, and shallow: a delightful man, but there was no substance to Brian whatsoever. He was constantly shifting his ground because he was unsure of himself in nearly all his dealings and, of course, in his personal relationships. He would be very involved with someone for a while, but then didn't want to know them. Very butterfly-like."

On several occasions Sommerville observed fierce arguments between "Eppy" and "Paulie," as John Lennon would affectionately refer to his musical soul mate. Brian Epstein was fearful of the effect on the fans that news of Paul's relationship with Jane might have; it had become public knowledge after a Fleet Street paparazzi had photographed the couple at the Prince of Wales Theatre, where they had been to see the show *Never Too Late*.

"I always had the impression that Brian used to worry about Paul, that he was a bit frightened of him perhaps because he was so strong-willed in his opinions about the exact details of how the Beatles' career should progress. Even though they could also be as thick as thieves about such matters, Brian was always circumspect when talking to Paul about things of any great importance. John and Brian always seemed to get on all right. But Paul would argue with Brian, and as far as I could see, Brian always gave in.

"There was a considerable difference of opinion over the Jane Asher situation. Brian made a terrible fuss about it, saying that it would offend the fans. But, in effect, Paul just told him to mind his own business. Brian was probably just being over-cautious, and Paul more far-sighted, knowing that that sort of thing didn't matter. But at the time it was a textbook rule of publicity that the artist must appear single and available."

Life at Forthlin Road already had become almost too much to put up with. Any time of the day or night Jim McCartney could gaze out of the windows at the front of the house and find the street filled with girls, ready to burst into sexual hysteria at the slightest provocation. A virtual prisoner in his house, Paul enlisted the aid of his next-door neighbor, Thomas Gaule, in his escapes. Gaule, who so often had provided Paul and his brother with their suppers after Mary had died, would lean a ladder against the back garden fence and Paul would climb down and make a hasty exit from the Gaules' front door to his car.

On tour Paul was becoming something of a master of disguise, donning false beards and hats so he could wander among the fans in the theater foyers, listening to what they were saying about the group. He prided himself on once, similarly clandestinely garbed, being able to travel by bus from Liverpool to Chester without being recognized.

In this not necessarily easy transition from council house tenant's son to houseguest in a West End townhouse, Paul found an ally in his photographer friend Dezo Hoffmann. Paul would meet Jane in Hoffmann's studio, in Wardour Street opposite Chinatown, and the trio would wander over to nearby Greek Street, to dine on borscht and strudel at the Budapest restaurant, Paul displaying the Celt within him in the large Gaelic coffees with which he invariably would end such repasts.

Paul's new home in the center of London was frequently besieged by fans, somewhat to the consternation of Jane's father, a quieter, more introverted man than his exuberant wife. Mr. Asher was understandably irritated by the fans who would call his home telephone number, listed in the directory because of his medical practice, and then hang up when it was not Paul who answered.

The house provided Paul, however, with a perfect launching pad for the program of self-improvement and education on which, with typical thoroughness, he had embarked. Jane Asher's intellectual background had proved an inspiration for him; never previously a great book reader, he now devoured culture, though culture of a more structured, formal type than what John Lennon was attracted to. "I don't want to sound like Jonathan Miller going on," he announced to the *London Evening Standard*, "but I'm trying to cram everything in, all the things that I've missed. People are saying things and painting things and composing things that are great, and I must know what people are doing."

Paul, however, refused to be led astray by the infinite possibilities for pomposity and self-deception, a traditional stumbling-block for the newly self-educated. His sense of absurdism remained intact: when told by the journalist of that *Evening Standard* interview that she was reading *The Naked Lunch* by William Burroughs, Paul retorted that he was reading *The Packed Lunch* by Greedy Blighter.

Brian Sommerville soundly dismisses the not infrequently made assertion that Paul McCartney's relationship with Jane Asher revealed the full extent of his social ambitions. "I think he took to the progression very naturally, more than any of the other three, a progression not far off from rags to riches.

"I don't think for one minute it was done consciously, as part of some plan or design. He just found himself in a set of circumstances, loved the girl, and fell naturally into those circumstances, as if he'd been brought up in the Bloomsbury Set all his life. To coin a cliché, Paul was a good mixer. Even in those days you could have popped him into any drawing room, as they say, and he would have got on well with everyone. He was a man who was not conscious of any class barriers—far from it."

In fact, Sommerville felt Jane Asher to be an ideal partner for Paul McCartney, so different from the often gold-digging groupies who flung themselves at him wherever he went.

"Jane was a very sweet, extroverted girl—not surprising that she was an actress. She was bright, very conversational, and full of fun. And she was extremely fond of Paul, but didn't show off about him; he wasn't a status symbol. In fact, I felt she wanted to keep it all very quiet and very personal. She wasn't at stage doors and parties all the time. Their relationship was kept very quiet, simply because that was the way they both liked it."

Sommerville, whose friends were fooled on several occasions by the phone calls Paul would make to them imitating almost uncannily the clipped accent of his publicity manager, had his first opportunities to observe Paul's public persona when he traveled with the group on the forty-date tour that began in Glasgow on October 5. Split into two legs by a visit to Sweden, the tour was further interrupted by an appearance on the TV program "Sunday Night at the London Palladium" on October 13; when fans rioted outside the theater, Fleet Street discovered Beatlemania. The always-conservative press breathed a collective sigh of relief when this acknowledgment was confirmed by the reception received by the group at the televised Royal Variety Show three weeks later, the occasion of Lennon's famous expression of wacky spontaneous wit (solidly rehearsed, in fact, and a cause of some concern to Paul that it was not *too* irreverent): "Those of you in the cheaper seats, clap your hands; the rest of you, just rattle your jewelry."

Reflecting his new status as a member of an alternative royalty, as well as his crash culture course, Paul peppered interviews with apothegms that were honest, eminently quotable, and revealing: "I don't feel like I imagine an idol is supposed to feel"; "For heaven's sake, don't say we're the new youth, because that's a load of rubbish"; "Security is the only thing I want. Money to do nothing with, money to have in case you wanted to do something"; and, probably with deliberate ambiguity, "What's wrong with us? Our parents used all the old clichés and look how we turned out."

Sommerville walked something of a tightrope when press requests were received to interview specific group members. Ringo was always available, though George was "sulky—if he'd set his mind against doing something, nothing would shift him." Though John could always be relied upon to say plenty, it was for interviews with Paul that the most requests came to him at the NEMS office in Argyll Street.

"Publicly, Paul was very much the frontman: pretty, seemed the most approachable, the most friendly. John seemed the most difficult, though I never found him so—in fact, he was a nice man was John. He could be as tactful as Paul in dealing with the press, but there was always a little touch of venom.

"Paul could rarely come out with the wit that John could, but he could talk very authoritatively on the music scene and other artists, and life in general.

"But they seemed to me to be making an equal contribution: if it was anybody's group at all, it was John's and Paul's. It was Lennon and McCartney, though Paul may have been more a driving force and John an artistic force. Paul seemed to have more exuberance and enthusiasm, while John was more hesitant about making decisions."

Behind the exuberance and enthusiasm that Paul presented, Sommerville was quite aware, lay a very different man. "The Paul which the public sees is not the real Paul. He *is* a built-in PR man:

157

the facade is there all the time. Behind it is a very serious man. What he gave off then was that pleasant little-boy-lost image. But behind it was a highly intelligent and extremely hard-working bloke. He knew what he was doing, and was very, very money-conscious. Not tight, but careful, extremely careful. He was very astute and business-like, and very organized. But the facade was this little-boy-lost wondering what it was all about and thinking 'Isn't this fun?'"

During the Christmas season at London's Finsbury Park Astoria, Sommerville had arranged for the Beatle to appear in *Melody Maker*, in that paper's "Blind Date" series, in which pop personalities would be played new releases upon which they would then comment, attempting to guess the name of the artist. It had been arranged that the journalist involved, Ray Coleman, would conduct the session in the Beatles' dressing room at the Astoria. For whatever reasons, however, Paul had set his mind against doing it at that time.

"Ray Coleman had arrived, so I said I'd take him for a drink and come back in half an hour. But Paul was giving every conceivable excuse not to do it—he could do it at the office the next day, he could go to the hotel where the others were staying. And I was arguing because, of course, Ray had a deadline. Paul wasn't being unpleasant, just obstinate. And we argued for about ten minutes.

"But Ray had met someone who worked for us in the corridor, and he invited him into the dressing room. And Paul saw him walk in. 'Oh, Ray—the "Blind Date" thing, yeah? Brian, why didn't you tell me he was here?' And he looked at me and winked.

"He had suddenly been confronted with the-man-from-the-paper. And the PR man inside him knew there was only one attitude he could present to him. It didn't matter how much the hired hand had to swallow the situation. Paul changed from being the man who just couldn't be bothered to someone who saw the importance of the situation. I don't think John and I would have got into one of those 'will-won't' situations.

"Another important aspect about Paul is that when you were trying to organize a photo session, he'd come up with ideas and suggestions. Instead of just posing, he wanted to be involved, to organize the photographer really. That wasn't a bad fault. Frequently when I suggested ways that a session could be done, Paul would come up with much better ideas. He wasn't just reacting to a situation, but constantly applying his thoughts."

With the Beatles, the LP the group had recorded in the summer, was released on November 22. It immediately replaced *Please Please Me* at number one. A week later came the fifth single, "I Want to Hold Your Hand." It also went straight to number one. Another song on which John and Paul had worked together, it had been written at the Asher house in Jane's music room.

On January 10, 1964, the Beatles smashed into the U.S. charts with the record. In ten days "I Want to Hold Your Hand" sold over 500,000 copies, the fastest-selling British record ever in the United States.

In Paris, where the group played a three-week engagement at the Olympia starting on January 15, they went through a practice run for the coming assault on America. Paul was by far the most popular of all the Beatles in France, says Dezo Hoffmann, who as ever accompanied the group on the trip. "There was a helluva big cry-out for Paul."

As in Hamburg, away from the critical eyes of Liverpudlians, the Beatles had blossomed, so this Parisian distancing from the massed eyes of the British public permitted Paul in particular to take a valuable step forward in his already considerable skill of projecting himself to the media. Not only was this French sojourn a dry run for the coming States trip but, because of the success of "I Want to Hold Your Hand," all the American media based in Paris were clamoring for interviews.

The very first one they gave was to a TV reporter from the Westinghouse Corporation, a political journalist who approached them in his customary grave style. Hoffmann, who was recording the event with his camera, observed how Paul immediately took the initiative. "This fellow didn't know who any of the Beatles were. But it was only Paul who seemed to realize—you could see it on his face—that the guy was a little mesmerized by them, as to who each of them was.

"He began by asking his questions in a very serious manner. Then came their replies and the whole atmosphere was reversed. The interviewer loved it; he was scheduled to talk to them for half an hour and ended up spending nearly two hours with them.

"And the most interesting thing of all was the way the character of Paul came out, purely subconsciously, because every time it was his turn to answer a question, he would say, 'Don't forget, I'm Paul.' And this wasn't because he was being egotistical and wanted to be recognized, but because he genuinely wanted to help the interviewer. He knew the guy didn't know which of them was which. And also it was a very professional attitude, because by now he was familiar with the methods by which tape was edited, and he knew it would be cut down very much, and by announcing himself he was making it easier for the editor.

"I remember Brian Sommerville being delighted when the interview was over. It was the best thing they'd done together up to that point. And that was all thanks to Paul, because he knew very well how important it was for America, and he was absolutely on the ball throughout it."

Paul was uncharacteristically subdued on the BEA flight to New York that left Heathrow Airport early on the morning of February 7, 1964. As if to benefit from its feeling of security, he buckled himself into his seatbelt and didn't unfasten it for the whole flight. "Since America has always had everything, why should we be over there making money? They've got their own groups. What are we going to give them that they don't already have?" he pessimistically demanded of Phil Spector, the record producer, who accompanied the Beatles in the first-class section of the plane.

Paul was always nervous and apprehensive before any momentous occasion; this time, however, it was an unexpected air of melancholy that settled over him as the plane moved steadily on toward the grandest occasion of them all, the summation of all that he and the other Beatles had worked for. For more than anything, it had somehow been the notion of America that had inspired them with its possibilities, its contrasts, its imagery: white rock and roll

160

and black R&B, Westerns, juvenile delinquent style, immense cars built like spaceships, the impression of vastness, the American Dream as filtered through the vision of the leafy suburbs of South Liverpool.

The question he posed to Spector was not based on fact: "I Want to Hold Your Hand" was at number one in the States, and "She Loves You" was hot on its trail. What was causing the strange sense of disquiet in Paul was that he knew that somehow all that he had worked for had been achieved. Which meant, in a way, that it was all over.

It was as legend has it: the ten thousand screaming girls at the airport; the madness outside New York's Plaza Hotel; the seventy million viewers who watched "The Ed Sulivan Show"; the nonsense of the British Embassy reception in Washington.

But it was when they flew south to Miami that Dezo Hoffmann first saw Paul McCartney at peace. The police sergeant in charge of their security at the Deauville Hotel, Buddy Bresner, invited the group to his home for supper. "And I saw how comfortable he suddenly seemed, with the two children there—the smallest was about four, the other about nine. And the unbelievable patience he had with those kids was incredible—they didn't let him alone for a moment. He sat there reading to them, in a way that was obviously not an inconvenience to him at all—he was completely at home.

"The others were embarrassed, especially John—he couldn't stand that sort of thing. The other three didn't know how to speak to those kids—they were uncomfortable, they had nothing in common with that age group. It was all right if kids were screaming in a concert hall for them, but they didn't have time for them privately. All John had time for was any girl he could make a date with.

"Paul was the only one who *always* had time for kids. He was in his element there. It was just something born into him. That's why I say he should have been a teacher—which, in a way, he was."

Whenever he was back home in Liverpool, Paul continued to pay visits to Rory Storm's mother, often now accompanied by Jane Asher.

"My mum said to him, 'What's it like being so rich?' " says Iris Caldwell. " 'I can only wear one shirt at a time and drive one car at a time,' he replied. She said, 'People say you've changed.' 'I haven't changed—I'm exactly the same as I always was. People's attitudes to me have changed, that's what it is,' " he told her.

"I think Paul got a lot of peace by becoming famous—it was a justification of all he had worked for: he was terribly insecure and felt wanted when he became famous. But for John fame brought pain."

Not every single ounce of the lavishings of adulation and critical praise coming the way of the McCartney family was directed at Paul. In a far, far more minor capacity Mike McCartney, who had renamed himself Mike McGear, was forging some sort of success with the Scaffold. The trio was part of an iconoclastic Merseyside literary movement, inspired in equal parts by the same Beat writers who so had affected Bill Harry and by the London satire boom: the humor delivered by these Liverpool practitioners of the art, however, was both earthier and more surreal, loaded with laconic Scouse irony rather than reliant upon lampooning. That it hardly interlinked at all with the city's more working-class music scene had been of considerable appeal to Mike McCartney; he had always been overshadowed by "our kid," as he forever sententiously referred to Paul, and but for the Scaffold, would have been virtually invisible.

As artistically gifted as his brother, though lacking his purposeful sense of direction, Mike also had not been blessed with a similar academic intuition. O-level art was the only GCE subject he had passed in the summer of 1961. Miserably for Mike McCartney, that was the year that the entrance requirements for full-time art courses were raised to five O-level passes. So instead of moving from the Institute to the Art College, he found himself working in the city center as an apprentice hairdresser at the Liverpool branch of the Andre Bernard chain. Though hardly the direction in which he hoped his life would proceed, this occupation at least offered an opportunity to present an infinitely neat, well-groomed appearance, as well as providing sufficient cash for the most up-to-date clothes.

Luckily for the Beatle's brother, in 1962 a fellow hairdresser introduced him to Roger McGough and John Gorman, members of the newly formed Merseyside Arts Committee. Still an ardent and skilled photographer, he was enlisted to take pictures of the various revues the Committee promoted around the city, particularly at the Everyman Theatre. Soon, Mike Blank—as Roger McGough dubbed him—found himself being given small parts in the various sketches that comprised these events. "Mike was invariably the straight man," says McGough, "although later he became the handsome one. He was quite good at reading and enjoyed being onstage. And that was Mike's role, really. He wasn't creative in a writing sort of way. He seemed very frustrated, though."

After a visit to one of these revues, *The Liverpool One Fat Lady All Electric Show,* in 1963 by an ABC-TV producer, the trio was offered a slot on a weekly TV satire program, "Gazette," starting in January 1964. Mike, desperate to maintain an identity separate from Paul, chose the rather too fashionably coy surname of "McGear."

As Beatlemania rampaged around the world, there was some satisfaction for Jim McCartney that his other son did not appear, as had usually been the case, to be altogether wallowing helplessly in the tidal wave of Paul's wake. Each week Jim would travel by bus to the TV studios in Manchester for the live broadcast of "Gazette." As often as not, he would be accompanied by Thelma Pickles, who had married Roger McGough.

"Jim and I always sat together and talked," she says. "He was the kind of man you'd like to have as a dad—he really was like the perfect dad. There was no side to him: he was completly honest and would always tell you what he thought, but never in a Bolshie way—there was nothing unpleasant, nothing nasty about him.

"I'm sure Paul got his not unfounded reputation for being the peacemaker—probably a genuine assessment—from Jim. When I say he was gentle, I don't mean he was soft; he was by no means soft. He had his standards, and he'd expect that anything he did, and anything his boys did, would be within those standards or principles.

"He had respect for other people, and the self-discipline he believed in was quite simple: that you would work hard and do your best. He would expect you to do your best, and if you didn't he'd be disappointed. But he was also one of those parents who wouldn't expect you to do more than your best.

"He was a very caring man, not an ounce of selfishness in him. If you spoke to him, he was interested in what *you* were doing, and how *you* were. He didn't only take an interest in Paul; he took an equally strong interest in what Mike did.

"I think it had been a great strain for him having to take on the role of both parents. But he knew he had to get on with it, and he did. And he did it supremely well."

John Gorman, the Scaffold frontman, had his difficulties with Jim McCartney. "Something that came as a complete surprise to me was Mike saying, 'You know when you talk to my dad? Can you call him Mr. McCartney, not Jim like you do.' 'But he's my friend . . .' 'But older people should be addressed as Mr. or Mrs.' 'But come off it, Mike, he's your dad, he's like one of us.' 'Well, I think it would be better if you called him Mr. McCartney. There's only one other person who calls him Jim, and that's John Lennon, and he doesn't like it."

All the same Gorman concurs completely with Thelma Pickles's view of the man. "He was very down-to-earth. I think that affected Paul and Mike very much to the good. He was an *extremely* honest man. He was very keen to bring it home to Mike and Paul that you play the game, and you don't try and be deceptive, and you keep things straight. Mike would never go on a train without paying, for example. It was a very healthy attitude, very sane in the world as it was, especially in Liverpool where everyone tries to get an edge over on everyone else."

Within these perfectionist attitudes with which Jim McCartney had imbued his boys, however, Roger McGough detected an undercurrent of great reserve, even a tangible uncertainty about the offering of affection and love. "There is no doubt that initially, there was that great reserve, even though you'd overlook it in Paul because he was so absolutely correct in the way he dressed, so clean and polite. And Mike was exactly the same: not a hair out of place, and if there was, it was studied.

"And this idea of always being so charming seemed to me as if it was because they were afraid of not being liked, whereas John Lennon would plow through people uncaringly, telling them to fuck off. And there would always be this covering up by Paul. It was as if John said the wrong thing, Paul would be working extra hard to cover up for it—'It's all right: he didn't mean it!' That was always part of Paul's way. But I don't think it's false or contrived in any way."

His brother's growing fame, moreover, led to a constant testing of Mike McCartney's sense of self. "It was very difficult for him," says McGough. "Whenever journalists wanted to talk to us, it was always 'Paul's brother' they wanted. We'd turn up to the interview and it would be, 'Right, Paul. Oh sorry . . . urrrhh . . . Mike.' And in the photo captions it was always 'Paul's brother Mike's group.'

"It was funny. John Gorman could be mistaken for Ringo's brother. 'One of you is a Beatle's brother, isn't he?' would come the question. 'It's John—he's Ringo's brother.' So John would talk about his brother Ringo for hours. So the sense of humor kept it at bay to some extent. I think Mike coped well—it was tremendously difficult for him."

John Gorman has another distinct memory. "Mike never stopped talking about his mother. And you could tell that for him it was far more than just a mother who had died: she was more than dead, she'd vanished forever from his life and he'd never be able to see her again. It was very deeply rooted."

On his return from America Paul traveled up to Liverpool in his new Aston Martin DB 6 to visit his sixty-one-year-old father and make the ultimate pop-star gesture: if Jim McCartney wanted to retire from his £10-a-week cotton salesman job, Paul would maintain him for the rest of his life and would buy him a new house "across the water," in Heswall, Cheshire, where in the twenties Jim had been a gardener for several cotton magnates. Jim accepted without hesitation. It was the happiest day of his life, he said later.

Not only had he grown weary of his poorly paid job, but he was becoming pestered not just by British Beatle fans but by advance parties of American girls who had slipped away from the chore of visiting Buckingham Palace and the Tower of London with their parents and taken a train up to Liverpool. Polite as ever, Jim frequently would invite them in for a cup of tea. "I'd say, 'there's the kitchen.' They'd go in and start screaming and shouting because they'd recognize the kitchen from photographs." Clearly, things were getting out of hand.

The matter of purchasing a property did not proceed with the relative simplicity that might reasonably have been expected. The sellers of the first house Jim chose refused to sell to him, worried about the constant harassment by Beatles fans that might befall their former neighbors.

No such opposition was made to the purchase of Jim's second choice, a five-bedroom detached house with its own wine cellar in Baskervyle Road; Rembrandt, as the house was named, cost £8,750 (about $21,500) and as much again was spent on renovation. The house had large grounds and a view over the Dee estuary.

To complete his obligations to his family, Paul also arranged for a £10-a-week covenant to be paid to his brother, facing hard times now that the "Gazette" TV series had ended.

The move from Forthlin Road was undertaken at midnight, all the furniture remaining in the house, on which rent continued to be paid for some months in an effort to prevent fans from setting out in search of the new McCartney residence.

In London, meanwhile, it was increasingly evident that the solid foundation provided by his domestic situation at the Ashers' was advantageous for Paul. And in turn, he was able to bring financial security to the house: in April, Peter Asher, with his friend Gordon Waller, topped the charts with "World Without Love," a song written by Paul while "sagging off" from Liverpool Institute.

Tony Barrow, the NEMS publicist, told the *Daily Telegraph Colour Supplement:* "Paul is now leading a very organized life. The other three don't know what they are doing. They wait for others to tell them. But Paul always knows—you ring him up and he will say, 'No, not Thursday, I am dining at eight. Not Friday, because I have got to see a man about a painting. But Saturday's okay.' It isn't that he's changed. But out of all of them, he has developed the most."

A breathing space, a time to reflect on all the madness, came in March, when the group began work on their first film, *A Hard Day's Night.* A memory of producer Walter Shenson suggests that perhaps some of this development of Paul's was thoroughly willful, a surrender to—or perhaps acceptance of—that relentlessly ambitious desire for progress that drove him to constantly endeavor to inspire the other Beatles to stick at their art and seek further peaks. At a dinner party at Shenson's house, Paul arrived with Jane Asher. As chance would have it, also present was Joan Sutherland, the opera singer. Paul, Shenson remembers, left Jane and his host and hostess and spent the evening wrapped in conversation with the diva.

A Hard Day's Night had its London premiere on July 6, 1964, the day before Jim McCartney's birthday. At the party that followed, at London's Dorchester Hotel, Jim McCartney was introduced to Princess Margaret. (The Princess had asked Paul what he had thought of the film. "I don't think we are very good, ma'am," he replied. "But we had a good director.") Then, as midnight chimed, Paul drew his father over to him. "Happy birthday, Dad," he said, and produced a painting—perhaps the one mentioned to the *Telegraph* magazine—of a horse, which he handed to Jim.

"Thank you, son. Very nice," muttered the somewhat confused father. (Later he was to tell Thomas Gaule about it. "I thought, 'It's very nice, but couldn't he have done a bit better than that?' "). Then Paul revealed that this was a painting of the £1,050 racehorse, Drake's Drum, that he had bought his father.

"You silly bugger," was Jim's joyous reply.

"My father likes a flutter [bet]," Paul said. "He's one of the world's greatest armchair punters."

Unsurprisingly, it was Liverpool that was the setting for the Northern premiere of *A Hard Day's Night,* three days later on July 10. A crowd of 150,000 lined the streets for the group's triumphant drive from Liverpool Starways Airport to the city center.

Roy Corlett, who as a junior reporter had so soundly sneered at the name the Silver Beatles when Paul had told him of it in the Jacaranda, was still on the newshound trail, on the staff of the *Liverpool Post and Echo.* "I went to the airport in the evening when they were due to be flying back to London. For some reason the plane was delayed, so they were taken up into the airport directors' office. I commented to Paul on what a tremendous reception they had had. 'Is there any particular moment you remember of the whole thing?' I asked. I'll always remember his reply. He said, 'As we drove along Mather Avenue there were all these people lining the road and waving. And on the corner of Booker Avenue, I suddenly saw Dusty Durband with his kids, and they were all waving, too. That was the best moment of the day, that one of the teachers from the Institute would actually turn out and wave at us as we drove into Liverpool.' "

The previous month Jane Asher had had her own film open, *The Masque of the Red Death,* in which she starred. Jane was discovering there were penalties to pay for going out with a Beatle, even from those of a similar, or higher, stellar status. On ITV's "The Celebrity Game" on June 28, she sat on a panel that included Zsa Zsa Gabor. When the panel was asked "Is it possible to fall in love at first sight?" Jane replied in the negative. "So she does not like the Beatle," purred Zsa Zsa. Jane responded with an icy glare.

The same week she appeared in ITV's "Play of the Week," *A Spanner in the Grassroots.* "The play is true to life," said Jane, "for it shows there are certain things wrong with both classes, and there is hope for the future in the intermingling of people without set ideas. But I never think of a play as anything like *my* real life. I don't think of myself as a certain class—this class thingummy is all so silly."

At the end of July both Paul and John had close shaves with death while playing onstage at the Stockholm ice hockey stadium when they each got severe electric shocks from their instruments. Paul's near-miss came right in the midst of "Long Tall Sally": while exploiting to the fullest the lessons he had learned from Little Richard, he suddenly felt a jolt of electricity surge through him, literally making his Beatlecut stand on end.

Like the Paris Olympia shows, the Swedish gigs were intended as a series of practice dates for the Beatles' first full-length tour of the United States, a 15,000-mile trek involving twenty-six performances.

For the Beatles the tour was something of a nightmare, though one that many would have given a limb to experience. Locked in their dressing rooms or hotels, there was no opportunity of seeing the country of their dreams; apart from the brief thirty minutes onstage, before which Paul inevitably straightened John's tie, there was little to do but take amphetamines (a contributory cause of the group's constant ready wit), down Scotch and Cokes, and indulge themselves with the hosts of girls who presented themselves.

Moreover, the stress wrought a fearsome weariness. On a day off in a small U.S. town, they managed to find a haven of relative peace. In payment for thus providing sanctuary, however, the local sheriff and a number of civic dignitaries came out to the Beatles' plane shortly before takeoff, demanding autographs and pictures.

Paul sat by the window, gazing at the arrival of this motley crew. "He was smiling like mad at them, nodding his head wildly up and down," says Derek Taylor, who had replaced Brian Sommerville as "publicity manager," "but he was saying to me, 'Get out there quick. Tell them we want to go out and meet them, but *you* won't let us because we're too tired. Go on.'"

Eight days into the schedule, however, the entire group, particularly Paul, had an epiphany-like experience that was to have a resounding effect; indeed, its reverberations were to continue in Paul's life for some time to come. Bob Dylan turned them on to marijuana for the first time.

It happened on August 28, after the first of two shows they played in New York, at the Forest Hills Tennis Stadium. The mighty but slight presence of Dylan had been invited down from on high, from his Woodstock aerie, to the group's hotel, the Delmonico, with a portentous formality more common among heads of state.

On his arrival—aptly enough in a suitably egoless blue Ford station wagon—Dylan was rushed past the screaming fans to the floor of the hotel on which the group was ensconced. Passing quietly through the outer rooms that contained lesser luminaries such as the Kingston Trio and Peter, Paul, and Mary, Dylan was led into the Beatles' inner sanctum. There, he was somewhat dismayed to find a babbling bunch rattling on thanks to amphetamines and displaying the effects of the expensive bottles of liquor that littered the room.

Dylan immediately defined his own position by demanding, when "Eppy" inquired what he would care to drink, "cheap wine," a bottle of which was sent out for. When speed was proffered, Dylan roundly declined the offer. Instead, he suggested, they smoke a joint. As always at such moments the four group members left it to Brian to announce the embarrassing admission: they had never smoked marijuana.

Dylan was astonished. What about the pot references in their music? You know, like "When I touch you I get high, I get high." John corrected the shaman: "The words are, 'I can't hide.' "

After thirty minutes of nervous preparation, during which blinds were drawn and towels stuffed against bolted doors, the room was deemed safe for this pioneering experience. At which point Bob Dylan whipped out his rolling papers and started rolling. And rolling.

The room was soon filled with giggling wrecks, scrabbling around on the floor while imagining themselves on the ceiling.

It was Paul, however, who was the most profoundly affected by the weed. He was thinking, he declared, *really* thinking for the very first time. He demanded that road manager Mal Evans follow him around for the rest of the evening, noting down every last word of his stoned ramblings.

He would never be the same again.

CHAPTER TWELVE

It was the purity of Paul's song "Yesterday," a purity that existed in symbiosis with a melody line of unparalleled beauty, that caused it to become an archetype of the ballad form.

Since "Yesterday" first appeared on the *Help* LP at the beginning of August 1965, it has been recorded by over two thousand artists. Yet it was one of the easiest pieces of writing Paul had ever done. Falling out of bed one morning, he went straight to the piano (on which he had started taking formal lessons) and—still close to his unconscious dream state—played as the song flowed from him with an ease that suggested divine inspiration. "It was one of the most instinctive songs I've ever written," he said later. "I thought it sounded so good that someone else must have written it already."

At first the tune had no lyrics. "Dusty" Durband recalls Paul visiting him at his home in Liverpool, and playing it on the piano. It had a working title, he told him, of "Scrambled Eggs," as befitted a song written at breakfast time, and some of the nonsense lyrics with which he was playing around went, "Scrambled eggs/ Oh, how I loved your legs."

With time, however, the same impetus that had provided the music suggested a source of lyrics: according to Thomas Gaule, the words of "Yesterday" are about nothing less than the death of Paul McCartney's mother. The lines "I said something wrong/ Now I long for yesterday" refer to his blurting out the question as to how they would manage without her money. With a poetic sense of justice, the event in his life that had most driven Paul McCartney in forever pushing the Beatles on to greater and greater triumphs became, when expressed through the group's music, its biggest success.

"I get made fun of because of it a bit," Paul said. "I remember George saying, 'Blimey, he's always talking about "Yesterday"; you'd think he was Beethoven or somebody.' But it is the one, I reckon, that is the most complete thing I've ever written.

"It's very catchy without being sickly, too. When you're trying to write a song, there are certain times when you get the essence, it's all there. It's like an egg being laid, it's so there, not a crack nor a flaw in it."

Paul, who considered himself "hip to the fact that people like a love song," knew intuitively that to do it justice, "Yesterday" needed more than the instrumentation provided by the Beatles' lineup. It was he who suggested to George Martin that perhaps a full orchestra should be used. Martin modified the notion; instead, would not a classical string quartet do the trick? And so, when "Yesterday" was recorded, Paul's guitar part was all that was in any remote way reminiscent of the Beatles' preceding music. Paradoxically, it was the decision of Paul to use strings on this most traditional of popular song ballads that permitted the musical revolution that was to take place from now on within the Beatles' music. It was "Yesterday" that opened the way for *Sgt. Pepper.*

Marianne Faithfull, a pop starlet who had already had several hits, was Paul's choice to record the inevitable cover; one night at a party he played her an acetate of his version. The inertia of her record company, however, led to Matt Monroe, a popular ballad singer, beating Marianne onto the charts—Monroe's cover became a Top Ten British hit. In America, Paul's own version became a number-one record, with some charts listing it under his own name, rather than that of the Beatles.

Marianne Faithfull was part of an elite set of the capital's hip culturati; as a woman, however, in those pre-liberated days, her role was strictly secondary to that of her husband's, John Dunbar, an art critic and close friend of Peter Asher's, and a young writer from Cheltenham called Barry Miles, later known simply as Miles. As befitted a coterie that personified the still innocent hedonistic code of what was becoming known as Swinging London, it swiftly embraced the company of that most desirable and accommodating of acquaintances, Paul McCartney, a close friendship developing between Dunbar and the Beatle.

Countless evenings would be spent at Dunbar and Faithfull's Bentinck Street apartment in Mayfair, the occasional glass of vintage wine being very much secondary to the endless joints of the most exclusive hashish. As a contrast to the leisurely, meandering, stoned discussions into which the assembled company was so often locked, there developed the most primitive of musical rituals: pots and pans would be brought from the kitchen on which the various cross-legged participants would beat out mantralike rhythms. A significant musical evolution was felt to have been arrived at when, rather as George Martin had just altered the Beatles' basic sound with the addition of string instruments, a decision was made to incorporate the effects obtained by rubbing the rims of glasses filled with varying amounts of water. With Paul in particular delighted with the effect, these experimentalists whiled away many hours of their youth reproducing the "singing" effects they had arrived at.

Miles was unsurprised that later, on his first solo album, Paul McCartney used such sounds, on a track with the original title of "Glasses"; Miles had always respectfully taken note of Paul's prodigiously retentive musical memory. "Anything musical that he learns goes immediately into his head and is liable to resurface years later, when for whatever reasons he knows that he needs it."

It was not only close friendship that linked Dunbar, Peter Asher, and Miles; there was also a business partnership in which they were dedicated to opening a bookshop and art gallery. On one of the many occasions when Miles called for Peter Asher at Wimpole Street, he was chatting with him up on the top floor of the house while Peter changed his clothes. Searching for a clean pair of socks, Peter wandered through into Paul's room, where he still kept much of his clothing. Instead of being orderly and organized, the room was approaching a state of chaos: piles of clothes —both dirty and never worn—littered the floor; poking from beneath the bed could be seen haphazard piles of gold records; and when, in search of his socks, Peter pulled open a cupboard door, Miles watched in amazement as something close to £100,000 in bundles of used notes tumbled out—part of the legacy, no doubt, of Brian Epstein's demand that promoters add under-the-counter cash to concert fees in an effort to elude the taxman. "Paul was far more of an old beatnik than he appeared," says Miles.

At the time, late summer of 1965, Paul McCartney was in America again, on the Beatles' third American tour. In Los Angeles, where the group had rented a house in Benedict Canyon for their week's stay, they had celebrated their arrival by dropping acid with Peter Fonda and the Byrds. The next day a summit meeting had been arranged with Elvis Presley; it contrasted pathetically with their meeting with Bob Dylan, a year previously. Nervous banter was the extent of their communication. Paul as ever trying to break the ice—thereby saving himself from embarrassment—informed Elvis he was coming along "quite promisingly" on the bass when that most influential of all their idols ran through Paul's part on "I Feel Fine." In response to an invitation from the Beatles, the next night several of Elvis's Memphis Mafia turned up at the group's house—though without Elvis. Like a proud, new houseowner, Paul politely showed these good ol' boys around.

The ritual Christmas release of a new Beatles' album, *Rubber Soul,* was undertaken again that year. The change of attitude that had taken place in the group since *Beatles for Sale* had come out the year before was expressed in one of the album's most easily overlooked songs, "The Word." On "The Word" the Beatles, fulfilling their function as spokesmen for their times, clairvoyantly proclaimed, "Spread the word I'm thinking of/Have you heard the word is *love.*" The individual harmonies and instrumental parts intertwined into a unity and wholeness that spoke of a philosophical oneness in the group that never before had been realized with such gentle strength and conviction. Significantly, the song was a joint composition of John and Paul's.

Within their souls the Beatles may have been united, but in practical matters this mood was not sustained. "Normal" Smith remembers the sessions as the group's most arduous and personally divisive. "With *Rubber Soul* the clash between John and Paul was becoming obvious. Also, George was having to put up with an awful lot from Paul. We now had the luxury of four-track recording, so George would put his solo on afterwards. But as far as Paul was concerned, George could do no right—Paul was absolutely finicky.

"So what would happen was that on certain songs Paul himself played the solos. I would wonder what the hell was going on, because George would have done two or three takes, and to me they were really quite okay. But Paul would be saying, 'No, no, no!' And he'd start quoting American records, telling him to play exactly as he'd heard on such-and-such a song. So we'd go back from the top, and George would really get into it. Then would come Paul's comment, 'Okay, the first sixteen bars weren't bad, but that middle . . . ' Then Paul would take over and do it himself —he always had a left-handed guitar with him.

"Subsequently I discovered that George Harrison had been

177

hating Paul's bloody guts for this, but it didn't show itself. In fact, I take my hat off to George Harrison that he swallowed what he had to swallow in terms of criticism from Paul.

"Mind you, there is no doubt at all that Paul was the main musical force. He was also that in terms of production as well. A lot of the time George Martin didn't really have to do the things he did because Paul McCartney was around and could have done them equally well. The only thing he couldn't do was to put symbols to chords; he couldn't write music. But he could most certainly tell an arranger how to do it, just by singing a part—however, he didn't know, of course, whether the strings or brass could play what he wanted.

"But most of the ideas came from Paul."

In the last quarter of 1965, Paul McCartney moved into his new house at 7 Cavendish Avenue—Jane Asher never "officially" moved in.

One day, "Normal" Smith went over to confer with Paul. By now the engineer had met Jim McCartney, and his view of the father differed not at all from that that was customarily voiced: "Such a super father—it seemed to me that even if he knew nothing whatsoever about music, he would still be behind Paul, that he would encourage him as best he could. The relationship was extremely good, the sign of a nice relationship."

Having made a mental note of Jim's pristine appearance and assuming, correctly, that here lay the inspiration for Paul's immaculately groomed facade, "Normal" understandably expected to find a home that was a further extension of this. But the engineer had not noticed the occasional hash burns that had begun to appear on Paul's favorite sweaters and shirts. In something of a reaction to his upbringing, Paul turned 7 Cavendish Avenue into a prototype for the English Rock Star Mansion. "When I went in there, I thought, 'Christ, this is a bit of a dump. We went into Paul's own room, his den, where he showed me his collection of brasses. And then we went into the main lounge where he'd got these new tinted spotlights, as well as a screen on which to show films that was supposed to come down from the ceiling—except that it had got stuck halfway down, and was all cock-eyed. And there was muck and filth all over this really nice house. The garden was a complete mess, not helped at all by his Old English sheepdog, Martha, who was shitting and pissing everywhere."

In accord with this resolutely modern notion of Martha "doing her own thing," Paul passed the first few days of the New Year of 1966 helping paint the premises in Southampton Row that would house Indica Books, the joint venture by Peter Asher, John Dunbar, and Miles. Paul had already helped catalogue the stock; he also designed Indica's wrapping paper. Perhaps significantly, the first single he wrote afterward was "Paperback Writer."

His evenings were often spent in similar company, at the appropriate "in" clubs, the Ad-Lib, the Scotch of St. James, or Sybilla's. One night at Sybilla's, Miles remembers, the bill for two rounds of drinks came to £8, "which in those days was ridiculous: Jane Asher was really frantic. But none of us ever had to pay because Paul would just sign the bill wherever we went. It was an understanding he insisted on right from the very start, so there was never any of that unpleasantness over money."

In March, the same month that Paul and Jane went skiing in Switzerland, Peter and Gordon released their single "Woman." The songwriting credit was to one Bernard Webb, said to be an English student at college in Paris. In fact, it was another Paul McCartney composition; Paul had insisted on the secrecy, wanting to test whether the record would be a hit without record buyers knowing he'd written it: it was the duo's first record to fail to enter the Top Twenty.

Most of the spring was again spent at Abbey Road—now only a short walk for Paul—working on the next album. In a music paper interview a week before his twenty-fourth birthday, Paul declared, "I don't like our American image. . . . I'd hate the Beatles to be remembered as four jovial moptops. . . . I'd like to be remembered, when we're dead, as four people who made music that stands up to be remembered."

Paul McCartney's birthday present to himself was a 183-acre dairy farm, High Park, outside Campbeltown, in Kintyre in Argyllshire. A peninsula, Kintyre is characteristically Scottish: beautiful and bracingly chilly, with its buildings constructed of gray granite. Moreover, the inhabitants' penchant for keeping very much to themselves guaranteed that the Beatle could enjoy at least a measure of privacy. Of crucial importance, an airport was located only half a dozen miles away. Paul informed the sellers that it had always been an ambition of his to own a farm in Scotland.

But as yet he was not to spend any time there. At the end of June a brief but backbreaking tour schedule was undertaken. First the group played in Hamburg, then flew, via Anchorage, Alaska, to Tokyo. Because of death threats from militant students, the Beatles were sequestered under armed police guard at the Tokyo Hilton; when it was discovered that Paul, adopting a false beard and hat, had roamed the streets of Tokyo for several hours, the police threatened to withdraw, leaving the group to the mercy of any terrorists.

Manila, in the Philippines, the final leg of this hectic series of dates, was even worse. Due to a series of misunderstandings the group failed to attend a party thrown in their honor by Imelda Marcos, wife of the president. As a consequence, their exit from the country was accompanied by punches, kicks, and abuse from a patriotic crowd stirred up to fever pitch by the official media. "I wouldn't want my worst enemy to go to Manila," commented Paul.

There was a month's brief hiatus, during which the *Revolver* album was released, to public and critical acclaim. Paul's haunting "Eleanor Rigby" earned special mention. Paul McCartney has always maintained that the song's central character was originally named Daisy Hawkins by him, and that later he changed it to Daisy McKenzie. In Bristol one day, where Jane was a member of the Old Vic, he saw a clothes shop, Rigby's, and changed the name to Daisy Rigby, then ultimately to Eleanor Rigby. Yet in the cemetery of St. Peter's Church, Woolton, lies the grave of an Eleanor Rigby, who was born on August 29, 1895, and died on October 10, 1939. The Rigbys, a prominent local family, lived exactly midway between Strawberry Fields, a Salvation Army children's home, and Aunt Mimi's home, Mendips. Is this a case of that renowned retentive memory of Paul's having subconsciously altered the origins of his source material?

On August 12, the Beatles' fourth nationwide American tour opened in Chicago. In comparison with the profound sense of menace that hung over the fourteen dates, the Manila incident could be forgotten as the mental aberration of the one-horse regime that it was. Before this tour John Lennon had made his "the Beatles are more popular than Jesus" remark. In the South bonfires of Beatles' records were burning, and death threats were received from the Ku Klux Klan. Despite John's humiliating apology for his misinterpreted remarks, a palpable fear settled over the fourteen-date tour. After rain caused a show in Cincinnati to be postponed for a day, Paul was discovered back at the group's hotel, vomiting violently from tension. It was hardly surprising that by the last date of the tour, August 29, 1966, in San Francisco's Candlestick Park, the Beatles had had enough: it was their last live show ever.

Taught by necessity to always pick up the pieces and plow on regardless, Paul used this new freedom to immediately set out on a further course of consciousness expanding that itself was an extension of the cultural awakening brought about by moving into Wimpole Street.

It was not easy for him: programmed for life by the attitudes and aspirations of his parents, he trod a delicate path through a new world in which everyone knew there were no rules. But those foundations were, in the end, to prove the salvation they had always been. When the psychedelic dream of the sixties turned out to have been a self-indulgent mirage, he was left as neither a burnt-out case nor a heroin addict, but a viable human being able to draw on those strengthening resources that had been established so early on. In contrast, the apparently free spirit of John Lennon was built on sandy ground, requiring him to forever leap credulously to ostensibly firmer footholds. Often this juxtaposition between the two—the fired craftsman versus the deep, authentic pain of the artist—made John appear the far more sympathetic character, in that somehow we intuitively sympathized

181

with his anguish, of which we had hardly any knowledge. But this was part of the mythology, for Paul's foundations were also John's. And John, in his confusion, was now reacting to Paul's seemingly endless abilities with both loving admiration and resentment, the source of which he was unable to trace. Paul was not an archetype, as John was. A private man, Paul lacked John's ability to produce apothegms that seemed poetically correct.

As part of Paul's inexorable efforts at self-awakening, on his return from America he journeyed to Africa, attended by the ever-faithful Mal Evans, who could be relied upon to venture forth and score bundles of prime African "bush." After returning to London, he set to work on what was to be the first solo project by a Beatle, the score for the film *The Family Way*, which starred Hayley Mills.

In November there appeared newspaper reports stating that two of the Beatles had had preliminary discussions with a certain Allen Klein, a New York accountant, about the possibility of him taking over their management affairs. Though these rumors were strenuously denied by Brian Epstein, they were not without substance. And, with an irony that was later to be keenly felt, one of these Beatle negotiators was Paul McCartney. Befuddled both by drugs and an increasingly desperate personal life, Brian Epstein was hardly in control of the Beatles' management. Moreover, the individual group members, who never ceased smarting from the miserly contract that they had signed with EMI Records, had learned with considerable rancor of the slick way that Allen Klein had substantially renegotiated the deal that the Rolling Stones had with Decca. Though Brian Epstein still remained shakily at the helm, that initial meeting with Klein had sown the seeds for a tragedy that was to run and run. Though he would later reject Klein as a managerial and financial guru, we may wonder whether at this relatively early stage Paul was not subconsciously seeking an escape route from the group—for that was what those discussions in November 1966 eventually led to.

Before the end of the year, however, Paul was again working closely, but—as always—critically, with Brian Epstein. Under the terms of the group's contract with United Artists, a third film was owed to the company. And Joe Orton, the fashionable playwright, was commissioned to provide a script. The meeting he had for this abortive project with Brian and Paul was hardly what Orton expected. Perhaps wishing to maintain a certain tension between himself and Brian, whose adoration of the legitimate theater was renowned, Paul, by now wearing one of the melancholy mustaches all the Beatles were sporting, was as disparaging about the form as Brian was worshipful. "The only thing I get from the theater is a sore arse," he quipped to Orton, hardly the remark that might be expected from a young man known for being so prominent at the most eminent of West End "first nights," and whose celebrated girlfriend was now a leading member of the Bristol Old Vic. (A month later Paul was to turn down a perhaps unrealistic invitation from the National Theater to write the music for the songs in its production of Shakespeare's *As You Like It*.)

Freed from the influences of Wimpole Street, was a dissatisfaction creeping into his relationship with Jane? If so, it was not apparent on the surface, for Paul and Jane still seemed the perfect pair, as they perseveringly picked through secondhand furniture on Portobello Road, seeking out the most homely, though distinguished, of bargains. Such pieces rested contentedly at 7 Cavendish Avenue, next to the bronze Paolozzi sculpture and the priceless collection of Tiffany glass.

Invariably, the question of their eventual marriage was posed by gossip writers. "Just say I laughed when you asked me that," Paul responded on one occasion as he waited in his Aston Martin for the electronic gates of his home to open.

Late in the year Paul went up to stay at his father's house for a few days. A friend of both his and John's, Tara Browne, the heir to the Guinness fortune, was already at the house, a guest of Mike McCartney's. One evening, after smoking a joint, Paul and Tara decided to take out a pair of mopeds and ride over to visit a member of the Mac clan, Aunt Bett.

Close to his aunt's home, Paul took a corner too fast and soared over the handlebars, landing on his face and badly cutting his upper lip. To minimize publicity, the family doctor was called and the wound was stitched up in the kitchen of Rembrandt, without an anesthetic. To this day a faint scar remains, though the mustaches that the Beatles helped make fashionable conveniently disguised the wound until the stitches had been removed.

On December 18, 1966, Tara Browne plowed his Lotus Elan into the back of a parked van in South Kensington and was killed. Yet another person close to Paul was dead. He and John wrote a song about the dead millionaire; "A Day in the Life" was included on the new LP on which the Beatles had just begun work.

1. Paul with Jane Asher at the October 1967 premiere of *How I Won the War*, which starred John Lennon. This photograph reveals no hint that the romance between Paul and Jane has only months to run. *(Pictorial Press)*

1

2

3

■ **1.** Never one to miss a promotional opportunity, Paul eats an Apple at the press launch for *Yellow Submarine* in July 1968. *(Pictorial Press)* ■ **2.** Paul relaxes with tea and a biscuit in a break from the recording of "All You Need Is Love" at Abbey Road in 1967. *(Pictorial Press)* ■ **3.** Paul and Jane leave Heathrow for Athens in July of 1967. *(AP/Wide World Photos)* ■ **4.** Paul in a decidedly sixties' psychedelic mood at the launch of the "All You Need Is Love" single. *(Pictorial Press)*

4

1

2

3

4

■ **1.** Sergeant Pepper promoted? Paul, in World War I uniform, in a *Magical Mystery Tour* scene in which he attempts to move a cow from the field of battle. *(AP/Wide World Photos)* ■ **2.** Paul and Jane Asher arrive at London airport on March 26, 1968, returning from their stay at the Maharishi Mahesh Yogi's Himalayan Meditation Center; their romance is nearly over. *(AP/Wide World Photos)* ■ **3.** In April 1967, Paul surprises Jane Asher by arriving on her birthday in Denver, Colorado, where she is appearing with the Bristol Old Vic theater group. Later that month in San Francisco Paul witnesses the events that inspire him to push for the Beatles to make *Magical Mystery Tour*. *(AP/Wide World Photos)* ■ **4.** Paul, Linda Eastman, and Linda's daughter, Heather, at Paul and Linda's wedding ceremony at the Marylebone Register's office, March 12, 1969. *(AP/Wide World Photos)*

1

■ **1.** This scene from the recording of *Let It Be* reveals none of the tension and acrimony present in the studio at that time. *(Pictorial Press)* ■ **2.** Linda's face registers her reaction at the moment of being busted for the first time in Gothenburg, Sweden, in 1972; Paul appears deliberately impassive. *(Joseph Stevens)* ■ **3.** This Linda Eastman McCartney photograph of her husband and daughter, Mary, was used on the cover of Paul's first solo album, *McCartney*. *(AP/Wide World Photos)*

2

3

■ **1.** Paul with the staff and pupils of the Liverpool Institute after Wings had played a concert for the school in November 1979. (*AP/Wide World Photos*)
■ **2.** Paul contemplates a bum note on the Wings 1972 European tour. (*Joseph Stevens*) ■ **3.** Paul and Linda write to fans of Wings. (*Joseph Stevens*) ■ **4.** The leisurely pace of the 1972 Wings tour of Europe was in marked contrast to the Beatles' whistlestop events. (*Joseph Stevens*)

CHAPTER THIRTEEN

In November 1966, the Beatles had returned to Studio One at Abbey Road. In far longer than it had once taken them to complete an album, however, they only recorded three songs.

The first was "Strawberry Fields Forever." Written by John, it was one of pop music's masterpieces, and the final version consisted of the first and second halves of two recordings, which had been painstakingly edited together by George Martin.

The next was "When I'm Sixty-Four." "It was the kind of vaudeville tune which Paul occasionally came up with," says

George Martin, "and he said he wanted 'a kind of tooty sound,' so I scored it for two clarinets and a bass clarinet."

Finally, there was "Penny Lane," another Paul song, celebrating the gently sloping Liverpool street that gives its name to the entire surrounding shopping area. As a snapshot picture of a district at a certain era, it is unsurpassed as a popular song. Watching a TV performance of Bach's *Brandenburg Concertos,* Paul had been struck by what he told George Martin was "this fantastic high trumpet," a piccolo trumpet, as the producer explained. "It's a great sound," Paul said, "why can't we use it?"

An eminent trumpet player, David Mason of the London Symphony Orchestra, was hired. "We had no music prepared," says George Martin. "We just knew that we wanted little piping interjections. As we came to each little section where we wanted the sound, Paul would think up the notes he wanted, and I would write them down for David. The result was unique, something that had never been done in rock music before, and it gave 'Penny Lane' a very distinct character."

The two major songs out of these three, however, were not destined to make it onto the LP for which they were being recorded. EMI was clamoring for a new single, and "Strawberry Fields Forever" and "Penny Lane" were released as double A sides.

Back in the studio, it was Paul's idea, says George Martin, that the group's new album should be linked by a song of his that the Beatles had just recorded—"just an ordinary rock number and not particularly brilliant as songs go," in Martin's opinion. "Why don't we make the whole album as though the Pepper band really existed," was Paul's suggestion, "as though Sergeant Pepper was doing the record. We can dub in effects and things."

Paul's idea that it should unify the record was inspirational: like a writer adopting a nom de plume, the Beatles, spiritually linked by lysergic acid, *became* Sergeant Pepper's Lonely Hearts Club Band, casting aside all former restraints and putting all their beings into their new identities.

The acid may have served as a uniting catalyst, but it also

ushered problems into Studio One. One night, Martin, blind to
the psychedelics his charges had ingested, noticed that an extraordinarily unhealthy appearance had descended over John Lennon.
Taking him up to the roof for some fresh air had no effect; besides,
there was the danger of the ninety-foot drop to the ground. "It
wasn't until much later that I learned what had happened. That
evening he had taken the wrong pill by mistake—a very large dose
of LSD. But Paul knew, and went home with him and turned on
as well, to keep him company. It seems they had a real trip."

The thoughtfulness Paul displayed in looking after John "was
typical of one of the best sides of his character," Martin thought.
"But during the making of *Pepper* he was also to give me one of
the biggest hurts of my life."

This was over the recording of "She's Leaving Home." "Paul
rang me to say, 'I've got a song I want you to work with me on.
Can you come round tomorrow afternoon? I want to get it done
quickly. We'll book an orchestra, and you can score it.'"

Martin, however, was booked for another session, with Cilla
Black, another NEMS artist. He politely suggested that the scor-
ing of the song must wait. But Paul's response was to call up
London's leading record producers, until he found one that was
available, Mike Leander. "The following day Paul presented me
with it and said, 'Here we are. I've got a score. We can record it
now.'

"I recorded it, with a few alterations to make it work better,
but I was hurt. I thought, 'Paul, you could have waited.'"

Having essentially directed the flow of the album since his
muse had offered the idea of becoming the Sergeant Pepper Band,
Paul was in no mood to brook the interference of a moment's
delay. He was, literally, inspired. His conceptual comprehension
of the LP continued to the last moment of editing. "When these
records are pressed, there's a run-out groove that takes the needle
to and fro to get the automatic change working," he said to
George Martin. "Why don't we put some music in there? Something silly?"

As if this was not enough, Paul then added, "And we never

record anything for animals. You realize that, don't you? Let's put on something which only a dog can hear." George Martin duly obliged this ultimate example of stoned whimsy.

Much of Paul's single-minded devotion to the Sergeant Pepper project arose from the fact that, for a time, he was once again a single man. On January 16, 1967, Jane Asher had flown with the Bristol Old Vic to America for a three-month tour. Thoughout the making of *Pepper* Paul had his eye on the calendar; there was an unbreakable deadline at the back of his mind: whatever happened, he intended to be in Denver, Colorado, on April 5 to surprise Jane on her twenty-first birthday. ("I want to be known as a Shakespearean actress—not as Paul McCartney's girlfriend," Jane had already told an American reporter.)

The arrangements for this private visit to America were carried out with scrupulous efficiency by the increasingly neurotic Brian Epstein, desperate to make amends for the largely imagined managerial errors that had almost lost him the Beatles to Allen Klein. At considerable effort and expense he rented Frank Sinatra's Learjet for Paul, and a luxury house was obtained for a month in San Diego—except Paul had meant to say he was going to San Francisco.

In California, the by-now customary summit conferences took place, with the Jefferson Airplane in San Francisco, and with the Mamas and Papas and the Beach Boys in Los Angeles. For Paul, however, the revelation of the trip was not such meetings of other stars, but the sight of San Francisco's thousands of hippies, who appeared so dedicated in the espousal of their life-style compared with London's King's Road kaftan wearers.

As it had been American music that had implanted in Paul's mind the song structures and riffs that he would later draw on at will, so now—thinking on a larger scale—it was a minor but hypnotically attractive American cultural eccentricity that moved Paul to plan a major scheme. Paul was *very* taken with the adventures of writer Ken Kesey and his drug-drenched companions, the Merry Pranksters.

On his return to London Paul went into the studio again, this time at Dick James Music. But now it was to produce an album for his brother and another third of the Scaffold, Roger McGough. Quite clearly, it was a work of fraternal duty rather than a labor of love. Despite having been managed for a time by Brian Epstein, who had secured them a recording deal with Parlophone, the Scaffold had hit hard times and were on the verge of splitting up. To give his brother every possible assistance, Paul wheeled in as many superstar names as he could—Jimi Hendrix, Graham Nash, Dave Mason, John Mayall, the odd Walker brother.

To Roger McGough, obliged by the Scaffold's increasing lack of success to retreat into his sensitive-though-droll Scouse poet persona, such an awesome lineup meant little. "My problem was not being a musician. So although I knew I was in the presence of heavies, I didn't know why: the language they spoke and things that entranced them I didn't appreciate."

All the same, McGough was intrigued to observe the martinet that emerged in Paul McCartney as he went about his production chores. "There was one extremely delicate track. And Paul's instructions before we went into this immeasurably poetic piece were just one complete sergeant-major's bark, 'AWRIGHT-YOU-READY-YOU-READY-C'MON-ONE-TWO-THREE-GO-O-O-OOOO!' We kept that in, because of the contrast."

McGough-McGear was not a hit. While the album was being made, Thelma McGough (née Pickles) stayed with her husband at 7 Cavendish Avenue, as she did on several other occasions. Perhaps the most notable feature of the house, she felt, was the large jar of grass on the mantlepiece, available for anyone to dip into. There were other signs of the times: the mirrored Indian cushions that Jane had bought on Portobello Road, the piles of the very latest records and books, the sunken bathtub in Paul's private bathroom, next to his vast bedroom and equally vast bed.

"It wasn't a showy house, though, but very well designed. Yet it was also very lived in. On the other hand the entire place seemed very designer-orientated—the beds had velvet headboards with matching wallpaper and curtains. I know Jim was always going on about the state of the garden, but the place was informal, not precious—a nice house."

The center of the house was Paul's music room, on the second floor. "Paul was always sitting upstairs composing and playing music. When people came around they were always up there."

The relationship between Paul and Jane continued to seem as ideal as their home. "They seemed to ideally complement each other. They both seemed fairly gentle and thoughtful, and seemed to get on really well. I never detected any friction whatsoever."

The press party for the launch of *Sgt. Pepper's Lonely Hearts Club Band* was held on May 19, 1967, at Brian Epstein's Mayfair home on Chapel Street. Paul, seated in a chair by the fireplace, found himself the focus of attention of a willowy American female photographer, to whom he had been introduced some days before at the Bag O' Nails Club, where they had watched a gig by Georgie Fame and His Blue Flames. Paul had taken her with him to the Speakeasy, where they had become separated, as Paul fell in with members of the Who.

At Chapel Street she sank to her knees in front of Paul, where she remained, shooting off roll after roll of film. Her name was Linda Eastman.

The alleged "drug" imagery of *Sgt. Pepper* earned it as much condemnation from the likes of radio stations as it gathered deserved critical acclaim. Yet John's "Lucy in the Sky With Diamonds" was not about LSD, as claimed, but influenced by a remark by John's young son, Julian; similarly, Paul's "Fixing a Hole" had nothing to do with junkies' needles, but had been written after he had repaired the roof on his Scottish farm. Ironically, however, such misinterpretations of the album were more or less in accord with the attitudes towards drugs that the Beatles were about to make public.

The day before his twenty-fifth birthday the image of Paul McCartney as the cuddly, cutest Beatle of them all came close to being irrevocably fractured. With wide-eyed, innocent wonderment appropriate to the Aquarian Age he admitted to *Life* magazine that, yes, he had tripped on acid. "It opened my eyes. We only use one-tenth of our brains. Just think what we could accomplish if we could tap that hidden part."

Perhaps Paul felt that such pioneering work out there on the new frontier of inner space would one day add a knighthood to the MBE that he had ambivalently accepted two years before. But though LSD may have put the Beatles in tune with each other for the epic construction of *Sgt. Pepper,* such a confession was severely out of sync with public opinion. A hysterical furor was unleashed by the report in *Life,* but Paul refused to recant: he compared taking drugs to "taking aspirin without a headache." "I don't regret that I've spoken out," he told the *Daily Mirror.* "I hope my fans will understand."

The Reverend Billy Graham offered him his prayers. "I am praying for Paul that he finds what he is looking for . . . he has reached the top of his profession and now he is searching for the true purpose of his life. But he will not find it through taking LSD."

Always the spokesman for the Beatles, Paul continued undaunted to broadcast proclamations appropriate to that peculiar year of 1967. "All You Need Is Love" had been rush-released after 400 million people around the world watched the Beatles perform it on the "Our World" TV broadcast. "We had been told we'd be seen recording it by the whole world at the same time. So we had one message for the world—Love. We need more love in the world."

Fine sentiments. But the folks in Bradford and Wigan, Minneapolis and Peoria, were very puzzled.

On July 24 a full-page advertisement appeared in the *London Times.* "The law against marijuana is immoral in principle and unworkable in practice," it insisted. It was signed by all four Beatles and by Brian Epstein, as well as by many writers, artists, and politicians.

But, in tune with the racing tastes of the age and the speed with which the Beatles were not only outdistancing but lapping the public, the group was only a month away from almost renouncing drugs altogether when that seditious proclamation was published in the top people's paper. For on Thursday, August 24, at the Hilton Hotel on Park Lane, the four Beatles attended an introductory meeting on Transcendental Meditation, given by the philosophy's founder, the Maharishi Mahesh Yogi. Conferring

191

afterward with the Maharishi, the group agreed to join him the next day in Bangor, North Wales, for a ten-day course of meditation. The morning after their arrival the Beatles held a press conference: in keeping with the teachings of the Maharishi, they renounced the use of drugs.

The next day, however, the brief moment of peace that the Beatles had attained was brusquely shattered: Brian Epstein was dead, presumably of an overdose of pills.

"What the Maharishi told us was something to do with individuality, some way whereby you could live without other people," said Marianne Faithfull, who with her boyfriend Mick Jagger had accompanied the Beatles to Bangor. "The strange thing about that was that at the moment they were being given a philosophy in which they could live their lives as individuals, at that very second Brian died, the one who'd wanted them to be as a group."

It was not only Brian Epstein who had wanted the Beatles to remain a group. The Beatles were almost desperately needed by Paul McCartney, who had a sense of purpose only when he worked with a team in close harmony, despite the fact that he had to control and drive that team. It was as much a question of self-preservation as a desire not to let the Beatles disintegrate that now drove him to seize the reins.

Accordingly, on September 11, it was on a Paul McCartney project that the Beatles began work. The Magical Mystery Tour was inspired by Paul's visit to San Francisco the previous April. In an effort to contrive an "on-the-bus-or-off-the-bus" attitude similar to the Merry Pranksters', a bus was rented, the Beatles and companions were installed, and the vehicle set off for the English West Country. That it is considerably easier to live a spontaneously hedonistic existence—in which all possibilities are pursued to the maximum—when untrammeled by a full camera crew and half the world's show-biz reporters seemed to pass Paul by— understandably perhaps, as his thinking, like that of all the Beatles, was still befuddled by the numbing news of the death of "Eppy." But the main difficulty with making a coherent, funny film out of this excursion was that so little happened.

To complete the fifty-minute TV film, a formidable cutting rate was necessary. Moreoever, the slot allotted for it by BBC Television was, considering the nature of the final product, the consequence of inconceivably crass thinking. Television schedules on the evening of Boxing Day (the day after Christmas) are comprised of appropriately mindless pap selected to permit the massed TV audience to snooze off the effects of the turkeys, trifles, mince pies, and liquor that it has consumed. A surreal piece of zonked lunacy was hardly likely to assist that desired somnambulistic state.

Magical Mystery Tour was slammed by the TV critics of the popular press. "If they were not the Beatles, the BBC would not have fallen for it," sneered the *Daily Mirror*. Of course, it was not *Magical Mystery Tour* at all against which the press was railing, but the very audacity of everything that the group had dared over the past year: the "drug lyrics" of *Sgt. Pepper,* the admission of doing acid, *The Times* anti-pot–law ad, the espousal of a vaguely Indian philosophy, viewed as particularly heinous by the xenophobic press. It was time to put the Beatles in their place.

In fact, *Magical Mystery Tour* was perfectly in accord with avant-garde TV trends. Had it been slotted in as one of the increasingly original, often similarly plotless "Wednesday Play" series shown by the BBC, it would not have been out of place. As it was, only Keith Dewhurst of *The Guardian* caught the correct tone. On Wednesday, December 27, he wrote: "If one asks where the Beatles were going on their *Magical Mystery Tour* (BBC-I last night) one has to give pompous answers: into their own half-grasped feelings; into the grain, the being alone moments, the glimpses out of the travelling window of living in Britain today; into a kind of fantasy morality play about the grossness and warmth and stupidity of the audience whose adoration has set the Beatles free among the dreamscapes whose poignancy their photography caught so well.

"One has to say these stodgy things because that in its fantastical way is what the film was about. Some of it was too condensed and some too private, but the whole was an inspired freewheeling achievement and 'I Am The Walrus' has a desperate poetry by which we will be remembered, just as an earlier desperation is remembered through Chaplin. Before the Beatles I saw Benny Hill, Petula Clark and an astringent moment of David Frost. Their professionalism made me feel that Boxing Day had come too soon. But the poetry beyond the professionalism of the Beatles was better than this. It redeemed in retrospect days of shallow rubbish and black thoughts about show business."

Finding himself on the newsstands that day in a minority of one, Dewhurst obviously decided to reemphasize his position in his column the next day: "My feelings on finding myself almost alone in praising the Beatles television film *Magical Mystery Tour* are amazement, and the sad conviction that as a mass the public is more stupid and ignorant than it is as individuals, and does not like to be told so. It particularly does not like something which it cannot understand but dimly feels to be a depiction of its qualities and its romantic view of show business. In deference to this the film should no doubt have gone out under some late-night banner like "Omnibus" or "Contrasts"—a bureaucrat's device which says switch over to the wrestling, this program does not concern you or your life in any way at all. My amazement is for the way in which the film has been dismissed as pretentious rubbish with no attempt to analyze content.

"The film is a deliberate parody of mass communication so it parodies the techniques. Most of its technical tricks are used now even in commercial films, and in shows like 'Top Of The Pops' every week. They are known, and that being so people should be able to accept them and advance through them to the images and the content of the film. Why, therefore, do people automatically deny that the content exists? Answer: because they don't want to know what it has to say. They don't want to have to face the fact that their idols and their modern mythology is a lot of mass-produced hooey and that most of us are fobbed off most of the time with utter banal rubbish. The film is about the predicament of people who have become such idols. They are trapped inside an image and a wealth machine which simply cannot express what they really feel. This is a valid modern theme and the Beatles seem most qualified to comment upon it. Maybe they will be entirely trapped: maybe like Chaplin they will never quite struggle in the way they would in the world of 'real art.' But the struggle itself is indicative and the film, whatever its faults, is a comment and a documentation. The Beatles' image of themselves as magicians is not conceited, because it is we who want them to be magicians. They know that they are not."

For Paul McCartney, who had been nurturing ambitions to direct, the negative reception was a severe setback. For Paul, so reliant for his sense of well-being on public acceptance, had experienced his first failure in a long time. He would not attempt to emulate *Magical Mystery Tour* for another fifteen years.

For the record: the production costs of *Magical Mystery Tour* were £40,000; in America alone, it grossed $2 million from college rentals; also in the United States the soundtrack album grossed $8 million in ten days—hardly a commercial failure. But considering the largely negative reaction it had received, it was perhaps inauspicious that the film was the first Beatles venture to carry the logo of a new company they had formed in an effort at minimizing the income tax they were obliged to pay. The name "Apple" had first come to the public's attention when the group had opened the Apple Boutique on London's Baker Street—the name had been an idea of Paul's (*"Apple. Apple Corps. Geddit!?!"*).

At the by-now annual gathering of the Mac clan at Rembrandt on New Year's Eve, Paul announced that he and Jane Asher had become formally engaged. Though seemingly out of tune with the new permissive times, such an acceptance of so solid a Northern working-class ritual was hardly out of character for Paul: that he had already been "walking out" with Jane for four-and-a-half years was closely in keeping with tradition.

The happy couple's joy on this occasion was somewhat marred by an egregious example of misconduct, in the eyes of the Macs, on the part of John Gorman. Before Christmas, the Scaffold's career had finally been untracked from its inertia; a song written by Mike McCartney, "Thank U Very Much," had become a Top Five hit. Understandably elated by this reversal of the group's fortunes, Gorman was in festive spirits. Yet he had no control whatsoever over the young lady who was his companion for the evening at Rembrandt. And, overcome with the emotion of this celebratory party, she contrived to somehow fall out of a second-floor window. "In fact, she was so drunk she just got up and staggered around. But, all the same, an ambulance came and took her away. And I was blamed for that, even though I was downstairs when it happened. I ended up going to another party in the hospital."

This incident was the last straw as far as Gorman was concerned for the somewhat self-righteously disciplined McCartneys. At a previous New Year's Eve party, Gorman had been accused of stealing a bottle of rum. "In fact, I'd taken it with me and hidden it in the bushes to drink on the way home. But Mike saw me with it, walking down the drive, and ran after me and tried to grab it from me. I said, 'Mike, it's mine—I haven't stolen it.' But he took it off me and went back inside with it.

"But with this girl falling out of the window, I'd well and truly blotted my copy-book: I was too immoral for the McCartneys—I wasn't allowed to go to their parties anymore. At all those parties it was quite in order for any members of the family to jump around and get drunk and let their hair down. But if any outsiders did it, it was considered the grossest breach of hospitality."

In March 1968, the Beatles released their seventeenth single, a song written by Paul. Like "Yesterday," "Lady Madonna" ("Lady Madonna/Children at your feet/Wonder how you manage to make ends meet") was entirely dedicated to Mary McCartney. By the time the record came out, however, the Beatles were in India, studying TM with the Maharishi. Though ultimately dissatisfying, this isolation in an indescribable country provided the peace for songwriting that had been removed by the assorted traumas that had occurred since the release of *Sgt. Pepper*.

At a press conference held on their return to London, Paul defined the discontent they had found themselves developing toward the Maharishi. "We thought there was more to him than there was, but he's human. And for a while we thought he wasn't, we thought he was . . . uhhh . . . "

CHAPTER FOURTEEN

"Lady Madonna" was the last record that the Beatles were obliged to provide Parlophone Records. From now on, all releases would appear on the group's own Apple label, for which luxurious premises had been obtained at 3 Savile Row. In late April Apple advertised in the music press, offering assistance to unknown artists. "It's ridiculous that people with talent like Dave Mason and Denny Laine have sometimes had to struggle to get their work accepted," commented Paul.

At the end of the month, perhaps as a tribute to his brass-band-loving grandfather, Paul visited the Yorkshire wool town of Bradford to conduct the prize-winning Black Dyke Mills Band; the tune in question was entitled "Thingummybob," which Paul had written as a theme song for a TV comedy series; in the autumn, "Thingummybob" was released on the Apple label.

On May 12 Paul and John flew to New York to officially announce the existence of Apple. On "The Tonight Show," on which Joe Garagiola substituted for the vacationing Johnny Carson, Paul thoroughly confused his host with his explanation of Apple as "a controlled weirdness, a kind of Western communism. We want to help people, but without doing it like a charity. We always had to go to the big men on our knees and touch our forelocks and say, 'Please can we do so-and-so . . . ?' We're in the happy position of not needing any more money, so for the first time the bosses aren't in it for profit. If you come to me and say, 'I've had such and such a dream,' I'll say to you, 'Go away and do it.' "

Admirable but fatal words, they were to leave the Apple Corps, and the Beatles' gradually dwindling millions, the prey of every spaced—and not so spaced—scamster who had ever had even the glimmer of a half-baked idea.

Not that this in any way occurred to Paul as he was leaving the studio; his thoughts were elsewhere, on the date he had made with that female photographer who a year before had so clearly signaled her intentions at the London *Sgt. Pepper* reception. Paul had never been faithful to Jane Asher. Unbeknownst to her, he maintained a bachelor apartment close to Claridge's Hotel in Mayfair; there he entertained young ladies of his fancy, including for a number of years John Dunbar's nanny, a far more down-to-earth, working-class girl than Jane.

For such an apparent young blade, there was something strangely middle-aged about Paul McCartney's amorous arrangements. Though of course his experiences with the Beatles had made him old beyond his years, at the same time the cossetted world of the rock and roll star had retarded his maturation. This was not something of which he was unaware, however: indeed, it is interesting to note the way that Paul McCartney managed to detect and avoid almost all the traps that lead to the eventual downfall of the rock and roll musician driven by little else but a manic sense of self.

All the same, after taking control of the Beatles, and of the Apple Corps, he had begun to express some attitudes not dissimilar to that of one of the Calvinistic Northern mill owners who would have sponsored the likes of the Black Dyke Mills Band: increasingly, his attitude—even to his brother—was one of "If you've got it, you'll make it," an attitude that was the exact contradiction of what he was offering Apple up as.

"It's funny," says Roger McGough, "it's as if Paul doesn't see his own talent: he seems to think what he's done anyone can do. But that comes down to the family: the McCartney clan attitude is to squash you if you get uppity—you mustn't be allowed to think you're good, and you must keep yourself down. A lot of it I think comes from Jim telling Paul, 'We're all the same, but if you've got a talent you've got to use it.'

"It's impossible for Paul to think that he's gifted. He thinks he's only like anybody else, and if you don't do it, you're just lazy. That goes a long way to explaining why he wouldn't be overgenerous, either in terms of support or finances. 'If I can do it, anybody can.' "

As carefully clandestine in New York as he was in London, Paul McCartney had ensured against any possible press leak that might alert Jane to his cheating on her. Instead of inviting Linda Eastman to his suite at the St. Regis Hotel, he arranged a rendezvous at the apartment of Nat Weiss, Brian Epstein's friend and attorney; the pair remained there together for several days.

Without her knowing it, Linda had a huge advantage working for her. A source of considerable contention between Paul and Jane—perhaps the cause of those adverse remarks about the theater to Joe Orton—was her insistence that having children would interfere with her acting career. Yet, now that Paul had everything he could possibly ever want, all that remained to fulfill his life was the presence of children, something he had always desired far more than the other Beatles, two of whom (John and Ringo) had already produced heirs. Linda could hardly have guessed at the effect she caused when she innocently produced Heather, her six-year-old daughter, for whom Paul gladly babysat while her mother departed to photograph a rock act.

Linda Eastman was no stranger to the feting of musicians. At the age of six, in 1947, she had been the inspiration for the hit song, "Linda," written by Jack Lawrence. It was at the suggestion of her father, Lee Eastman, a celebrated show-business lawyer, who—a neat twist—had changed his surname from Epstein, that Lawrence wrote the song, giving Eastman the publishing rights in exchange for gratis legal work.

At the luxurious Eastman home in Scarsdale, New York, or at their Park Avenue apartment, on whose walls hung her father's impressive art collection, Linda and her younger brother John had grown up accustomed to the sight of such dinner table guests as Tommy Dorsey, Hoagy Carmichael, Hopalong Cassidy, and Robert Rauschenberg. The sense of competitiveness in life was firmly instilled in her.

Because of the connection of her own family with Linders' department stores, Louise Eastman, her mother, was independently wealthy. When Linda was eighteen Louise was killed in a plane crash: Linda Eastman fitted the pattern of so many people in Paul McCartney's life who had had to bear sudden, tragic loss at a relatively young age.

At the University of Colorado, where she studied art and history, Linda met and married a geologist named John See, with whom she had Heather. When the marriage split apart she moved to Tucson, Arizona, and studied photography. Then, armed with a Pentax, she moved back to New York, taking a job as an assistant on *Town and Country* magazine, a launching pad to further her ambition of becoming a photographer. One day in 1966, an invitation to a Rolling Stones party aboard a yacht came into the office; Linda seized the invitation and was the only magazine photographer present at the event.

"Linda's very special," said Danny Fields, at the time the editor of *Datebook* magazine. "She has this quality I find in Libra ladies . . . men have a tendency to dance for them, to perform, to

200

please them. And the pictures she got that day—there were the other pictures, the official pictures of the Stones taken by some professional news photographer, and then there were Linda's pictures. The Stones were *doing* things, striking poses, being arrogant and beautiful and fantastic and sexy. They did it, they danced for her camera, and she always had this quality. She took the best portraits of beautiful people of anyone. The publicity group shots she did were okay, and that's most of her stuff that's been published, but her portfolio of close-ups was just astonishing."

A free spirit, Linda fitted in far better with the world of rock and roll than with that of publishing; she was a familiar figure in the photographer's pit at the Fillmore East, and her rock-star boyfriends included Steve Winwood, Eric Burdon, and Tim Buckley. Though hardly the most fashionable of dressers, there was something indubitably sexy—a sexiness never caught by the camera—about the innocently seductive way she clad her tall, leggy frame in preppy fashions. Besides, Paul's heart had always gone out to blondes.

Paul always needed to be with a woman. When he was with one, the tension lines on his forehead and around those liquid, slow-moving eyes would vanish; that cherub's face, so much harder in real life than in photographs, would visibly soften.

It was to an empty house that he returned when he came back to England: Jane Asher was on a British provincial tour with the Bristol Old Vic. Within days he had encountered a female playmate to substitute for Jane until her return: Francie Schwartz, one of the many supplicants for Apple largesse at 3 Savile Row, somehow contrived to wangle her way into an audience with Paul, and thence into his bed. For three weeks this casual but mutually convenient arrangement continued. But then Jane suddenly returned home, her season having been unexpectedly cut short.

"The eyes and ears of the world" was how Paul described the obsessive girl fans, later immortalized in a George Harrison song as the "Apple Scruffs," who shadowed the every movement of the Beatles. He should have heeded his own precise perception in so defining them, for when one of the girls, Margo Stevens (such a regular at Paul's gates that she was permitted by Rosie the housekeeper to take Martha the sheepdog for walks), frantically pressed the Entryphone to warn Paul that Jane was coming up to the front door, he didn't believe her. "Ah, pull the other one."

Inside the house Jane found Francie Schwartz, wearing only Paul's dressing gown. A short while later the girls outside saw Jane rush out and drive off. Then they saw her mother arrive, and leave with what were obviously Jane's possessions. A month later, on a BBC-TV talk show, Jane publicly announced that her engagement had ended, but that it was not she who had broken it —which, of course, she hadn't.

Unsurprisingly, rife as it was with bad karma, Paul's romance with Francie Schwartz soon fizzled out. Paul then had a brief fling with another girl, Maggie McGivern, taking her on holiday with him to Sardinia.

In the late summer Paul called Linda Eastman in New York and invited her over to London. The Apple Scruff girls saw the pair arrive together at Cavendish Avenue in Paul's Mini-Cooper. In the house they saw various lights go on and off, until one went on in what the girls called the Mad Room, Paul's music room. They could tell Paul was happy: he sat on the windowsill with an acoustic guitar, singing a new song to them called "Blackbird."

The changes that had occurred in Paul McCartney's relationships that summer had been preceded by only a few weeks by those in John Lennon's life.

The much-abused Cynthia Lennon had returned from a holiday in Greece to encounter a scene very similar to that Jane Asher discovered: wearing nothing but John's dressing gown was a Japanese artist he had known for some time named Yoko Ono.

Paul heard that the split between John and Cynthia was irrevocable soon after he and Jane had parted. Knowing Cynthia as he did, and sensing the pain she was suffering, Paul drove down to Kenwood to see her, taking with him a single red rose and a song he had written on the journey for Julian Lennon called "Hey Jude." "How about it then, Cyn?" he joked wearily. "How about you and me getting married now?" Cynthia was touched by Paul's show of loyalty and support.

When John first heard the heartfelt plea for a lost love that was "Hey Jude," the sentiments seemed to measure up so exactly to his own feelings that he thought Paul had written it for him. John later remembered: "I took it very personally. I said, 'It's me!' He says, 'No, it's me.' I said, 'Check, we're going through the same bit.'"

At the Abbey Road sessions to record the new songs the Beatles had written in India—of which "Blackbird" was one—there was a palpable tension, not the least cause of which was the permanent, intrusive presence of John's new female companion. Yoko Ono was as severely disruptive to the need of John and Paul to work together in the studio as had been Stuart Sutcliffe nearly ten years earlier. She was, moreover, a constant reminder of the way things had changed in their lives, and of the intense difficulties and internal battles that had been caused by the chaotic events of the previous twelve months. Provincial at heart, Paul had grown up with and understood Cynthia: like a good Northern woman, she had been prepared to take a backseat as the men enacted their version of going down to the pub together. It had always been Paul who had been John's real soul mate, and a very real love existed between them. Now this was being supplanted by the kind of woman who, ironically, the social revolution the Beatles had helped create gave the freedom to exist (although, of course, Yoko had been unique before her time).

Unable to bring themselves to collaborate, the music suffered, John's songs missing the mellifluous melodies that Paul so often offered as an emollient, and Paul's sweet songs lacking the acidic textures of John's tough middle-eights. The total recording time was five months: after three months George Martin went on vacation and left his engineer, Chris Thomas, in charge. "Paul was the first to walk in. He said, 'What're you doing here?' 'Well, don't you know?' He said, 'Well, if you can produce us, do so: if you can't, then fuck off.'

"Actually, I thought the atmosphere was all right. Yet every day, in the middle of a song, they'd have to have a meeting about who to hire and fire at Apple. Yet when they started playing it was a really great atmosphere: they'd really rock out. And they were very funny: Paul was very quick, but John was out on his own.

"But when I worked with Paul later, I realized how much he'd been leading the Beatles. He is staggeringly gifted—he can be so precise, perhaps too precise. He's tremendously strong, but he knows perfectly well that the old cliché of all masterpieces consisting of ninety-five percent hard work is perfectly true. And he puts in that hard work because he just loves doing it. He *is* a brilliant musician, more so than Lennon was—Lennon's thing was something else altogether."

However, the resulting double album, *The Beatles* (a.k.a. the White Album) was something of a failure. In the main, it consisted of rough sketches of songs that sounded as though they had been conceived for separate solo records.

Ringo had lent John and Yoko his apartment in Montague Square, in the West End; there for much of the time the couple remained, growing gradually addicted to heroin, except for those increasingly eccentric, brief forays they would make into the outside world.

Paul, for his part, occupied his time in attending to the smallest details of the major project at hand, in this case, the successful launching of the Apple record label. He worked with EMI and Capitol; he instructed Derek Taylor, the press officer, to cease tripping at work; and he produced a record by a young Welsh girl called Mary Hopkin.

Mary Hopkin caught the attention of Twiggy, the model who was the personification of the Swinging Sixties, when she saw the girl's appearance on the weekly TV talent contest, "Opportunity Knocks." Twiggy contacted her friend Paul and suggested he offer the girl a deal with Apple.

So impressed with this seventeen-year-old was Paul that he knew her voice was exactly suited for "Those Were the Days," by songwriter Gene Raskin, which for months he had been searching for the right artist to record. He also decided that he would produce the record and take Hopkin under his wing. "He was a good producer, because he was very diplomatic, which is important," says Mary Hopkin. "Being a performer himself, he understood my hang-ups. He was very easy to work with, but that was partially because I had no definite ideas of my own. As I found out what I wanted to do, I became more difficult to work with."

Although Paul personally designed the sleeve of her first LP, and suggested its title, *Post Card,* being the personal protégé of a Beatle as busy as Paul McCartney also led to the inevitable difficulty of Mary Hopkin being squeezed in whenever Paul had half a day to spare: seven months were to elapse before he produced her next single, "Goodbye." "There was a lack of songs for me to record, so Paul sat down and wrote it in about ten minutes. But it did get a bit difficult with him, because he wanted me to record a song called 'Que Sera' that Doris Day had once done, because Paul said it had been his favorite song when he was a child. It embarrassed me so.

"But he carried me along on this great wave of enthusiasm. One minute we were sitting in the garden with Linda at Cavendish Avenue, and then he was on the phone to Ringo asking him to drum on it, and then we were in the studio in half an hour and it was done. But I hated it so much I refused to let it be released in Britain."

"Those Were the Days" was scheduled for release on August 16, 1968, intended as the prestigious opening of an almost equally major Apple front to "Hey Jude," which came out on the same day. The Hopkin single, which eventually sold four million copies worldwide, was almost as large a hit as the Beatles' record, and followed it to number one in Britain. For the time being at least, Apple Records seemed to have made an indelible commercial mark.

A month later, however, the purposeful yet idealistic image presented by Apple suffered an almost pulverizing setback: with characteristic spaced-out innocence, John Lennon and Yoko Ono foisted on a bewildered, often appalled public, an album of avant-garde music entitled *Unfinished Music #1: Two Virgins,* with a cover shot of the happy couple, arms intertwined, entirely in the nude. It was Art, said John. EMI Records refused to handle the album; but Paul, even though he had been dismayed at the sleeve, consented to contribute a somewhat ungrammatical and ambivalent sleeve note: "When two great Saints meet, it is a humbling experience. The long battle to prove he was a Saint." *Two Virgins* was not a great seller.

This was not the only matter of controversy with which John was involved that autumn. On October 18, at Ringo's Montague Square apartment, he became the first Beatle to be busted when the drug squad of Detective Sergeant Pilcher, later celebrated in the underground press for his superstar busts as "the groupie cop," raided the premises, discovering an ounce and a half of cannabis, but not the heroin of which John and Yoko were now rather more fond. Possibly as a consequence of the stress of having been arrested, Yoko lost the baby she was carrying.

When, hot on the heels of the *Yellow Submarine* animated-cartoon film and LP, the White Album was released at the beginning of December, it seemed as though both the group and the company were back on a clear course. Everything was as it had always been: it was Christmas and, regular as the seasonal lights being switched on in Regent Street, around the corner from Apple, there was a new Beatles record. But its release concealed an internal rot of which none of its participants was unaware.

Still Paul soldiered on, gathering and ordering the troops for yet another effort. For his own complex psychological reasons as much as anything, he still insisted on perceiving the Beatles as a unity. And on January 2, 1969, the group gathered at Twickenham film studios in West London for yet another film project, tentatively titled *Get Back*. As had been *Magical Mystery Tour*, this was Paul's scheme; chastened, however, by the negative response to that effort, he this time entrusted the professional leadership to a director of some repute, Michael Lindsay-Hogg, who had worked in the mid-sixties on the then-revolutionary "Ready Steady Go" rock and roll TV series. Nonetheless, Paul attempted to place his own stamp on the director's approach to the documentary, invoking the attitude of Andy Warhol. "You should get really close up, like right into one of John's eyes. Can you do that? That direction rather than John and the moon."

The idea was almost breathtakingly simple: on film the Beatles would record a new album at Twickenham, which would be followed by a concert—an act, hoped Paul, that would galvanize and channel the group away from the negative energy that had built up since they'd stopped performing live. More regular live shows, he hoped, would result. For his part, Paul desperately needed the immediate approbation and resultant self-love that came from the applause of an audience. Recently, his needs rising, Paul had stopped his car outside a pub north of London and bounced inside to the piano, rolling off a selection of favorites to an audience who could hardly believe their luck.

But, as ever when he was fighting his insecurity, Paul was at his rambling, hectoring worst as the cameras rolled at Twickenham, more like the worst kind of British middle-management official promoted to a position beyond his abilities than the bluff, paternalistic but pleasant Northern mill owner he was at 3 Savile Row. At least he pointed out some truths, but it was the manner not the matter of his speech that grated. "We've been very negative since Mr. Epstein passed away. We haven't been positive. That's why all of us in turn have been sick of the group, you know. There's nothing positive in it. It is a bit of a drag. It's like when you're growing up and then your daddy goes away at a certain point in your life and then you stand on your own two feet. Daddy has gone away now, you know, and we are on our little holiday camp. You know, I think we either go home or we do it. It's discipline we need. It's like everything you do, you never had discipline. Mr. Epstein, he said, sort of 'Get suits on' and we did. And so we were always fighting that discipline a bit.

"But now it's silly to fight that discipline if it's our own. It's self-imposed these days, so we do as little as possible. But I think we need a bit more if we are going to get on with it."

"Well, if that's what doing it is, I don't want to do anything," replied George, as though responding to an instruction from a teacher at the Liverpool Institute. When Paul asked the "lads" if they would like to play a live show, George's response after a moment was, "You're so full of shit, man."

The deep resentment that George had secretly borne Paul for so long surfaced at another of these sessions. "I always seem to be annoying you," Paul suddenly realized, years too late.

"All right," George replied, "I'll play whatever you want me to play, or I won't play at all if you don't want me to play. Whatever it is that pleases you, I'll do it."

Driving home to Esher for lunch that day, George announced to Pattie, his wife, that he had left the group, that the Beatles were finished. But after a few days at home he turned up at an Apple business meeting as though nothing whatsoever had happened.

Paul's ceaseless bickering at George was largely inspired by jealousy: aware of his musical abilities, Paul felt hampered by the limitations of the bass and desired quite desperately to be the group's lead guitarist, not only for the expression of his own talents, but also for the increased status that of late had turned the guitarist into the heroic figure of rock music. It was only expediency, after all, that had caused him to become a bass player in the first place; no one else had been prepared to take up the instrument when Stuart Sutcliffe left the group. Yet in this desire to play guitar, Paul was yet again ignoring his own abilities, not taking into account that he was regarded by many musicians as the finest bass player in the world, and ignoring the way so many of the Beatles' songs were structured around his hypnotic bass lines.

For *Get Back*, Paul's favorite fantasy, one encouraged by Lindsay-Hogg, was that the film's climactic concert should be in a Tunisian amphitheater. He had also fancied making the entire film on an ocean liner—so often parsimoniously penny-wise, Paul did seem at times to also be considerably pound-foolish, as they say in England, much like Brian Epstein had been, in fact. Then, on a rather more practical level, Apple staff were instructed by him to inquire as to the availability of the Roundhouse in North London, a converted railway engine turntable popular with the most drug-wrecked rock audiences.

In the end, of course, the Beatles' final concert took place in an aptly apathetic way, by the equipment being lugged up to the roof of 3 Savile Row, with the windswept group playing until the police arrived and pulled out the plugs.

CHAPTER FIFTEEN

On the morning of March 12, 1969, Paul McCartney married Linda Eastman at Marylebone Registry Office. As at the weddings of John and Ringo before him, Paul's bride was pregnant at the ceremony. Unlike John, however, it was not considerable feelings of misgiving that Paul felt, but a genuine joy in knowing that his own child was on the way.

Having forgotten to buy a ring, Paul had had to call up a jeweler the previous evening, from whom he had bought one for £12. None of the other Beatles were present, and the only guests were

Mal Evans and Peter Brown, the group's invaluable overseer at Apple. The ceremony was delayed when the train carrying Paul's best man, Mike McCartney, broke down, and he was unable to make the scheduled time of 9:45 A.M. Fortunately, no other weddings had been booked that day at the registry office.

Unsurprisingly, considering the erratic but indubitable spiritual awakening that Paul had undergone over the past two years, the ceremony was followed by a blessing at a Roman Catholic church in St. John's Wood.

Despite the champagne that flowed back at 7 Cavendish Avenue, this wedding of the world's most eligible bachelor was not the most romantic of occasions. Baying in angry confusion at the security gates of Paul and his new bride's house was the once so submissive selection of girl fans: in their perplexed anguish they rammed open the gates and pushed burning newspapers through the letterbox until the police were called.

Paul had spent the previous evening in the studio, working with George Harrison and keyboardist Billy Preston—who the Beatles had first met when he was playing with Little Richard in Hamburg—on a track called "Thumbin' a Ride" for Jackie Lomax, an Apple artist who had been a former member of the Merseybeat group the Undertakers. Paul had found the song for Lomax to record on the B side of a Coasters single in his own collection. And on his wedding night Paul returned to the studio to complete the production. (Though Lomax was actually the protégé of George Harrison, George was that night indisposed, having that day become the second Beatle to be busted by the industrious Detective Sergeant Pilcher.)

A sense of urgency hung over the Lomax session. In the middle of January John Lennon had told journalist Ray Coleman that "Apple is losing money. If it carries on like this, we'll be broke in six months." Though it was only what all the Beatles knew—the endless party at 3 Savile Row was rapidly draining the group's financial resources—Paul had unleashed on Coleman a tirade as they passed on the stairs one day at Apple: "This is only a small company and you're trying to wreck it. You know John shoots his mouth off and doesn't mean it."

John's remark, however, had an instant effect: Allen Klein, whose reversing of the Rolling Stones' financial fortunes had once so impressed Paul, immediately contacted the group to offer his services. John Lennon liked the way that Klein punctuated his every other word with the expletive "fuck," taking this as an indication of funky forthrightness rather than the "street" affectation that was obligatory in the circles in which Klein moved. With typical bluntness, the same day that John met Klein he dashed off a memo to Sir Joseph Lockwood, the managing director of EMI Records: "Dear Sir Joe: From now on Allen Klein handles all my stuff."

To Derek Taylor in the Apple offices he declared, "I don't give a bugger who anybody else wants, but I'm having Allen Klein for me."

So a clumsy situation was created for Paul McCartney. For not long after meeting Linda, she had introduced him to her father and brother; their knowledge of show-business law, especially that of music publishing copyrights, had been particularly reassuring to a young man who had been attempting to make some sense of the labyrinthine business structure Brian Epstein had left for them. Furthermore, Paul was very taken by the air of well-connected dignity the Eastmans oozed; he asked Lee Eastman if he could suggest someone who could establish some sort of order in the group's affairs. Lee, naturally, recommended his son, John Eastman. Of his own accord Paul, stimulated by the fresh insights into the world of music publishing he had gained from his new contacts, purchased several thousand shares in Northern Songs.

In London, John Eastman met the other Beatles; even though the young Manhattan lawyer also often used the word "fuck," John Lennon did not react favorably to his smooth, sophisticated demeanor. All the same, the younger Eastman was engaged by Apple.

One of his immediate suggestions was that the Beatles themselves should buy NEMS, Brian Epstein's management company. As was contractually correct, NEMS was continuing to take 25 percent of the Beatles' earnings, a situation that would persist for nine more years. Early in 1969, however, punitive tax demands obliged the Epstein family, the inheritors of Brian's company, to offer NEMS to an agile City of London merchant bank, Triumph Investment Trust, the personal fiefdom of Leonard Richenberg, a former economics adviser to the British Treasury.

But on hearing of the interest in the company shown by the Beatles, Epstein's brother Clive decided it would be only fair to give Apple first option. Accordingly, John Eastman met with Sir Joseph Lockwood, who agreed to offer the Beatles an advance against future royalties of one million pounds, the price of NEMS.

It was at this juncture in the negotiations that John Lennon met Allen Klein. Klein argued against the acquisition of NEMS; to earn a million pounds in royalties after tax, he pointed out, would require considerably more than that sum of money to be made in the first place. John Eastman's role was relegated to that of Beatles' legal adviser. No wonder the reaction of Linda Eastman, on hearing of Klein's successful wooing of John Lennon, had been simply, "Oh shit!"

The opinion of his wife-to-be simply confirmed the instinctive mistrust Paul had for Klein, a considerable change of heart from his feelings of eighteen months earlier.

Klein asked Clive Epstein to defer the sale for three weeks. Growing edgy at this procrastination, however, Clive Epstein sold out to Triumph two weeks later. Allen Klein and John Eastman blamed each other for this failure, a considerable setback for the Beatles, who would now lose a quarter of their earnings to a shrewd merchant bank: in a few weeks, furthermore, 1.3 million pounds of royalties were due to be paid to NEMS.

First, Klein tried to browbeat Richenberg into selling the company back to the Beatles. Then he informed Sir Joseph Lockwood that he was to no longer pay royalties to NEMS. With steely Zen detachment Sir Joseph took the middle path: nobody, he declared, would receive any money until the dispute was settled.

Over champagne at Claridge's, a more genteel meeting took place between Richenberg and Lee Eastman. Eastman senior fared no better than had Klein. Eventually, however, at a meeting with Klein and the Beatles at 3 Savile Row, a financial settlement was

214

made with Richenberg whereby Triumph relinquished its entitlement to the 25 percent.

Paul's attorneys at first told Klein that they had received instructions that their client's signature would not appear on the necessary contracts until Klein agreed to take no fee. Satisfied with the settlement, however, Paul quickly changed his mind.

Eight days after Paul and Linda had plighted their troth, John Lennon and Yoko Ono were similarly married, in a civil ceremony in Gibraltar.

More than any boardroom bitterness or studio squabbling, the close proximity in time of the weddings symbolized the irrevocable split between the two men. It also explained much of the subsequent acrimony, particularly on John's part: for he had been free to marry Yoko since November 8 of the previous year when his divorce from Cynthia had been finalized. Yet it seems no coincidence that John remarried only a week after Paul's wedding. No matter how much he loved Yoko, the Gibraltar ceremony seems like something close to an on-the-rebound reaction to the loss of his first great love, Paul McCartney, whose matriarchal sense of order but paternal sense of purpose had provided John with a stabilizing influence. As Paul had sought a mother figure, so John had found a substitute for both his father, the missing Alf Lennon, and his errant mother, Julia, in the vastly complex figure of Paul McCartney. In later years John would admit that Paul had been the first love of his life, and Yoko the second.

While Paul was honeymooning in America, and John in Amsterdam, in a bed-in, further stock exchange shenanigans were taking place. In fact, John and Yoko's Bed Peace happening was a contributory cause of these; like half the world, Dick James, the Beatles publisher and managing director of Northern Songs, had become increasingly confused by John's unpredictable behavior. In the case of James, furthermore, there was a responsibility owed to his three thousand shareholders, many of whom were becoming equally alarmed as the value of their shares fluctuated in response to John's odd actions.

But it was not until the appearance of Allen Klein, whom he seriously mistrusted, that Dick James made a decision: he would sell his 23 percent of Northern Songs to Lew Grade's ATV for the offered price of over a million pounds. This gave ATV, already a minority shareholder, 35 percent of the stock: the company then put in a bid of £9.5 million for the rest of Northern Songs.

Though John and Paul were furious with Dick James, there was nothing underhanded in what he did. Indeed, his hesitancy had been that of an honorable man, as had been his original offer to Brian Epstein. "As soon as John and Paul were back, I met them at Paul's house to explain why I'd done what I had. Linda made tea and didn't enter into the discussion, though Yoko did. I apologized and explained, and I think they understood. But we were *all* upset."

In the subsequent negotiations by Allen Klein to allow John and Paul to take over Northern Songs, a troubling detail came to light that unsettled the fragile bond of common purpose that had temporarily drawn the pair back together. Whereas John still had the original 644,000 shares he had been allotted when the company went public, he discovered that Paul now had 751,000, the result of his acquisitions the previous year.

"It was a matter of investing in something you believed in instead of supermarkets and furniture stores," Paul tried to explain to John. "I had some beanies and I wanted some more."

"This is the first time any of us have gone behind each other's backs," was John's stunned reply.

Notwithstanding Klein's efforts, ATV took control of Northern Songs on May 20, 1969. The same day it was announced that Allen Klein had become the Beatles' business manager. Paul, who had been having nightmares in which Klein appeared as a dentist chasing him with a drill, had been outvoted by the other three. John Eastman remained Paul's representative; "a warm, workable relationship," he described it to the press.

One of Klein's first managerial actions was to take his new troop up to Manchester Square, to visit Sir Joseph Lockwood and demand higher royalties. Sir Joseph politely asked that they leave the building. As they did, tails between their legs, Paul McCartney made schoolboy-like faces at the EMI managing director, as if to exonerate himself in Sir Joseph's eyes from this folly.

On May 30 the first Klein-era Beatles single was released, "The Ballad of John and Yoko." Though virtually a Lennon solo project, Paul provided the drumming.

Early in July, Ringo was invited to dinner at 7 Cavendish Avenue. He noticed that whenever he passed a favorable comment on an action of Klein's, Linda would start crying. "Oh, they've got you, too."

By now it had been decided that *Let It Be*, as the Lindsay-Hogg documentary had been retitled, would have a full cinematic release in the New Year, which meant that those hours of music recorded by the Beatles could not come out until then. In a move that seemed out of keeping with the attitude within the group—but was very much in keeping with the attitude within the man—Paul urged the Beatles to record another LP, to be released before *Let It Be*. Utterly disinclined to venture into the Apple offices, Paul, under considerable stress, knew as always that work would be his only salvation. At home he was under virtual siege, the once-passive hordes of Apple Scruffs having turned vicious with his marriage to Linda. Now, like a rampaging teenage gang in an urban-wasteland horror film, they wandered at will in his overgrown garden, from time to time breaking into the house and stealing souvenirs. Carol Bedford, one of the girls, remembers a fine example of the chauvinist Northern man emerging in Paul. Questioning her about a break-in, which she, unknown to him, had committed, Paul wondered aloud just how the culprit could have entered the house. When she suggested that perhaps it had been done via the ladder that was at the back of the house, Paul was dismissive: "Girls can't climb ladders." Linda McCartney, she says, seemed always threatened by the Scruffs, and in their presence would cling onto Paul's arm with even more ferocious possessiveness than she usually did.

One day, Paul and Linda kept watch on 7 Cavendish Avenue from the garden of the house across the street. After he saw a girl open the security gate with a subtle kick and creep up the pathway, he tore after her. Violently he grabbed the trespasser just as she was lovingly laying a bunch of flowers on the front steps: it was Margo Stevens, who so often and so caringly had walked Martha on Hampstead Heath. "He could see how much he'd frightened me. He stopped shaking me and started stroking my hair."

Predictably, Paul exorcised his problems through writing a song about them: the intrusions made into his home by the Scruffs, with whom he had had to open diplomatic negotiations to secure the return of a treasured photograph of his father, were celebrated in one of his best rockers in years, "She Came in Through the Bathroom Window." It was recorded among the new collection of songs on which the Beatles were working, for an album that would be called *Abbey Road* (named for the EMI studio), although Olympic Studios in Barnes and Trident in Soho were also used. Whereas at the White Album and *Let It Be* sessions the four Beatles were forever augmented by the dark, silent, all-knowing presence of Yoko Ono, the *Abbey Road* dates had a balance of sorts in the light, airy Linda McCartney, heavily pregnant and dressed in unfashionable smocks and sandals.

Most days Paul would stroll the prettily opulent, peaceful streets that lay between his house and Abbey Road. One evening, after the other three Beatles had long since driven up in their expensive vehicles, John could be made out pacing up and down the front steps, gazing with increasing impatience along the route that Paul usually took.

Suddenly he was called to the phone by George. Then he was seen racing down the front steps and running as fast as his unfit body could carry him in the direction of the McCartney residence. Paul had called to say that he would not be coming to the studio that evening—he and Linda had realized it was the anniversary of their first meeting and had decided to have a romantic, candlelit dinner at home.

Arriving outside 7 Cavendish Avenue, John, like a man possessed, clambered over the tall security gate. When Paul responded to his thumping on the front door by opening it, John pushed him aside, rushing in and screaming at Paul for his thoughtlessness. "It's the anniversary of me and Linda meeting," Paul reiterated lamely.

"So what!" snapped John contemptuously. "I don't cancel studio bookings for my anniversaries with Yoko. How dare you inconvenience so many people!"

John glanced around him in furious frustration. Then his eyes alighted on something. Striding over to the wall, he removed a painting, one that he himself had done and given to Paul in earlier, genuinely loving times. It was Paul's favorite painting, as John well knew. John stuck his foot through it and stormed back to Abbey Road.

There were other, equally unpleasant scenes at the time of the recording. Late one afternoon the Apple Scruffs were gathered in front of 3 Savile Row, the "eyes and ears of the world" having learned that all four Beatles had arrived at the building for a meeting in John's office, which faced the street. The girls had a clear view of what was obviously a formidably bitter argument. As the arm-waving grew more frantic and the already twisted grimaces turned even more distorted and ugly, there was a sudden flurry of movement: Linda McCartney had been saying something to either John or Yoko—now John was leaping toward her, his clenched fist about to land a punch. Only the lightning-quick intervention of Paul, suddenly slipping between them, saved Linda from the blow and John from the remorse with which he would have inevitably been burdened.

Soon after, Paul and Linda left the building. A local wino named Billy, who the Beatles had met when they were recording at nearby Trident, approached Paul and asked for money. On being handed a £5 note, Billy offered his thanks by bursting into a raucous, drunken version of "Hey Jude," dissipating the tension and allowing Paul a nervous laugh as he climbed into his Mini-Cooper.

But nothing else could be seen as auspicious. Even on those occasions when the Beatles seemed to be as one mind, as on one particular occasion when they all left Abbey Road together, things just could not go right. By the time Paul had helped the seven-months-pregnant Linda into his Mini, the car was surrounded by at least two dozen fans. They parted willingly to let the Beatle open the driver's door and climb into his seat, but then the gap closed again around the vehicle. Starting the car and honking his horn, Paul tried to move slowly forward, but still the crowd would not clear. Suddenly, in a state of near-panic, Paul jammed his foot down on the accelerator pedal. As the car leapt forward, the fans did move back, but not quickly enough. Unbeknownst to Paul, as he and Linda raced out of the gates of Abbey Road, they left lying on the ground a girl whose foot the car had run over; another girl, who had run after the departing couple, had to be taken to the hospital after one of the heavy iron gates slammed into her head, knocking her out.

Considering the omnipresent bad vibes, *Abbey Road* can be considered even more of a great record than it already is, though no doubt the tension assisted the creative processes. John was not satisfied, however: his ire risen to the full, he railed against songs like Paul's "Maxwell's Silver Hammer," deriding it as an example of Paul's "granny music."

When the album was released at the end of September, Paul, continuing to be ever-conciliatory but increasingly desperate in his efforts to prevent the group from splitting, attempted to persuade the others to undertake a tour of small clubs, turning up unannounced, if necessary. George and Ringo agreed. John, however, had just returned from playing with the Plastic Ono Band in Toronto; he was as contemptuous as he was of any idea coming from Paul. "I might as well tell you, I'm leaving the group. I've had enough, I want a divorce, like my divorce from Cynthia."

Allen Klein was horror-struck, not because of the nature of the news, but because if it leaked out it could severely damage his efforts to secure a better royalty rate from Capitol, efforts that seemed close to fruition. The four members were urged in no uncertain terms to silence. Soon Klein favorably concluded these renegotiations. Later he claimed that this rise in the American royalty rate swung Paul over to his side. On the contrary, Paul said, it made him distinctly uncomfortable to have wrested so much more money from the company when the group was in such obvious disarray.

On August 28, a daughter, unsurprisingly named Mary, was born to Linda and Paul. As soon as a lull appeared in the Beatles' ever-bitter affairs, Paul, Linda, Heather, and the new baby disappeared to the peace of the Campbeltown hills.

Now, like an augury that had been misread by a befuddled seer, a most strange, yet somehow understandable, rumor swept the world: that Paul McCartney was dead.

It emanated from one source, a Detroit disc jockey on station WKNR-FM named Russ Gibb, who claimed to have received an anonymous phone call claiming not only that was Paul dead, but that he had died several years previously: this was the reason the Beatles had stopped touring. The proof, he claimed he had been told, lay in the *Abbey Road* cover photograph: this was a symbolic representation of Paul's funeral procession, and Paul was quite obviously dead because he was walking in his bare feet and smoking a cigarette in his right hand when everyone knew he played with his left—obviously this Paul McCartney was a double. If any further substantiation were required for this mass of "solid" evidence, it lay in the number of the Volkswagen (a Beetle!!!) parked behind the group: its license plate, 28 IF, was the age Paul would have been *if* he were still alive. (In fact, Paul was twenty-seven.) And what is more, said Gibbs, his caller had advised him to play backward the end segment of "Strawberry Fields Forever": there he would find the clincher—John solemnly intoning "I buried Paul."

Conspiracy theorists had a field day. Paul had been killed in a car crash and was the subject of "A Day in the Life": this was why he faced backward on the back cover photo of *Sgt. Pepper*. (In fact, Paul couldn't make the session, so Mal Evans donned the "Pepper" uniform and, feeling it might otherwise confuse the fans, turned his back to the camera.) There was more: Billy Shears was an actor called William Campbell, who had undergone extensive plastic surgery to play his part so the group would not have to fold. Death discs appeared: "Saint Paul," "Dear Paul," "The Ballad of Paul," and—the best title—"Paulbearer."

The only truth in all this nonsense was that the *Abbey Road* cover photo *was* lifeless. Perhaps this meant that the Beatles as a group were dead. . . .

And the only thing close to Campbell in Paul's life was Campbeltown (obviously another clue), a few miles down the road from High Park. There, one day, following the sounds of Martha's barking, Paul found himself facing a full complement of *Life* magazine reporters and photographers, dispatched by the publication to verify the official statement made so many times a day by Derek Taylor that Paul was not in the hereafter but only in Scotland.

Paul's response to this intrusion upon his privacy was to heave a pail of water over the nearest *Life* photographer. Fleeing the unexpected but most certainly corporeal wrath of their subject, the *Life* team descended to Campbeltown. In hot pursuit in his Land-Rover came Paul McCartney, miraculously transformed into the PR man who had always broken the ice with the press and offered them cups of tea. In exchange for the film of his uncharacteristic display of fury, Paul offered a full interview with exclusive Linda McCartney pictures of himself and his new baby. "Rumors of my death have been greatly exaggerated," he told the magazine. "However, if I was dead, I'm sure I'd be the last to know."

At the beginning of 1970 John Lennon employed the explosive talents of Phil Spector on the production of a new single from the Plastic Ono Band, "Instant Karma." It was a huge worldwide hit. In gratitude John gave the mysterious Spector the tapes recorded for *Let It Be;* he could sort them out to the best of his undoubted abilities.

In March Paul finally arrived back at the Apple offices from Scotland. Under his arm were the tapes of a solo album, *McCartney,* that he had made on his farm. The release date he demanded was April 10.

In his absence, however, the *Let It Be* album, now completed by Phil Spector, had been scheduled for the same month: two such significant releases would cause a glut on the market. Besides,

Ringo's *Sentimental Journey* LP was intended to come out immediately after *Let It Be*.

In an effort at amelioration, Ringo visited Paul McCartney at Cavendish Avenue. Paul's long period of tranquillity in Scotland seemed only to have brought out a paranoid venom almost on a par with that John Lennon had displayed a few months previously. "I'll finish you all now!" he screamed at the hapless drummer. "You'll pay!" He told Ringo to put on his coat and get out. With his customary good nature only temporarily ruffled, Ringo decided to do what he had always done, to take a backseat. If it meant that much to him, Ringo decided, Paul's album could come out before his.

Paul got what he wanted: an April 10 release date for *McCartney*, a generally slight effort on which Paul played all the instruments, and on which Linda shared several of the vocals.

Paul, however, had not yet heard the remix of *Let It Be*. When he did, he was appalled, particularly by the treatment meted out to his ballad, "The Long and Winding Road." Spector, never able to do things by halves, had added horns and violins and a pseudo-celestial choir. Paul demanded of Klein that the original version be returned to the album, but the request went unheeded.

Paul gave up. He phoned John and told him he was leaving the Beatles. John sounded pleased. "That makes two of us who have accepted it mentally."

On the day that *McCartney* went on sale, a press release was sent out by Derek Taylor. "Paul McCartney has left the Beatles because of personal, business, and musical differences. They do not want to split up," continued the official statement from this most thoughtful of PRs, "but the present rift seems to be part of their growing up . . . at the moment they seem to cramp each other's styles. Paul has called a halt to the Beatles' activities. They could be dormant for years."

Tucked into review copies of the *McCartney* album sleeve was an interview by Paul with himself. In these morose, never quite precise, and somehow pugnacious words there was something immeasurably depressing.

Q: *Are all these songs by Paul McCartney alone?*

A: Yes, sir.

Q: *Did you enjoy working as a solo?*

A: Very much. I only had to ask me for a decision and I agreed with me. Remember Linda's on it too, so it's really a double act.

Q: *The album was not known about until it was nearly completed. Was this deliberate?*

A: Yes because normally an album is old before it comes out. (Aside) Witness "Get Back."

Q: *Are you able to describe the texture or feel of the album in a few words?*

A: Home. Family. Love.

Q: *Will Paul and Linda become a John and Yoko?*

A: No, they will become Paul and Linda.

Q: *Is it true that neither Allen Klein nor ABKCO Industries have been or will be in any way involved with the production, manufacturing, distribution or promotion of the record?*

A: Not if I can help it.

Q: *What is your relationship with Klein?*

A: It isn't. I am not in contact with him and he does not represent me in any way.

Q: *What do you feel about John's Peace effort? The Plastic Ono Band? Giving back the MBE? Yoko's influence? Yoko?*

A: I love John and respect what he does—it doesn't give me any pleasure.

Q: *Are you planning a new album or single with the Beatles?*

A: No.

Q: *Is this album a rest away from the Beatles or the start of a solo career?*

A: Time will tell. Being a solo album means it's the start of a new career and not being done with the Beatles it's a rest. So it's both.

Q: *Is your break with the Beatles temporary or permanent, due to personal differences or musical ones?*

A: Personal differences, business differences, musical differences but most of all because I have a better time with my family. Temporary or permanent? I don't know.

Q: *Do you foresee a time when Lennon-McCartney becomes an active songwriting partnership again?*

A: No.

Q: *Did you miss the Beatles and George Martin? Was there a moment, e.g., when you thought: "Wish Ringo was here for this break"?*

A: No.

On May 8 *Let It Be* was released. When the *Let It Be* film had its premiere in both London and Liverpool on May 20, none of the Beatles turned up.

But there was some measure of consolation for Paul McCartney: the title song of this very last album proper by the Beatles had as its subject the woman whose memory had provided all the drive and effort and will to succeed without which the group would never have done what it did—Mary McCartney.

The Beatles had been the life force of all that was positive and genuine in the sixties. As if further proof were needed that this already mythological era was irrevocably dead, the last day of 1970 found Paul McCartney issuing a High Court writ: he sought that the partnership, The Beatles and Co., formed in April 1967, be dissolved and wound up, and that a receiver be appointed.

His announcement the previous April that he had left the group had had motives that were characteristically ambivalent: the expression of an honest, heartfelt emotion, it just happened to come, as these things did with Paul McCartney, at a time when it could provide the maximum publicity for his first solo album.

Public reaction to Paul's declaration had been largely one of disbelief; the detail of which Beatle had actually made it was of scant importance compared with the fact that it had been made at all, that the Beatles, into whose collective life had been interlocked the existences of countless millions, were now dead. In substantial part it accounted for that palpable sense of weary uncertainty with which so many people who had, to some degree, grown up during the sixties approached the new decade—they were in mourning, not simply for the loss of the Beatles, but for the death of what they had perceived themselves to be.

The excoriating specifics of litigation, however, wonderfully concentrated these benumbed minds on the cause of their discomfort. Thus came a sacrificial scapegoat in the shape of the man who had requested that the writ be served: it was all Paul McCartney's fault.

In subsequent years, in many quarters he was to become an object of utter derision. Such sentiments might equally have been leveled at the consistently confused, cosmic buffoonery of John Lennon. Reversing roles with the new, private Paul McCartney, John Lennon became the most ardent of self-publicists, though he never seemed to achieve Paul's discipline of thinking before he spoke.

Save for his most ardent fans, Paul's reclusiveness could conjure up no sympathetic sense of romance comparable to that attractive aura of mystery that had been a by-product of the marvelous music once produced by John Lennon. For to a very large extent Paul McCartney's creative energies seemed possibly spent as he produced records that, apart from a handful of classic songs, were often self-indulgent and insubstantial. It was even more to his disfavor that these first solo albums sold far more copies than those by John.

The fact that, despite Paul's apparently glowingly rosy domestic situation, he spent the first couple of years of the seventies in a turbulent, perplexed state of creative and personal crisis was hardly considered at all. And if it was, it was thought to be just what he deserved.

From his standpoint, Paul McCartney had no choice but to serve the writ: it was the only means he had of freeing himself from Allen Klein, whom he mistrusted and disliked. In subsequent years the other Beatles were to acknowledge that Paul's caution, which at the time appeared to be the product of a self-serving paranoia, had not been misplaced. By then, however, Paul's character had been so thoroughly besmirched that such admissions were of little interest.

The case opened at the High Court on February 18, 1971. For Paul McCartney it had the desired effect: on March 10 a judgment was made in his favor; a receiver was appointed to handle the assets of the Beatles, and Allen Klein was prevented from further management of the group's business.

John Lennon reacted by reverting to the explosive character he had been at Quarrybank School: he drove to 7 Cavendish Avenue, hurled a brick through a ground-floor window, and raced off in his Rolls-Royce, laughing.

Already Paul was embroiled in a further legal entanglement. In February he had released a new single, "Another Day," with Linda McCartney credited as his co-writer. As such a new partnership meant that only half the songwriting royalties would go to Northern Songs, Lew Grade, whose ATV had taken control of the Lennon and McCartney publishing company, set about to prove that such a co-credit was merely a devious ruse.

"Another Day" had been recorded in January in New York, the first of many occasions when Paul would manipulate the English tax laws to his advantage by recording outside of the United Kingdom. The session was part of a lengthy booking at A&R Studios. Twenty-one songs in all were recorded, thirteen of which found their way onto his next solo LP. *Ram*, miserably, was an even more marginal work than *McCartney:* its most interesting feature was the back-cover shot of two beetles screwing, a somewhat unelevating piece of symbolism.

The drumming on *Ram* was by a New York session player, Denny Seiwell. Apart from the disintegration of the Beatles, Paul's major dilemma for the past two years had been how best to make the difficult transition from bachelor rock and roller to rock-and-rolling family man. The solution, he had come to realize, was not in regarding his family as a substitute group, but in forming a further group of which his family could be part.

Accordingly, Seiwell was enlisted, as was guitarist Denny Laine, whose previous group, the Moody Blues, had once supported the Beatles on a British tour. Linda, Paul announced, would be his keyboard player.

Wings was never quite right, however, not even its name. And its first album, *Wild Life*, released in time for Christmas, 1971, was Paul McCartney's least successful album ever. Believing, probably with some justification, that this was due to a lack of public awareness that this was Paul McCartney's group, he preceded the group name with his own for their next album release. Yet the real cause of the relative commercial failure of *Wild Life* was its unremitting mediocrity.

With work as the only antidote he understood for any form of adversity, Paul McCartney plowed on. In the first month of 1972, a second guitarist was recruited for Wings, Henry McCullough, a former member of the Grease Band. McCullough's style of playing was as astounding as his attitude toward life was undisciplined.

In February a Wings single was released, "Give Ireland Back to the Irish." Not only was it promptly banned by the BBC, but, in keeping with Paul's low standing in critical opinion, it was considered a cynical effort to enlist a similar fashionably radical following to that which John Lennon enjoyed. Paul's Irish background, however, gives the lie to such charges of wilfull manipulation.

The same month, on February 9, 1972, at Nottingham University, Paul McCartney stepped out onstage with Wings to give his first proper live appearance since the Beatles played their last date in San Francisco in 1966. As he'd suggested the other Beatles do after the release of *Abbey Road*, Paul returned to live performance through a series of unpublicized, low-key dates. Wings had turned up at Nottingham University the previous day and offered their services on the condition that there would be a complete press embargo on news of the show.

"Eric Clapton once said that he would like to play from the back of a caravan, but he never got around to doing it," said Linda. "Well—we have! We've no manager or agents—just we five and the roadies. We're just a gang of musicians touring around."

His appetite for live work whetted, Paul arranged for a full European tour. Scheduled to begin on July 9 at the Chateau Vallon Centre Culturelle, the shows were promoted by John Martin, who had booked the Woodstock festival and was now running the Rainbow Theatre, London's principal rock venue. Because of the relatively small-capacity halls in which Paul insisted the tour begin, Martin lost a fortune, as did Paul McCartney himself. This notwithstanding the fact that—the gypsy feel of the short British tour having established a precedent—the group traveled between most of the dates in an open-topped, converted double-decker bus.

Following the release in May of a truly execrable single, "Mary Had a Little Lamb," dedicated to daughter Mary, arduous rehearsals began at the Manticore rehearsal studios, owned by Emerson, Lake and Palmer, in Fulham, West London.

To document the tour and provide press photographs, Joe Stevens, a New Yorker working in London for the underground press, was hired. Because of British work permit difficulties, Stevens was working under the sly sobriquet of "Captain Snaps"; a company was formed between the two McCartneys and Captain Snaps to divide up profits from sales of his pictures. At the suggestion of Linda, whose rock photography techniques at the Fillmore East Stevens had assiduously studied, the company was named Women's Tango Lessons Ltd.

"The first time I went to their rehearsals at Manticore," says the photographer, "I had a load of contact sheets with me that I'd just picked up of Marc Bolan and Alice Cooper.

"Paul and Linda went nuts. Paul said, 'Tell me about Bolan: I never get to go to any gigs; I don't know what any of these new people are like.' I explained that the last time I had seen Marc

Bolan at Wembley the drummer in Paul's ex-group was shooting a film called *Born to Boogie*. He didn't know anything about that at all. I told him that Marc Bolan didn't leave the audience alone for a second, that he boogied endlessly, and was on the edge of the stage all the time, watching everyone in the audience and shaking his butt until they were in a frothing frenzy. And at the beginning of the tour a few times I'd seen Paul after the show, and he'd say, 'Am I doing my Bolan okay for you?'

"That first day, though, and at all the subsequent rehearsals, Paul seemed very spaced, not just on grass, but distanced from what he was about to get into. I got the impression that the idea of this tour would be that it was rock-and-roll therapy for him. All the plugs from his switchboard had been pulled out, and he had to be courageous and put them back in. And he had to show his family what he had been and still was."

For Linda McCartney, the photographer who Captain Snaps was replacing, the rehearsals and early dates were a harrowing ordeal: "Suddenly she had become a keyboard player in some sort of Beatles operation. At the first gig she was terrified. But married couples or lovers will do pretty much anything for each other, and she was in that boat. So she got her courage together.

"At the Fillmore East I'd once seen her watching Joe Cocker onstage, with Henry McCullough backing him, in fact. And I saw that his honesty and that passion he had that was almost killing him was bringing tears to her eyes. And when Paul was at the electric keyboard doing "Maybe I'm Amazed," she'd sit next to him, and she had the same exact expression on her face—except now she was in the show.

"I asked her about it and she said, 'When that's going on, it's not your husband, it's just amazing music from an amazing performer, and you're sitting next to him, and you can actually touch him.' "

Quickly Captain Snaps established a close rapport with Paul and his wife. After five days on the road, however, he suddenly learned what the boundaries were that had to be observed. "We're crawling up this mountain at about four miles per hour. I've got my feet up on the table, and Paul and Linda are sitting opposite

1. A scene from the "Pipes Of Peace" video, 1983. *(AP/ Wide World Photos)* **2.** Not one of the better days in the life of Paul McCartney: on January 18, 1980, in handcuffs, he is led from jail in Tokyo to the public prosecutor's office to answer to charges of smuggling marijuana. *(AP/Wide World Photos)* **3.** Irrepressible Paul and Linda pose with an elderly Barbadian lady on January 16, 1984, after being fined two hundred Barbadian dollars each for possession of marijuana. After flying back to London from the island, Linda is busted again at Heathrow customs. *(AP/Wide World Photos)*

■ **1.** Paul in a pensive mood. (*Joseph Stevens*) ■ **2.** In a state of shock on December 9, 1980, Paul leaves his farmhouse near Rye in Sussex to travel to London after hearing of the murder of John Lennon. (*AP/Wide World Photos*) ■ **3.** Paul McCartney chats with Julian Lennon—who inspired the song "Hey Jude"—on the set of NBC-TV's "Friday Night Videos," on November 7, 1984. (*AP/Wide World Photos*)

1

3

2

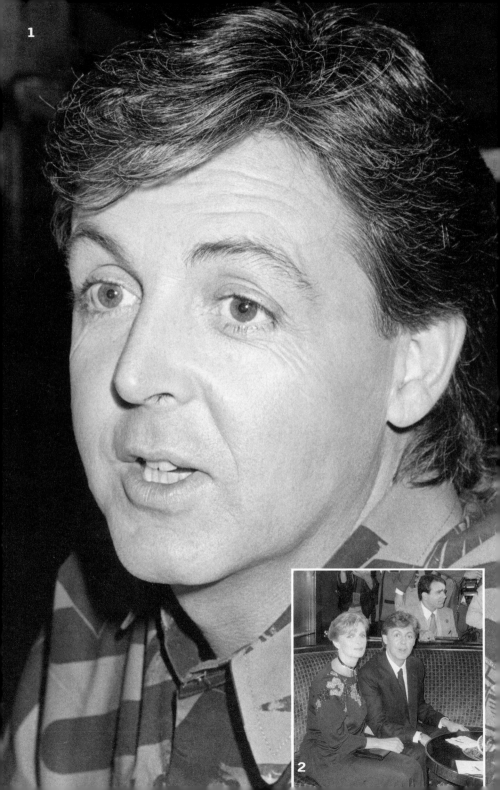

1

2

3

■ **1.** A 1984 shot of Paul. The years are beginning to become etched on his face. *(Mike Guastella/Star File)* ■ **2.** Paul and Linda at the New York premiere of *Give My Regards to Broad Street*. *(Vinnie Zuffante/Star File)* ■ **3.** Paul in the studio. *(L.F.I./Retna Ltd.)*

1

2

3

1. The relaxed Easthampton, N.Y., vacationer in August 1981. *(Vinnie Zuffante/Star File)* **2.** The McCartney family in April 1980: Paul and Linda with James, Stella (left), and Mary (front). *(AP/Wide World Photos)* **3.** Paul goes to some lengths to identify with one of his principal musical influences at the 1982 London Buddy Holly Week—he just happens to own the Buddy Holly song-publishing catalogue. *(Richard Young/Retna Ltd.)*

1

■ **1.** Paul resorts to the characteristic thumbs up, the habitual device he employs against demanding fans. *(Pictorial Press)*

and we're smoking joints and eating yogurt, and Linda says, 'You having a good time?'

"I said, 'Yeah, it's really great working for the Beatles.' I didn't know just how badly that was going to go down. In a few minutes, Linda got up and started making some food in the little kitchen, and called me over, 'Listen, don't ever do that again. Paul doesn't like to talk about the Beatles, and he certainly didn't appreciate that remark at all—it's not very funny. If you want to continue working with us, you'd better cool it.' "

For having so offended those rigid, yet rarely declared, McCartney rules of propriety, Captain Snaps was banished, like a naughty child, to the road crew's bus for a week before being allowed back with the McCartneys and the rest of the group.

When the tour had wended its way through France and the edge of Germany to Switzerland, there was a ten-day break. Paul and Linda had long since arranged to fly to New York for a surprise birthday party being thrown for Mick Jagger after a Rolling Stones performance at Madison Square Garden.

On August 10, 1972, seven dates into the second leg of the tour, at Gothenburg in Sweden, Captain Snaps observed that the hall contained an unusually large number of police, many leading what looked to be drug-sniffing dogs.

By now, confident of the group's playing and audience reception, Wings was playing a far lengthier show than the one with which the group had begun the dates. This seemed to be making the police restless: in the middle of "Long Tall Sally," the final encore, the cops pulled the vocal plugs on the PA, so that only the instruments could be heard. "Just like the Beatles, Snaps," Paul yelled down to the photographer, in a reference to the days when his old group could only be seen and not heard.

When Paul and Wings stepped off the stage at the end of the number, it was to the sound of the Stones' "Exile on Main Street" that the audience filed out. As the photographer stood by the mixing console, a message came over the walkie-talkie of the Wings security guard standing next to him: get Captain Snaps back to the dressing room immediately.

"I rushed over there, and it was right in the middle of their first pot bust: Linda is being mauled by a cop, but she has a big smile when she sees me: 'Snaps, get up on that bench and start taking pictures—cover of the *Daily Express* tomorrow morning!' I said, 'What's going on?' She said, 'Just get the pictures.' "

Typically, the McCartneys were working this adverse situation to their own advantage. "Paul is grimacing a lot, but he's also mugging for the camera—he's definitely working the whole thing for the maximum publicity. And it did get the cover of the *Daily Express.*"

Captain Snaps was somewhat amazed by this bust, however, as he knew the McCartneys had run out of smoke. He knew they had some waiting for them at their hotel, but as they'd been late arriving in Gothenburg they had gone straight to the soundcheck. "In fact, they'd asked me to go over to the hotel and get it, but there wasn't any time."

During the five hours that Paul and Linda spent locked in the same cell at the Gothenburg police station, they learned of the events that had led to this minor downfall. The Swedish police had a transcript of a tape of an international phone call Linda had placed to the McCartney office, MPL Productions in London's Soho Square. In it she had asked for two cassette boxes of grass to be sent to a hotel en route. The tape transcript clearly noted her calling out to Paul, "Where shall they send it? Do you have a copy of the itinerary?" and of Paul's reply, "Send it to Gothenburg, to the hotel."

The McCartneys were given an on-the-spot fine of £800, with a warning that further charges might be brought, though no more was heard of these.

In Stockholm the next night Captain Snaps arrived late at the Wings show: the group was already onstage. "Linda was a lot more confident by now. She asks me to pass up to her this package of pictures of the bust that I've got with me, and with gaffer tape she sticks them all over the keyboards. The other photographers went wild. So they were definitely not shying away from this problem."

Not only were the McCartneys not shying away, they seemed

if anything quite intent on making things even more difficult for themselves. The year ended for Paul McCartney and Wings as it had begun, with a single being banned by the BBC, in this case "Hi Hi Hi," which received the double accolade of a banning both for sexual and drug references.

It wasn't long before Paul was in court again on another bust: In March of 1973 the nosy Campbeltown constabulary sneaked up to take a look at Paul's High Park greenhouses. Simple but poignant mitigating circumstances for the presence of pot plants were pleaded by his lawyer at the subsequent trial: Paul, he said, had received seeds in the mail from a fan and was unaware that they were for cannabis plants. "My client has had a keen interest in horticulture for many years." Considering the state of the garden at 7 Cavendish Avenue, Jim McCartney could have had a word or two to say about that. Paul was fined £100.

The thoughts of the diarist of the *Campbeltown Courier* on this matter were sharp and to the point: "How nicer it would have been to be told that a substantial sum had been donated to the swimming pool fund."

The same month Wings returned to the Top Ten with "My Love," a single distinguished by Henry McCullough's searing guitar parts. An amiable, garrulous Irishman who liked a relaxing drink, McCullough found that he too clashed from time to time with the McCartney Code of Conduct. Perhaps the most obvious example of this occurred at a recording of the weekly "Top of the Pops" TV program while "My Love" was at the peak of its success.

Having demolished most of a bottle of brandy during a series of interviews at the group's publicist's offices before arriving at the BBC, McCullough began to find his coordination disintegrating as he stood under the hot lights of the "Top of the Pops" set. As, on camera, the group mimed to their hit, Paul could not avoid hearing a curious gurgling noise as they reached McCullough's principal guitar part. Glancing around, he was aghast to see that, as the guitarist continued to mime, he was also vomiting over the rear of the "Top of the Pops" rostrum.

* * *

With the group's second LP, *Red Rose Speedway*, set for release in May, Paul McCartney decided it was at last time to offer his thoughts to the world in a series of interviews.

At the offices of his publicist, Tony Brainsby, at Atherstone Mews in South Kensington ("If you put an *R* at the front and a *D* at the back of Atherstone it spells Ratherstoned," callers would chirpily be informed), Paul played the professional Northerner to the hilt, thriftily extolling the virtues of the secondhand coat he had picked up in a Liverpool market "for thirty bob" and, in a now habitual affectation, snapping the filter tips off the cigarettes he chain-smoked before lighting them.

His always adept interview technique now reached hitherto unsurpassed levels. Though many words emerged from his mouth, little was said at all, and what substance there was was always directed to the matter at hand: the selling of *Red Rose Speedway*. In complete contrast to the soul-baring extravaganzas that had become the norm for John Lennon interviews, Paul McCartney gave away nothing of himself whatsoever. Reading an interview with him became a frustrating experience.

It was not as frustrating, however, as listening to a Wings record. Paul McCartney's dilemma within the group seemed to be that, astute as ever to changing tastes, he was intent on creating a serious rock band with songs that, on the whole, were more suited to the whimsical, tongue-in-cheek side of the Beatles. The gravity of his mission, moreover, appeared to have led to the omission of an essential component. Where *was* the humor in the music? Had the years of litigation caused his wit to wither?

To cement this promotion of *Red Rose Speedway*, a British tour was finally set up, to begin on May 11 in Bristol, the day after the British screening of the by now unsurprisingly banal "James Paul McCartney" TV special, part of a deal done with ATV to mollify Lew Grade.

Dave Robinson, an energetic though impoverished Irishman, was the manager of Brinsley Schwarz, a cult band with some status as doyens of the pub-rock grassroots movement, an early forerunner of punk. Through his friendship with Henry McCullough,

236

Robinson made his way up to the "Top of the Pops" "My Love" session the week after Henry had thrown up.

"Henry said he'd put in a word with Paul about the Brinsleys doing the support slot, but of course he never actually got round to it. I went up to 'Top of the Pops' with a prepared speech in my head. But Paul answered the door and looked very groovy, and my prepared speech fell to pieces. Anyway, Paul gave me the name of the guy putting the tour together, but that fellow was a general downer. So I really hustled and got Paul on the phone and he agreed to it.

"When we were on the tour Paul was a real gentleman, a great bloke. We got full soundchecks, which was so unusual for a support act."

Later Robinson was to found Stiff Records, and even later still was to become managing director of Island Records. In a similarly lowly position in Brinsley Schwarz lurked one Nick Lowe, at the time a talented ex-mod recovering from his acid-casualty phase. Robinson could not help but notice a certain difference in attitude between the bass player with Brinsley Schwarz and the bass player with Wings.

"Nick Lowe kept blowing it, because he wouldn't turn up for the soundchecks: he'd be down at the pub. I began to think the Brinsleys had no future, because I saw McCartney's work rate. At a Wings soundcheck he'd be so diligent: 'The harmonies weren't right on the second song last night!' I told the Brinsleys they had to emulate that attitude, especially Nick Lowe.

"The tour re-established my faith in the fact that groups get better by touring. Paul worked very hard—I've never seen such a work rate. But I asked him what the fuck he was doing on the road. He said he was just a bassist and needed a band. He also knew the problems of being a young guy on the road, and that's why he said he had Linda there.

"He also said that all this business about making it was bullshit. He kept making it to the top, he said, and he'd find there was another top to make it to. Then he'd get there. Then he got to the very top . . . and discovered there was nothing there. That's when he decided to be just himself."

Both Wings and Brinsley Schwarz traveled in the same bus to all the dates. "I think," says Nick Lowe, "that our position as pub rockers appealed to McCartney because he very much wanted to foster this local band image for Wings—'we're just a band.' And we were just a slightly larger-than-life version of a local band.

"There was always this veil in front of him: you always got the impression that he was thinking about something else to what he was telling you. And whatever happens, he's having a nice day all the time: if any nastiness crops up, it's like he never sees it.

"I don't think this veil was anything to do with smoking pot, although he did seem to smoke it pretty much *all* the time. I used to put it down to a skill he'd developed in dealing with being so incredibly famous. Because he's one of those people who can appear slightly off-putting, because whichever way they turn their head, you've seen a photograph of them. So they look like a hologram of themselves.

"After I'd noticed this, I asked him one night—a real klutzy question—when he became aware that he was the possessor of this instantly recognizable persona. And when he had realized, had it worried him at all?

"He said he'd become aware of it in the mid-sixties. At the start it was a laugh, and then after America he realized it was getting beyond a joke. But he said, 'I had to come to terms with it.'

"Then he said something that can sound very conceited, but it didn't come across like that at all when he told me. He said, 'I've found that the richer I've become, and the more famous, I've been able to afford to have people as a buffer between me and the public, so I don't really have to get involved with them. And I've found that all I had to do was to wink at them, or give a thumbs-up, and not only have I made their day, but I've got myself out of lots of trouble.' Which, in fact, is a very honest answer. I was most surprised.

"Actually, he was very kind to me—me personally. He gave me a lot of encouragement, especially when the Brinsleys broke up. And I always got on well with Linda. She's always been the one who is the favorite to knock, but I always thought she was a charmer. I don't know whether I would have liked to be in a band with the lead guy's missus, but I always got on great with her. Both of them have been much-maligned people."

It was on this tour that Nick Lowe became aware of one other aspect of Paul McCartney: "He never, *ever* used to take a piss. On those long journeys that we used to do, everyone would be dying to go when we stopped at service stations. But old Macca would never get out of the bus. We used to think, 'Why on earth doesn't he need to have a piss?' How extraordinary! What training! It must have come from all those hours in the van with the Beatles."

There was, noted Nick Lowe, an undeniable frisson of friction between Henry McCullough and Linda McCartney: it was as though McCullough, essentially a rock and roll trouper of the old school, felt guilty about the money he was making with music that was not really his style, and accordingly exorcised his discomfort with himself on the easiest target. "He used to be terribly rude to Linda sometimes, in front of us, which must have been very embarrassing for her."

It came as no great surprise to anyone in the know when McCullough quit the group after the tour. More unexpected was the sudden departure of Denny Seiwell, who was missing his family and New York.

These exits could not have come at a worse time. Wings was scheduled to record in Ginger Baker's studio in Lagos, Nigeria. With only Denny Laine accompanying them, the two McCartneys flew down to Lagos: Paul had decided he would personally play all the instruments for which they didn't have musicians.

If that was not sufficient strain, Lagos itself proved to be something that the McCartneys had not bargained on. The climate —humid, dank, unbearably hot—was bad enough: at one stage Paul thought he was having a heart attack and had to be taken to a hospital by Linda. Then there were the rumblings of discontent from the local musicians who accused Paul of trying to rip off their music: he'd done all right so far without it, why should he steal it now? was his retort. Worst of all, one night Paul and Linda got lost in the backstreets of Lagos and were held up by a gang of robbers at knifepoint. And it seemed the incident might not end with just theft. "Don't hurt him: he's Beatle Paul," screamed Linda, as the knives hovered perilously close to her husband. Confused, the gang fled with their takings.

The result of all this tension, however, was by far the best music and album Paul McCartney had made since the breakup of the Beatles. *Band on the Run*—its "if we ever get out of here" line comes from some words George Harrison once uttered at one of the interminable Apple boardroom meetings—became justifiably Paul's biggest post-Beatles seller, eventually getting to number one in Britain for ten weeks, a full seven months after it was released in November 1973. It was the seventh best-selling LP in the country in the seventies. In the United States, it stayed in the Top 200 for seventy-three weeks, and was number one for four.

Perhaps in an attempt to recapture the vitality of that record, Paul, Linda, and Denny Laine went to Kingston, Jamaica, before it was released to record with that eccentric genius of the mixing desk, Lee "Scratch" Perry. Paul had long been a great fan of reggae.

Jamaica, Paul said was "like paradise. I like peasants—people-people. We're peasants, too, from all corners of the globe, a gang of peasants who want to be in a musical entertainment. This is the whole idea. It's like in medieval days. A few people just got together and made some music to make themselves happy, and then to make people happy off it. And that's really all it is for me.

"I occasionally want to make some little political statement, occasionally want to do a kids' song, but we're not too heavily into that stuff. The main thing, still, is just the music."

Though a close friendship came from the time they spent with "Scratch" Perry, there was no real recorded result, only a single by Linda, "Seaside Woman," that was released under the name Suzy and the Red Stripes six years later.

Shortly after *Band on the Run* slipped from the number-one album slot in Britain, EMI released a single by a group called the Country Hams of a song called "Walking in the Park With Eloise"—it had few sales. The Country Hams were the new Wings lineup—Paul,

Linda, Denny Laine, drummer Geoff Britton, and guitarist Jimmy McCulloch—augmented by Chet Atkins on guitar and Floyd Cramer on piano. The song had been written by Jim McCartney many years before, and the record was his son's tribute to his father. The sessions took place in Nashville, and formed part of two months' solid work intended for the next Wings LP. In the end, however, hardly any of this music was ever released.

Paul had also been in the studio in London with his brother, producing a solo LP for him, *McGear*. Almost predictably, the record—a somewhat grandiose, overblown affair—had a front cover photograph of their mother. Dressed in her nurse's uniform, she could have easily been mistaken for a nun.

Mike McCartney had finally left the Scaffold; the group had become incorporated in a larger revue, Grimms. One night Mike had a drunken fight with Liverpool poet Brian Patten, and walked off the tour bus for good. According to Roger McGough, this was not necessarily a bad thing. For Mike McCartney's increasing spaciness was proving immensely irritating to John Gorman. "I tended to be the mediator between the two. It was immensely difficult to pin Mike down, to be rational about anything. He was dreamy and dozy, and would spend a lot of time on what we would consider were irrelevancies, not trying to get an overview on things.

"And there was always this dissatisfaction within him: 'That record wasn't successful, let's get a new record company; that tour didn't go right, let's get a new manager.' Not 'What we need are the best songs.'

"To my mind, what he should have done was to get a band together, and do the clubs, and work it. But Mike thought it was all to do with the marketing, and what you wore on 'Top of the Pops.' I think he thought Paul's brother couldn't play those sort of clubs, so everything had to be done in the studio and on TV.

"Had Mike remained around the Beatles, doing photography, perhaps it would have been better for him. But he wouldn't have wanted to go around just taking pictures of the Beatles, because he would have had to do something for himself. It was not easy for Mike McCartney."

* * *

The next Wings LP, *Venus and Mars,* appeared at the end of May 1975, but had almost none of the energy or creative tension of its predecessor. Though it may have been psychologically crucial for Paul McCartney to wrap himself in the security blanket of a band of musicians, it was patently not to the advantage of his craft. *Wings at the Speed of Sound,* released the following May, was similarly shallow.

Though neither record was wholly unredeemable—they each contained a number of strong songs—they lacked the consistency of spirit that made *Band on the Run* marvelous. Paul McCartney seems to have missed the point that, apart from Laine's contributions, *Band* was essentially his solo album. As such, it was the successor to, and the logical development of, the disappointing *McCartney* and the weak *Ram,* which had been the necessary backward steps before he could progress forward. Now he had proved that he had overcome the initial hurdles and could make good solo records.

So why didn't he continue to do that? Certainly there was that almost desperate desire to be part of a group. And he needed the stimulus he gained from playing onstage with such an outfit. But those who have worked with Paul McCartney since the Beatles mention a major flaw in his abilities: so prolific is his songwriting that he is unable to separate the mediocre from the truly great— a task that had been John Lennon's. So it seems he may well not have realized just how good a record *Band on the Run* was, or even exactly why it was so good.

It often seems that what separates the enduring groups from the one-hit wonders is the personal development of the individual musicians as human beings. Clearly, it requires a certain wisdom of the soul to accurately perceive and avoid the multifarious traps that await the young and successful. The good guys never really change. And those who knew the Beatles in Liverpool, like Bill Harry, are adamant that ten or twenty years after Hamburg the Beatles were still essentially the same people.

Paul, however, as he didn't quite admit to Nick Lowe, did fall for one trap: he surrounded himself with yes-men. Who around him was going to tell an ex-Beatle that what he'd just written was a heap of shit?

Crippled by arthritis, Jim McCartney had for some time been fighting to stay alive. "I'll be with Mary soon," he said shortly before he breathed his last, and on March 18, 1976, he died.

Paul was too distraught to go to the funeral.

On the first day of summer that year, Paul McCartney appeared with Wings in Los Angeles. It was ten years since he had last played live on the West Coast, at the Beatles' final performance. At the Los Angeles Forum, the group played five shows. This was the most comprehensive world tour by a rock band to date, consisting of sixty-four dates and split into five legs, starting and ending in Britain, with European, Australian, and American stages.

The shortcomings of Paul McCartney's solo and Wings' records had always been magnified by the almost unsurpassable standards he had set for himself with the Beatles. Yet in the not unduly demanding standards of mid-seventies rock it was deemed that an LP was of high quality if it contained four strong numbers, a yardstick Paul McCartney invariably met. As a consequence, he had more than enough music for a strong two-and-a-half-hour show; he even included five of his own Beatle songs.

Yet for those Los Angeles dates, the music was certainly secondary: Paul was aware that, as with most stadium rock shows, it was the very fact of the event that was of paramount importance to the audience. And he performed accordingly, constantly hamming it up for the groundlings in the pit, his between-numbers raps delivered in an accent that was a parody not just of Liverpudlian but of the professional Northerner that he was himself. Of course it worked. These were artistically and aesthetically dull affairs, but the audience adored the shows—after all, a Beatle was onstage.

All the shows were taped, and at the end of 1976, a triple live album entitled *Wings Over America* was released. In a hardly dignified manner, Paul reversed the songwriting credits of the five Beatles songs so that they read "McCartney-Lennon," an act of smug pettiness that recalls those times when he would rip small tears in his parents' lace curtains.

In Europe the shows had been superior affairs, with Wings providing some of the most stirring rock that audiences had ever seen. In the figure of Jimmy McCulloch—so like a younger version of his almost namesake, Henry McCullough—lay the personification of the group's creative tension. Celebrated as a guitar hero at the age of sixteen for his work with Thunderclap Newman, McCulloch had become like a caricature of the Glaswegian rock musicians who could be found gathered together in London's drinking spots. There was something irrevocably doomed about most of these often unpredictably violent figures as they destroyed their lives and talents with endless quantities of alcohol and drugs.

It was to Paul McCartney's credit that he invested considerable energy in attempting to straighten out Jimmy McCulloch. His efforts went largely unappreciated. Several dates on the European tour had to be canceled when the guitarist cut his hand in a drunken brawl in Paris.

After work on the next studio LP, in the Virgin Islands and New York, McCulloch and drummer Joe English left the group. In 1979 McCulloch was found dead in his bathtub from a heroin overdose.

On November 11, 1977, a new Wings single was released. "Mull of Kintyre" refers to the tip of the Scottish peninsula on which Campbeltown is sited. The record, which featured the bagpipes of the Campbeltown Pipe Band, became the biggest-selling single in Britain ever, with total sales of 2.5 million. With the exception of the United States (where it peaked at a disappointing number thirty-three), it was a worldwide hit, six million copies eventually being sold.

London Town, the album recorded in the Virgin Islands and New York, followed; there was a Wings greatest-hits LP; and in June 1979, there was the gnomically cosmic LP titled *Back to the Egg*, with guitarist Lawrence Juber and drummer Steve Holly now members of the group.

In August Paul attended a party to celebrate his three entries in the then-latest edition of the *Guiness Book of Records:* most successful composer of all time, holder of the greatest number of gold discs, and the world's most successful recording artist.

At the end of the year Wings again toured Britain, and the year ended for Paul McCartney and Wings at Hammersmith Odeon, at a benefit concert for Kampuchea, on the last night of a four-day series of charity shows for that beleagured nation. One of the finest lineups of British rock talent ever assembled, it included Queen, the Who, the Clash, and the Pretenders, as well as Wings. The shows had been organized by Paul, who had been contacted by UN Secretary General Kurt Waldheim. Notwithstanding the crucial role that he himself had played, some fifteen months later, Paul McCartney furiously telephoned the director of London's Capital Radio, demanding to know why the station was playing a Wings bootleg. Paul was politely informed that the music he had heard comprised one side of the live double album recorded at those Hammersmith Odeon benefits.

Paul had always wanted Wings to tour Japan, but his pot convictions had prevented him from obtaining a Japanese visa. After lengthy negotiations one was eventually obtained, and eleven Japanese dates were booked for a tour starting in the middle of January 1980.

Under the circumstances. it was rather unwise of Paul to arrive on January 16 at Tokyo Airport with half a pound of marijuana in his suitcase. For this first arrival of the ex-Beatle to Japan in fourteen years, an array of TV cameras waited to record the event, the recording equipment even being permitted into the customs hall. Perhaps it was such an unavoidable media presence that prompted the Japanese customs officials to approach their work with a zealousness that, under different circumstances, Paul would have found admirable. With the TV cameras capturing every detail, the customs men swiftly discovered his hardly concealed stash.

Paul was led away in handcuffs. At the police station, where he discovered to his dismay that he was facing a possible seven years' hard labor for drug smuggling, Paul attempted to explain to his inquisitors that smoking pot was better than smoking "ciggies." This wonderful example of what can only be seen as a slight reality-perception problem was not appreciated.

Paul McCartney was imprisoned for eleven days before the old adage that multi-millionaires are unlikely to serve time was borne out. After subtle diplomatic efforts from the British government, he was released and put on a plane back to London.

As is the nature of crises, particularly those accompanied by enforced incarceration, his plight had caused Paul to undergo considerable reflection upon his life. On his return to London, he traveled straight to Campbeltown, where he began work on the somewhat belated follow-up to his very first solo album. *McCartney II* was released in May of 1980; it included a track entitled "Frozen Jap."

Four months after the LP's release Paul was recording again, this time at Air, by London's Oxford Circus. The studio is owned by George Martin. For the first time since *Abbey Road*, Martin was to produce Paul McCartney, another decision Paul had made in that Tokyo jail. It is said, however, that before George Martin agreed to work with Paul, he demanded to first hear the demo tapes of the songs. And in the corridors of EMI Records a tale is told of a conversation at this time between Martin and the EMI managing director: "How many songs has Paul got?" Martin was asked by the MD. "Thirteen." "But how many has he really got?" "Three." "Send him away to write some more."

The recording lasted from October 1980 to March 1982. The result, *Tug of War*, was an album almost on a par with *Band on the Run*. (On April 27, 1981, it was officially announced that Wings had ceased to exist; for what it's worth, the group's recording career had lasted longer than the Beatles'.)

On December 9, 1980, two months after work on the record had started, it was a haggard-looking Paul McCartney who came into the studio for the start of the regular morning sessions. "Do you want to cancel it for today?" Martin asked him. Paul shook his head: his answer to every difficulty had always been to work his way out of it. And so it had to be with the death of John Lennon.

For much of the time, Paul McCartney lives with his wife and children in a house called Waterfalls outside Rye in Sussex. It is a sixty-mile journey from London and, although he is the sixth richest person in Britain, with an estimated fortune of £400 million (he has learned much from the Eastmans: Paul's wealth has been increased considerably by his shrewd acquisitions of music-publishing companies, including the songs of Buddy Holly), he sometimes travels second-class on the train up to his offices in Soho Square. A similarly unostentatious attitude is applied to his home life; Waterfalls may have acres of grounds, but the circular house, with its rooms like the wedges of a cake, has none of the suggestions of the rock-star residence of 7 Cavendish Avenue. As Jim and Mary McCartney would have liked, it is a family house, though perhaps his parents would have disapproved of the clutter with which it is strewn. Like a typical working-class Northern man, Paul expects Linda to rise early and cook his breakfast and get the kids off to school while Paul feeds and waters and exercises his horses before traveling up to London by train or car. For relaxation he has become a bird watcher.

Paul no longer smokes cigarettes and has given up alcohol, and it is a strictly vegetarian family. The final conversion came one day at High Park when Linda, who is prone to outbursts of endearingly scatterbrained cosmic buffoonery of which John Lennon would have been proud, looked out of the window in horror at some grazing lambs as the family was about to begin a lunch of roast mutton. The McCartneys are hardly oblivious of crises of conscience: in 1983 they delivered Christmas hampers from Fortnum and Masons, having first carefully removed the meat, to the women nuclear protesters at the cruise missile base at Greenham Common in Berkshire. Paul gives away large amounts to charity each year, but if there is the least hint of publicity the offer is withdrawn. And in their own subtle way, his singles with Stevie

247

Wonder and Michael Jackson have contributed immeasurably to the cause of racial harmony.

In 1983 work began on a film, *Give My Regards to Broad Street*, Paul's follow-up to his only real failure with the Beatles, *Magical Mystery Tour.* So desperately intense and inescapable was the prepublicity that you might have been forgiven for imagining the film was not all it might be. And so it turned out, a venture that —like so much of his post-Beatles music—had simply not been thought out. The soundtrack album, however, on which Paul was accompanied by some of the finest players in the world, was on a par with *Tug of War.* The most superlative moments during the making of the film did not find their way into either the completed movie or onto the album: Paul, Ringo, Chris Spedding, and Dave Edmunds passed a couple of hours at the end of a day's shooting running through a set of songs drawn from the era of The Cavern and Hamburg. It seemed the best time Paul had had making music in years.

At the beginning of 1984 there was yet another bust, in Barbados this time; Linda compounded the error by bringing grass back to London. At her trial the next day she was threatened with a custodial sentence for any further offences.

In November 1984, the same month that *Broad Street* opened in London to critical scorn, Sussex police claimed to have uncovered a plot to kidnap the McCartneys, Paul's greatest fear since the death of his former soul mate.

Still, however, the McCartneys strive to exist as a normal family, as unpolluted as is possible by the endless complications and self-delusions that afflict the infinitely rich and famous. As a consequence Paul McCartney seems to have found for himself a not inconsiderable measure of happiness and peace.

And none to soon: at the age of forty-three it is as though Paul McCartney has finally passed the furthest outposts of youth and stepped into middle-age. Gone now are those boyish good looks: in their place is a face deeply etched with lines. Though these days it is parted on the side, his thick thatch of hair is almost as much a moptop as it was twenty years ago, except that it has been turned silvery-gray by time. Rock and roll is the language of eternal youth, of a post-war generation of Peter Pans unable to grow up; once Paul McCartney was a principal purveyor of such an attitude, but now he can certainly no longer suggest it by his visual appearance.

Unfortunately, this commendably undisguised evidence of aging only emphasizes the significant lack of maturing in his musical career. Once the expressed peak of his life's achievement was to become a composer of full-length musicals. Yet so huge an artistic failure was *Give My Regards to Broad Street* that we must question whether he any longer has within him the creative resources to make such a transition.

In fact, the failure of the film is said to have come as a deep shock to Paul McCartney. This may be all to the good: at least it should have placed him under intense pressure. And on such occasions—like the recording of *Band on the Run*, for example, when he no longer had an effective group—Paul McCartney is capable of coming up with some of his greatest work.

To achieve this, however, he must break free from the comfortable fetters of the cloyingly coy world he presents himself as living in. But has Paul McCartney become too rich and too successful to be able to confront himself? Is he so surrounded by sycophants that he is unable to perceive the reality of the Dream Castle he has built on foundations of sand?

And is this mere carping? Should we demand more of Paul McCartney than we would of ourselves? After all, he himself seems content with being the greatest popular songwriter of all time, a man with a supreme comprehension of the form of the popular song, and of the nature of his craft. (Even if he himself may wonder what ironies were at work to permit Michael Jackson to purchase, for forty million dollars, the entire publishing rights to the Beatles' catalogue.) Hardly an unsuccessful achievement for a boy from a Speke council estate: one, certainly, of which Mary McCartney would be proud.

At the time of this writing he is—ever the workaholic—recording again, working on yet another Paul McCartney album, at the studio he has built on the grounds of Waterfalls. And in his domestic life he is as assiduous as in his work, striving to bring up his children in a manner that would have been approved of by Mary and Jim, haranguing striking teachers at the local school that they attend.

In July 1985, Paul McCartney performed his first live concert since the end of 1979, when he closed the London segment of the LiveAid concert. It was not an easy return to the stage: those waiting in the wings reported that he went white as a sheet as—his microphone failing during his one song—he was soundly booed and hissed by the audience.

Yet no matter how miserable the circumstances of the performance became, it was revealing that, for Paul McCartney, only one number was suitable for performance at rock's latest most holy event. With those memories of mother Mary lodged so ineradicably within his soul, there was just no question over the choice of material: "Let It Be."

Bedford, Carol. *Waiting for the Beatles.*
London: Blandford Paperbacks, 1984.
Braun, Michael. *Love Me Do: The Beatles' Progress.*
London: Penguin, 1964.
Brown, Peter and Steven Gaines. *The Love You Make: An Insider's Story of the Beatles.*
London: Pan Books, 1983.
New York: McGraw-Hill, 1983.
Carr, Roy and Tony Tyler. *The Beatles: An Illustrated Record.*
London: New English Library, 1975.
New York: Harmony, 1978.
Coleman, Ray. *John Winston Lennon.*
London: Sidgwick & Jackson, 1984.
New York: McGraw-Hill, 1984.
Davies, Hunter. *The Beatles.*
London: Heinemann, 1968.
DiLello, Richard. *The Longest Cocktail Party.*
London: Charisma Books, 1972.
New York: Pierian, 1983
Editors of Rolling Stone. *The Ballad of John and Yoko.*
London: Michael Joseph, 1982.
Garden City, N.Y.: Doubleday, 1982.
Fong-Torres, Ben, ed. *The Rolling Stone Rock'n'Roll Reader.*
London: Bantam Books, 1974.

Gambaccini, Paul. *Paul McCartney In His Own Words.*
London: Omnibus Press, 1976.
New York: Delilah Books, 1983.
Harry, Bill. *The Beatles Who's Who.*
London: Aurum, 1982.
New York: Delilah Books, 1982.
Harry, Bill, ed. *Mersey Beat: The Beginnings of the Beatles.*
London: Omnibus Press, 1977.
Hoffman, Dezo. *With the Beatles: The Historic Photographs of Dezo Hoffman.*
London: Omnibus Press, 1982.
New York: Delilah Books/Putnam, 1982.
Leach, Sam. *Follow the Merseybeat Road.*
Liverpool, England: Eden Publications, 1983.
Lennon, Cynthia. *A Twist of Lennon.*
London: Star Books, 1978.
Martin, George. *All You Need Is Ears.*
London: Macmillan, 1979.
New York: St. Martin's Press, 1979.
McCabe, Peter and Robert Schonfeld. *Apple to the Core.*
London: Sphere, 1972.
New York: Pocket Books, 1972.
McCartney, Mike. *Thank U Very Much: Mike McCartney's Family Album.*
London: Sidgwick & Jackson, 1981. (Published in America as *The Macs.*)
New York: Delilah Books, 1981.
Miles. *John Lennon in His Own Words.*
London: Omnibus Press, 1981.
New York: Quick Fox, 1981
Norman, Phillip. *Shout: The True Story of the Beatles.*
London: Hamish Hamilton, 1981.
New York: Simon & Schuster, 1982.
Schaffner, Nicholas. *The Beatles Forever* (rev. ed.)
London and New York: McGraw-Hill, 1978.
Sheff, David and G. Barry Golson. *The Playboy Interviews With John Lennon and Yoko Ono.*

London: New English Library, 1982.

New York: Playboy Press, 1981.

Stannard, Neville. *The Beatles: A History of the Beatles on Record: The Long and Winding Road, Volume I.*

London: Virgin Books, 1982.

New York: Avon Books, 1982.

Stannard, Neville. *The Beatles: A History of the Beatles on Record: Working Class Heroes, Volume II.*

London: Virgin Books, 1983.

New York: Avon, 1984

Taylor, Derek. *As Time Goes By.*

London: Sphere Books, 1974.

Tremlett, George. *The Paul McCartney Story.*

London: Futura, 1975.

Williams, Allan and William Marshall. *The Man Who Gave the Beatles Away.*

London: Coronet, 1975.

Woffinden, Bob. *The Beatles Apart.*

London and New York: Proteus Books, 1971.

Abbey Road, 218, 219, 221–222, 230, 246
"All You Need Is Love," 191
"Another Day," 229
Apple Boutique, 195
Apple Corps, 195, 197, 198, 199, 204, 205, 212, 213
"Apple Scruffs," 201
Asher, Clare, 151, 153
Asher, Jane, 150–152, 153, 154, 155, 156, 159, 162, 167, 168–169, 178, 179, 183, 188, 190, 195
Asher, Margaret, 151, 153, 155, 202
Asher, Peter, 151, 153, 166–167, 175, 176, 179
Asher, Richard, 151, 155
Atkins, Chet, 241

Back to the Egg, 244
"Ballad of John and Yoko, The," 217
Ballard, Arthur, 74
Band on the Run, 240, 242, 246, 249
Barrow, Tony, 153, 167
Beach Boys, The, 188
Beat Brothers, The, 109–110
Beatles, The:
    at Abbey Road Studios, 128–129, 134–135, 146–147, 152–153, 179, 185–188, 203, 218
    in America, 160–161, 169–171, 176–177, 181, 198, 199
    break up of, 223, 227–229, 252

    at The Cavern, 107, 110, 112, 113–114, 129, 135–136
    clashes within, 85–86, 95, 98–99, 108, 177–178, 207–208, 215, 218–219, 220, 223
    drugs and alcohol and, 97, 121, 169, 170–171, 176, 178, 182, 183, 186–187, 188, 189, 190–192, 193, 204, 206, 212
    on "The Ed Sullivan Show," 161
    fans of, 106, 134, 156, 166, 212, 217–218, 219–220
    haircuts of, 95, 120
    in Hamburg, 88–89, 91–100, 106–110, 124–125, 144, 145, 180
    in India, 196, 203
    naming of, 82, 88
    NEMS royalty settlement by, 214–215
    in Paris, 159, 169
    publishing interests of, 144–145, 216
    violence and, 117–118, 134, 152, 180
Beatles, The (White Album), 204, 206, 218
Bedford, Carol, 217
Bed Peace, John and Yoko's, 215
Best, Mona, 75–76, 133–134
Best, Pete, 75–76, 92–93, 95, 100, 101, 104, 107, 111, 118, 128, 131, 133–134
Black Dyke Mills Band, 198, 199
"Blackbird," 202, 203

Blank, Mike, *see* McCartney, Peter Michael
Bolan, Marc, 231–232
Brainsby, Tony, 236
Bresner, Buddy, 161
Brinsley Schwarz, 236–238
Britton, Geoff, 241
Brown, Ken, 75–76, 93
Brown, Peter, 212
Browne, Tara, 183, 184
Byrds, The, 176

Caldwell, Alan, *see* Storm, Rory
Caldwell, Iris, 54, 75, 79, 130–132, 150, 162
Caldwell, Mrs., 130, 143, 162
Cass and the Casanovas, 81, 82, 111, 119
"Catswalk," 79
Cellarful of Noise, A (Epstein), 128
Chadwick, Les, 121–123
Charles, Ray, 99, 124
Clapton, Eric, 231
Clash, The, 245
Cochran, Eddie, 44, 81
Cocker, Joe, 232
Coleman, Ray, 158, 212
Coleman, Syd, 127–128
Corlett, Roy, 46, 78, 82, 168
Country Hams, The, 240–241
"Cry for a Shadow," 110

Davies, Hunter, 251–252
Davis, Rod, 41, 42, 44
Day, Doris, 205
"Day in the Life, A," 184, 221
Dewhurst, Keith, 193–194
Dick James Music, 144, 188–189
Donegan, Lonnie, 35–36, 41
Dunbar, John, 175, 176, 179, 198
Durband, Alan "Dusty," 29–30, 45–46, 52, 62–63, 64, 69, 87, 89, 103, 138, 168, 174
Dylan, Bob, 170, 176

Eager, Vince, 84
Eastman, John, 200, 213, 214, 216
Eastman, Lee, 200, 213, 214
Eastman, Louise, 200

Eckhorn, Peter, 100, 104, 107
Edmunds, Dave, 248
Edwards, J. P., 28, 41
"Eleanor Rigby," 180
EMI, 125, 127–128, 182, 186, 204, 206, 213, 218, 240, 246
English, Joe, 244
Epstein, Brian, 110, 114, 117, 118, 119–122, 124, 125, 126, 127, 128, 132, 134, 137, 143, 145, 153–154, 170, 176, 182–183, 188, 189, 190, 191, 192, 199, 207, 208, 213, 214, 216
Epstein, Clive, 214
Evans, Arthur, 30–33, 55, 56, 63, 70
Evans, Hal, 171, 182, 212, 221
Evans, Mike, 113
Everly Brothers, The, 47, 59

Faithfull, Marianne, 175, 192
Family Way, The, 182
Fascher, Horst, 98, 99, 108, 125
Fields, Danny, 200–201
"Fixing a Hole," 190
Fonda, Peter, 176
Fourmost, 153
"From Me to You," 149, 150
"Frozen Jap," 246
Fury, Billy, 83–84, 85

Gabor, Zsa Zsa, 168
Garagiola, Joe, 198
Garry, Len, 41
Gaule, Tom, 37, 72, 77, 89, 154, 167, 174
Gentle, Johnny, 86
Gerry and the Pacemakers, 81, 107, 144, 153
Get Back, 206–207, 208
Gibb, Russ, 221
"Give Ireland Back to the Irish," 230
Give My Regards to Broad Street, 248, 249
"Goodbye," 205
Gore, John, 25–26
Gorman, John, 152, 163, 164, 165, 195–196, 241
Grade, Sir Lew, 216, 229, 236
Graham, Billy, 191

Grease Band, The, 230
Griffiths, Eric, 41, 58–59, 109
Guitar, Johnny, 96, 132–133

Haley, Bill, 34
Hanton, Colin, 41, 53, 58–59, 69, 76
Hard Day's Night, A, 167–168
Harrison, George, 58–60, 77, 79, 87,
   106, 212
   Paul resented by, 177–178, 208
   Paul's school friendship with, 54–57
Harrison, Harry, 55, 56
Harrison, Louise, 54, 55, 56, 60
Harrison, Pattie, 208
Harrison, Peter, 56
Harry, Bill, 74–75, 78–80, 81, 85–86,
   110–113, 118, 152, 242
Help, 173
Hendrix, Jimi, 189
"Hey Jude," 202–203, 205, 219
"Hey Little Girl," 128
"Hi Hi Hi," 235
Hoffman, Dezo, 137–140, 155, 159–
   160, 161
Holly, Buddy, 47, 82, 97, 146, 247
Holly, Steve, 244
Hopkin, Mary, 204–205
Howard, Frankie, 139–140
Howes, Arthur, 145
Hutch, Johnny, 78, 85
Hutchins, Chris, 150

"I Am the Walrus," 193–194
"I Feel Fine," 177
"I Lost My Little Girl," 47
In His Own Write, (Lennon), 44
"Instant Karma," 222
"I Want to Hold Your Hand," 159, 161

Jackson, Michael, 248, 249
Jagger, Mick, 192, 233
James, Dick, 215–216
James, Ian, 37, 38
Jefferson Airplane, The, 188
Jim Mac's Jazz Band, 10
Johnny and the Hurricanes, 145
Johnny and the Moondogs, 70
   Carroll Levis audition of, 76–77

Johnson, Bella, 2, 21
Johnson, Olive, 2, 21
Jones, Raymond, 114
Jopling, Norman, 143
Juber, Lawrence, 244

Kaempfert, Bert, 109–110
"Keep Looking That Way," 79
Kelly, Arthur, 54, 56
Kelly, Brian, 104
Kenwright, Bill, 64
Kesey, Ken, 188
Kingsize Taylor and the Dominoes,
   107, 145
Kirchherr, Astrid, 95, 96–97, 98, 108,
   122, 124, 131
Klein, Allen, 182, 188, 213, 214–215,
   216–217, 220, 223, 224, 229, 252
Koschmider, Bruno, 88–89, 93, 94, 97,
   98, 99, 108
Kramer, Billy J., 152, 153

"Lady Madonna," 196, 197
Laine, Denny, 197, 230, 239, 240, 241,
   242
Leach, Sam, 105, 106, 108–109, 110,
   116–117, 118–119, 120, 121, 122–
   123, 124
Leacock, Steven, 52
Leander, Mike, 187
Lennon, Cynthia, 71, 80, 108, 130, 149–
   150, 152, 202–203, 215
Lennon, Freddie, 60
Lennon, John:
   at Art College, 49, 74–75
   "Beatles/Jesus" remark of, 181
   Cynthia's marriage to, 149–150
   death of, 246–247
   drug arrest of, 206
   education of, 23, 40, 48–49, 51
   George's first meeting with, 57
   as Johnny Silver, 87
   mother's death and, 60–61, 65, 74
   Paul's first meeting with, 40–41,
      43–44
   personality of, 48–49, 51, 61–62, 67,
      115–116, 165, 181–182
   prose writings of, 44, 110–111, 112

Lennon, John *(continued)*
  as Quarrymen leader, 40–45, 47–49,
    53, 57–60, 62, 94
  in split with Paul, 215, 229
  Wooler attacked by, 152
  Yoko's marriage to, 215
Lennon, Julia, 60–61, 215, 252
Lennon, Julian, 149, 190, 202
Let It Be, 217, 218, 222–223, 225
"Let It Be," 4, 225, 250
Lindsay-Hogg, Michael, 206, 208, 217
Little Richard, 53, 60, 105, 112, 124–
    125, 169, 212
LiveAid concert, 250
Lockwood, Sir Joseph, 213, 214, 216–
    217
Lomax, Jackie, 212
London Town, 244
"Long and Winding Road, The," 223
"Long Tall Sally," 113, 169, 233
"Looking Glass," 79
"Love Me Do," 79, 113, 134, 137, 141,
    143, 144
"Love of the Loved," 128
Lowe, Nick, 237, 238–239, 242
"Lucy in the Sky With Diamonds,"
    190
Lynch, Kenny, 145

McCartney, 222–223, 229, 242
McCartney, Elizabeth, 8
McCartney, Florence, 11, 12
McCartney, James, II, 8
McCartney, Jim, 46–47, 57, 58, 151–
    152, 154
  birthday gift from Paul to, 167–168
  character of, 120, 163–164
  death of, 243
  early life of, 8–12, 83
  as husband/father, 17–21, 23, 26, 31–
    32, 33, 37, 38, 80, 89, 103, 120, 178
  marriage of, 13–14
  Paul's birth and, 14, 15–16
  Paul's music and, 71–72, 86–87, 111–
    112
  retirement of, 165–166
  song by, 240–241
  wife's death and, 2–5

McCartney, Jin, 3, 9, 26, 72, 152
McCartney, Joseph, 8–10, 12
McCartney, Linda, 190, 199–201, 202,
    205, 213, 216, 217, 218, 219–220,
    222, 223, 224, 229, 231, 232–233,
    234, 237, 238–240, 241, 248
  Paul's marriage to, 211–212
McCartney, Mary Patricia, 1–5, 12–13,
    14, 15–16, 17–18, 19, 21, 60, 64, 73,
    196, 225, 250
McCartney, Paul:
  birth of, 14, 15–16
  Cavendish Avenue house of, 178–
    179, 183, 189–190
  children and, 161, 199–200
  difficulties with Epstein, 154, 182–
    183
  drug arrests of, 233–235, 245–246,
    248
  drug use disclosed by, 190–191
  early childhood of, 18–21
  early musical influences on, 34–36
  education of, 23–30, 38–39, 49,
    51–52, 62–63, 65–66, 67–70, 87,
    103
  fame and, 162, 199, 237, 238
  fans and, 88, 106, 135–136, 154–155,
    212, 217–218, 219–220
  money and, 117, 157, 176
  moped accident of, 183–184
  mother's death and, 1–5, 60, 61, 64,
    65, 124, 131, 174
  musicality of, 45, 99, 129, 176, 178,
    204, 208
  new life of, 247–250
  personality of, 20, 26–27, 29–30, 32–
    33, 38, 66–68, 79–80, 116, 131–132,
    140, 165, 181–182
  press cultivated by, 82–83, 112–113,
    157–158, 159–160, 222
  as prettiest Beatle, 88, 95, 97, 111,
    139, 190
  as prose writer, 44, 112–113, 206
  in Quarrymen, 44–45, 47–49, 52, 53,
    57–60, 62
  rumored death of, 221–222
  Scottish farm of, 179–180, 190
  at scout camp, 30–33

McCartney, Paul *(continued)*
  self-interview of, 223–225
  as Teddy Boy, 36–37, 57, 70
  women and, 37–38, 98, 136–137, 150,
    198, 201
McCartney, Peter Michael:
  birth of, 17
  in duo with Paul, 46–47
  early childhood of, 18–21
  education of, 23–30, 55, 162
  mother's death and, 2–5, 165
  as photographer, 113
  with Scaffold, 152, 162, 189, 195–
    196, 241
  at scout camp, 30–33
McCartney II, 246
McCulloch, Jimmy, 241, 244
McCullough, Henry, 230, 232, 235,
  236–237, 239, 244
McFall, Ray, 107
McGear, 241
McGivern, Maggie, 202
McGough, Roger, 152, 163, 165, 189,
  199, 241
McGough-McGear, 189
MacMillan, Harold, 142
McNally, John, 105–106
Magical Mystery Tour, 192–195, 206,
  248
Maharishi Mahesh Yogi, 191–192,
  196
Mamas and Papas, The, 188
Marsden, Gerry, 78
Martin, George, 128–129, 134, 135,
  138, 144, 146, 151, 174, 175, 178,
  185–188, 203, 225, 246
"Mary Had a Little Lamb," 231
Mason, Dave, 186
"Maxwell's Silver Hammer," 220
Mayall, John, 189
"Maybe I'm Amazed," 232
Miles, Barry, 175, 176, 179
Mimi (Lennon's aunt), 42, 43, 44, 48,
  49, 58, 59, 60, 65, 180
Mohin, Bill, 3, 13
Mohin, Dill, 3
Mohin, Mary Patricia, *see* McCartney,
  Mary Patricia

Mohin, Mary Teresa, 12–13
Mohin, Owen, 12–13
Mohin, Rose, 13
Mohin, Wilf, 13
"Money," 113
Monroe, Matt, 175
Moody Blues, The, 230
Moore, Tommy, 82, 85, 86, 87
Moores, John, 80
"Mull of Kintyre," 244
"My Bonnie," 109–110, 114, 116
"My Love," 335

Nash, Graham, 189
Nerk Twins, 77
Northern Songs, 144, 215–216, 229

"One after 909, The," 79
Ono, Yoko, 202, 203, 204, 205, 206,
  215, 218, 219, 224, 252
Orton, Joe, 183, 199
"Our World," 191

Palmer, Eddie, 118
"Paperback Writer," 179
Parlophone Records, 125, 128–129,
  189, 197
Parnes, Larry, 81, 84, 85, 87, 95
"Penny Lane," 186
Petty, Norman, 146
Pickles, Thelma, 61–62, 135–136, 145,
  163–164, 189–190
Pilcher, Detective Sergeant, 206, 212
Plastic Ono Band, The, 220, 222,
  224
Please Please Me, 159
"Please Please Me," 144, 145–146, 147,
  149
Pobjoy, William, 48–49
Poole, Brian, 121
Post Card, 205
Presley, Elvis, 34–35, 41, 99, 137, 142,
  146, 176–177
Preston, Billy, 212
"P.S. I Love You," 113, 134

Quarrymen, The, 33, 40–45, 47–49, 52,
  53, 57–60, 62, 70, 75–76, 77–78

Rainbows, 77
Ram, 229–230, 242
Raskin, Gene, 204
Red Rose Speedway, 236
Revolver, 180
Rhone, Dorothy, 80, 108, 110, 123, 130, 135, 150
Richard, Cliff, 75, 110, 111, 129, 138
Richards, Ron, 134
Richenberg, Leonard, 214–215
Robinson, Dave, 236–237
Rolling Stones, The, 143, 182, 200–201, 213, 233
Rory Storm and the Hurricanes, 78, 81, 96, 107, 111, 132, 133
Rubber Soul, 177

Schwartz, Francie, 201–202
Searchers, The, 105, 107
See, Heather, 200, 221
See, John, 200
Seiwell, Denny, 230, 239
Sentimental Journey, 223
Sgt. Pepper's Lonely Hearts Club Band, 175, 186–188, 190, 191, 193, 196, 198, 221
Shapiro, Helen, 144
"She Came in Through the Bathroom Window," 218
"She Loves You," 153, 161
Sheeley, Sharon, 81
Shenson, Walter, 167
Sheridan, Tony, 100, 109–110, 111, 114
"She's Leaving Home," 187
Shotton, Pete, 40, 41, 42, 44, 45
Silver Beatles, The, 82, 85–87, 168
Sissons, Peter, 38–39, 40, 41, 46
"Slow Down," 105
Smith, Norman "Normal", 128–129, 134–135, 146–147, 177–178
Sommerville, Brian, 153–154, 156, 157–158, 160, 169
Spector, Phil, 160–161, 222, 223
Spedding, Chris, 248
Starr, Ringo, 101, 132–133
Steele, Tommy, 73, 84, 129
Stevens, Joe (Captain Snaps), 231–235
Stevens, Margo, 201–202, 218
Stewart, Les, 75–76

Storm, Rory, 54, 57, 75, 79, 123, 130, 131, 132–133
"Strawberry Fields Forever," 185, 186, 221
Sutcliffe, Millie, 124
Sutcliffe, Stuart, 74–75, 78–79, 80–81, 85–86, 87, 92, 94–95, 98–99, 100, 108–109, 124, 131, 203, 208
Sweeney, Jack, 33, 62–63, 65–66, 68, 69, 70, 89, 140

Taylor, Derek, 169, 204, 213, 222, 223
Taylor, E. R., 48
Taylor, Kingsize, 83, 124
"Thank U Very Much," 195
"Thingummybob," 198
"Thinking of Linking," 79
Thomas, Chris, 203–204
Thomas, Margaret, 24
"Those Were the Days," 204–205
Tug of War, 246, 248
Twiggy, 204
"Twist and Shout," 146
Twitchy, 60

Undertakers, The, 212
Unfinished Music #1: Two Virgins, 205–206

Vaughan, Ivan, 38, 39–41, 43, 45, 47, 65, 86
Venus and Mars, 242
Vincent, Gene, 44, 81
Voorman, Klaus, 94–95

"Walking in the Park With Eloise," 10, 240
Waller, Gordon, 167, 179
Walters, Lou "Wally," 101
Ward, Muriel, 27
Watson, Jimmy, 137, 138
Webb, Bernard, 179
Weiss, Nat, 199
Weissleder, Manfred, 145
Whalley, Nigel, 41, 53, 58, 60–61, 107, 109
"When I'm Sixty-Four," 185–186
White, Andy, 134–135
Who, The, 190, 245

Wilde, Marty, 84
Wild Life, 230
Williams, Allan, 73, 78, 80–81, 85, 87–89, 91, 92, 96, 99, 100–101, 105, 107, 109
Williams, Beryl, 78, 92
Williams, Danny, 144
Wings, 230–246
Wings at the Speed of Sound, 242
Wings Over America, 243–244
"Winston's Walk," 79
With the Beatles, 113, 159

"Woman," 179
Women's Tango Lessons Ltd., 231
Wonder, Stevie, 247–248
Woodbine, Lord, 73, 91, 92
Wooler, Bob, 104–105, 107, 113–114, 152
"Word, The," 177
"World Without Love," 167

"Years Roll Along," 79
Yellow Submarine, 206
"Yesterday," 173–175, 196